The Parliament
of Great Britain:
A Bibliography

The LexingtonBooks Special Series in Libraries and Librarianship

Richard D. Johnson, General Editor

The Parliament of Great Britain: A Bibliography
Robert U. Goehlert and *Fenton S. Martin*

Prizewinning Books for Children
Jaqueline Shachter Weiss

The Feminization of Librarianship in France
Mary Niles Maack

The Parliament of Great Britain: A Bibliography

Robert U. Goehlert
Fenton S. Martin
Indiana University

LexingtonBooks
D.C. Heath and Company
Lexington, Massachusetts
Toronto

Library of Congress Cataloging in Publication Data

Goehlert, Robert U.
  The Parliament of Great Britain.

  Includes index.
  1. Great Britain. Parliament—History—Bibliography. 2. Great Britain.
Parliament—Bibliography. I. Martin, Fenton S. II. Title.
Z7164.R4G57   1982   [JN508] 016.32841   82-47920
ISBN 0-669-05700-2

Published simultaneously in Canada

Printed in the United States of America

International Standard Book Number: 0-669-05700-2

Library of Congress Catalog Card Number: 82-47920

Contents

Introduction

Our aim in compiling this volume was to produce a comprehensive bibliography on the Parliament of Great Britain. While a wealth of material has been written about the Parliament, no extensive bibliography has been published as a guide to the literature. While Hailsham's *Parliament: A Reader's Guide* (7),[a] Hyland's *King and Parliament: A Selected List of Books* (8), and Palmer's *Government and Parliament in Britain: A Bibliography* (12), remain useful guides to the literature, they are twenty or more years old and are briefer than this volume. In order to provide a guide to the broad spectrum of sources and fill the need for an extensive bibliography on the Parliament, we conducted a systematic search of the literature. The bibliography is designed to assist both the general reader and serious students and scholars.

The primary focus of this bibliography is on the history, development, and legislative process of Parliament, not with national politics and government policy in general. Consequently, secondary and peripheral materials on the ministries and government, political parties, the crown and royalty, commissions, foreign affairs, campaigns and electioneering, and current events are not included. Our aim was to include all scholarly research material published in English over the last one-hundred years. We did not include any foreign-language materials, as most of the literature on Parliament is in English, and the majority of foreign-language studies are comparative in nature. Those who desire more general information about specific events and issues and the day-to-day activities of Parliament should explore the primary documents of Parliament, newspaper accounts, and magazine material indexed in the *British Humanities Index* and *Social Sciences Index*. While there are many fine British newspapers, three stand out as most useful for following parliamentary politics. These are *The Times, The Guardian,* and *The Daily Telegraph.* By using the *Index to the Times* and Palmer's *Index to the Times Newspaper* to identify the dates for important events, one can then use any of the British newspapers, even though they are not indexed. By identifying the time frame, the researcher need only browse through other newspapers to see if they have articles on the topic. There are several magazines indexed in one or the other index that are especially useful for journalistic accounts of important events and developments on parliamentary politics. Among the more important magazines are *The Economist, New Statesman, Observer Magazine, New Society, Spectator, Listener,* and *Encounter.* Also, although some bio-

---

[a]The numbers in parentheses refer to the item number in the bibliography. See the entry for complete bibliographic information.

graphical materials are included in the bibliography—especially when they contain substantial sections on the workings of Parliament—as a rule, auto-biographies, biographies, and diaries of Members of Parliament are excluded.

The bibliography includes books, edited volumes, original essays in compilations, journal articles, research notes and review essays, and dissertations and theses completed in the United Kingdom, the United States, and Canada. It includes only a select number of British documents. Generally we did not include documents as the number that would have to be included would be enormous. In addition to the nonparliamentary publications of the H.M.S.O., the journals of the two houses and the reports of the parliamentary debates are most important. In the introduction we have listed the major indexes and guides to British documents (items 16–57). Those interested in identifying documents should examine those bibliographical tools.

For each entry in the bibliography we have attempted to provide as complete a citation as possible, including the author's entire name, the use of full numbers for the pagination of journal articles, and the pagination for monographs. We have also included the pagination for all but a few U.S. dissertations. No paginations are given for British theses, as the tools we used to identify them did not provide the pagination. If a dissertation were published as a commercial monograph, usually only the latter citation is provided. If an article on the same topic as the author's dissertation has appeared, usually only the citation to the article is included. Though the bibliography emphasizes monographs and journal articles, dissertations and theses were included to provide continuity and coverage for topics not otherwise available in the literature.

While many of the monographs included in the bibliography have been reprinted, the original publisher and date are given. The reason for using the original publishing information and not the reprint date is to provide the user with the time frame in which a work was published. With the exception of the dissertations and theses cited in the bibliography, the bibliography includes only published materials, assuring easy accessibility of the materials listed. Consequently, the bibliography does not include conference papers and other typescript volumes. Most, though not all, of the U.S. dissertations and theses are available from University Microfilms International on microfilm or xeroxography. To determine whether a U.S. dissertation can be ordered from University Microfilms, the user should consult the appropriate volume of *Dissertation Abstracts International* or *Comprehensive Dissertation Index*. To determine the availability of British theses for photocopying, interlibrary loan, or consultation, the user should examine the introductory pages to *Index to Theses Accepted for Higher Degrees by the Universities of Great Britain and Ireland*.

One of our goals in compiling the bibliography was to include materials from all subject disciplines in the humanities, social sciences, and law. In order to be as comprehensive as possible, we searched ten indexes and abstracting services. These indexes are

Annual Bibliography of British and Irish History

Australian PAIS

British Humanities Index

Humanities Index

Index to Legal Periodicals

International Political Science Abstracts

Public Affairs Information Service Bulletin

Social Sciences Index

United States Political Science Documents

Writings on British History

As a result of our search, we have included citations to over two hundred journals. Though the majority of journals contained fewer than ten citations each, there were a number of journals that regularly contained articles on the Parliament. These core journals are listed in order of importance.

Parliamentary Affairs

English Historical Review

Parliamentarian

Political Quarterly

The Table

Institute of Historical Research Bulletin

Political Studies

Historical Journal

American Political Science Review

English Review

Modern Law Review

Public Law

Journal of Modern History

Contemporary Review

History Today

Royal Historical Society Transactions

Law Quarterly Review

Public Administration

British Journal of Political Science

Political Science Quarterly

The U.S. and Canadian dissertations cited were identified by using *Comprehensive Dissertation Index* and *Dissertation Abstracts International.* British theses and dissertations were identified by using Roger R. Bilboul's *Retrospective Index to Theses of Great Britain and Ireland, 1716–1950* and *Index to Theses Accepted for Higher Degrees by the Universities of Great Britain and Ireland and the Council for National Academic Awards.* We also checked Peter S. Bell's *Dissertations on British History, 1815–1914: An Index to British and American Theses* (117). In the case of British theses, degrees for Ph.D., D. Phil., and B. Litt. are cited as such; for the degrees of M.A., M.Sc., M. Phil., and M. Litt., we have cited the degree as a Master's thesis. In the case of Wales, Ireland, and the University of London, the author's college is given when known.

To identify books on Parliament, we searched various sets of the *Subjects Catalogs of the British Museum, National Union Catalog, Books in Print, British Books in Print, American Book Publishing Record, Cumulative Book Index, Publishers Weekly, Public Affairs Information Service Bulletin,* and the *Universal Reference System, Political Science Series.* Four journals regularly carry book reviews and listings of works on parliaments throughout the world. These are *Parliamentary Affairs, Paliamentarian, Legislative Studies Quarterly,* and *Inter-Parliamentary Bulletin.* Many of the monographs included in the bibliography have been reviewed in those journals. To find reviews of the monographs cited in the bibliography, the reader can also consult *British Books News, Current Book Review Citations, Book Review Index,* and *Book Review Digest.*

We also checked numerous bibliographies on Parliament published in books or articles. These were identified by using the *Bibliographic Index.* Some of the major bibliographies consulted include the following:

Inter-Parliamentary Union's *World-Wide Bibliography on Parliaments* (10)

Palmer's *Government and Parliament in Britain: A Bibliography* (12)

Westergaard's *Modern British Society: A Bibliography* (115)

Brown's and Christie's *Bibliography of British History 1789–1851* (118)

Davies's *Bibliography of British History: Stuart Period, 1603–1714* (126)

Graves's *A Bibliography of British History to 1485* (127)

Hanham's *Bibliography of British History 1851–1914* (129)

Mowat's *Great Britain Since 1914* (135)

Nicholl's *Nineteenth-Century Britain, 1815–1914* (136)

Pargellis's and Medley's *Bibliography of British History: The Eighteenth Century, 1714–1789* (137)

Read's *Bibliography of British History; Tudor Period, 1485–1603* (138).

The bibliography is classified according to ten major topics: (1) Origins and Development of Parliament, (2) Legislative Process, (3) House of Commons, (4) House of Lords, (5) Organization of Parliament, (6) Pressures on Parliament, (7) Reform of Parliament, (8) Parliament and the Electorate, (9) Members of Parliament, and (10) Support and Housing of Parliament. Preceding the bibliography proper we have included a section titled Reference Works. We tried to include a wide selection of reference tools useful in the study of Parliament and British history and politics in general. In addition to the items mentioned elsewhere in the introduction, there are several items especially important for the student or researcher of Parliament. Wilding's and Laundy's *Encyclopedia of Parliament* (14) and Abraham's and Hawtry's *Parliamentary Dictionary* (100) are especially useful for finding definitions of parliamentary terms, important dates, significant events, and other kinds of reference questions. We have included a variety of sources for election statistics (58–71). In addition to the various volumes Craig has compiled on parliamentary election results (59–66), we have included several international almanacs of elections results, most notably, Mackie's and Rose's *International Almanac of Electoral History* (69), Rokkan's *International Guide to Electoral Statistics* (70), and Rose's *Electoral Behavior: A Comparative Handbook* (71). These latter compendiums are invaluable for cross-nation studies of election and voting behavior. In the section titled Biographical Directories we have included directories both to individuals and groups and to institutions. The single most important directory is Stenton's *Who's Who of British Members of Parliament* (98), which now consists of four volumes covering 1832 to 1979. *Dod's Parliamentary Companion* is also indispensable for current information. Finally, there are several historical handbooks that are also useful for finding information about Parliament, including dates of sessions, select committees, and so on. The most useful are Cook's and Brandon's *British Historical Facts, 1830–1900* (143) and Butler's and Sloman's *British Political Facts, 1900–1975* (142).

For general works on Parliament there are a number of important books. (To assist the user, we have indicated the section of the bibliography in which these works and others are located.) Jenning's *Parliament* (216) and Mackenzie's *The English Parliament* (226) are both standard works that should be on the reading lists of all students. While some older volumes, including Strathearn's *Our Parliament* (192), Howarth's *Questions in the House: The History of a Unique British Institution* (210), Ilbert's *Parliament: Its History, Constitution, and Practice* (213), Young's *The British Parliament* (270), and Laski's *Reflections on the Constitution: The House of Commons, the Cabinet and the Civil Service* (502), are still valuable works, there are also several more recent books that provide a good introduction to the Parliament. These are Raison's *Power and Parliament* (248), Rush's *Parliament and the Public* (255), *Parliamentary Government in Britain* (2461), Miller's *The End of British Politics* (2399), and Ashford's *Policy and Politics in Britain: The Limits of Consensus* (2247). Bradshaw's and Pring's *Parliament and Congress* (467) provides an excellent comparison of those two legislative bodies. Finally, there are two sets that deserve special mention. *The Parliamentary History of England to the Restoration,* otherwise known as the *Old Parliamentary History,* is twenty-four volumes covering the Commonwealth and Restoration periods. The other set is *The Parliamentary History* compiled by William Cobbett and J. Wright. This thirty-six-volume set covers the legislative history from the Norman Conquest to 1803. Although both sets are not free from errors, they are valuable reference works.

There are many excellent works on legislative processes and procedures. Griffith's *Parliamentary Scrutiny of Government Bills* (543) is a classic on parliamentary procedures. Also useful as general introduction to the legislative process are Jenning's *The Law and the Constitution* (555) and Walkland's *The Legislative Process in Great Britain* (582). For an authoritative work, one should consult May's *Treaties on the Law, Privileges, Proceedings and Usage of Parliament* (683). John Kersell's *Parliamentary Supervision of Delegated Legislation: The United Kingdom, Australia, New Zealand and Canada* (597) and his article titled "Upper Chamber Scrutiny of Delegated Legislation: Great Britain and Australia" (598) are the two best expositions on delegated legislation. To get an understanding of Private Member Bills, Bromhead's *Private Members' Bills in the British Parliament* (604) is the single best monograph. For Private Bills there are two recommended books, Clifford's *A History of Private Bill Legislation* (605) and William's *The Historical Development of Private Bill Procedure and*

Standing Orders in the House of Commons (611). There are three works that
focus on budgetary practices: Britain's *The British Budgetary System* (615),
Einzig's *Control of the Purse: Progress and Decline of Parliament's Financial Control* (628), and Robinson's *Parliament and Public Spending: The
Expenditure Committee of the House of Commons, 1970–1976* (647). In
addition, Chubb's *The Control of Public Expenditures: Financial Committees of the House of Commons* (617) gives in-depth coverage to the Estimates Committee. For information regarding the rules and practices in
Parliament, the standard work is Chester's *Questions in Parliament* (662).
A good work on parliamentary privileges is Kilmuir's *The Law of Parliamentary Privilege* (708).

There are five books that together provide a survey on the House of
Commons. These are Campion's *Parliament: A Survey* (739), Palgrave's
The House of Commons (768), the Study of Parliament Group's *The Commons in Transition* (775), Walkland's *The House of Commons in the Twentieth Century* (781), and Norton's *The Commons in Perspective* (2412). In
addition to the works already mentioned on the legislative process, there are
two more works that are detailed studies on the functions and duties of the
House of Commons; they are Campion's *An Introduction to the Procedure
of the House of Commons* (792) and Redlich's *The Procedure of the House
of Commons: A Study of Its History and Present Form* (811). While there
are a number of excellent histories about the House of Commons, we will
single out only two standard works: Neale's *The Elizabethan House* (823)
and Porritt's *The Unreformed House of Commons* (858). Finally, William's
The Clerical Organization of the House of Commons (865) provides a comprehensive introduction to the Clerk of the House and the support staff.

For the student and scholar alike, Pike's *A Constitutional History of
the House of Lords* (947) is an indispensable work. Another authoritative
work on the the House of Lords is Bromhead's *The House of Lords and
Contemporary Politics, 1911–1957* (1036). For further readings on the
House of Lords, there are Bailey's *The House of Lords: A Symposium*
(914), Marriott's *Second Chambers* (942), Robert's *The Function of an
English Second Chamber* (950), and Morgan's *The House of Lords and the
Labour Government, 1964–1970* (1037).

On the organization of Parliament, there are a select number of impor-
tant works. To understand the committee structure of Parliament, there are
Morris's *The Growth of Parliamentary Scrutiny by Committee* (1064) and
Coombes's *The Member of Parliament and the Administration* (1091).
Though dated, Dasent's *The Speakers of the House of Commons from the
Earliest Times to the Present Day* . . . (1126) and MacDonagh's *The Speaker
of the House* (1134) are still valuable historical studies. A more contemporary study is Laundy's *The Office of the Speaker* (1130). The role of Par-
liament as an ombudsman is best explained in Gregory and Hutchesson's

The Parliamentary Ombudsman: A Study in the Control of Administrative Action (1160).

For a concise introduction to the pressures of the executive on Parliament, there is Eaves's *Emergency Powers and the Parliamentary Watchdog: Parliament and the Executive in Great Britain, 1939–1951* (1191). Two essential works on judicial appeal are Blom-Cooper's and Drewry's *Final Appeal: A Study of the House of Lords in Its Judicial Capacity* (1272) and McIlwain's *The High Court of Parliament and Its Supremacy* (1292). While there is a growing body of literature on lobbying and interest groups in Britain, a good starting point for the literature is Stewart's *British Pressure Groups: Their Role in Relation to the House of Commons* (1317).

Though there is a sizable body of studies on the reform of Parliament, we have selected five books as a general survey in the field. They are Cannon's *Parliamentary Reform, 1640–1832* (1334), Crick's *The Reform of Parliament* (1343) and *Reform of the House of Commons* (1425), Finer's *Adversary Politics and Electoral Reform* (1352), and the Hansard Society for Parliamentary Government's *Parliamentary Reform: A Survey of Recent Proposals for the Commons* (1361).

There is a vast literature on Parliament and the electorate. While we were selective in what we included for the bibliography, attempting to provide historical coverage over several centuries, we did include many standard works. Butler's *The Electoral System in Britain, 1918–1951* (1684) is a seminal work on elections. Butler's and Stokes's *Political Change in Britain: The Evolution of Electoral Choice* (1479) is another authoritative work. Also worthy of mention are Ranney's *Pathways to Parliament: Candidate Selection in Britain* (1521), Ross's *Elections and Electors: Studies in Democratic Representation* (1527), and Cook's and Ramsden's *By-Elections in British Politics* (1746). In regard to the role of parties, there are three classic works, all of which should be read by anyone interested in parties. They are Rose's *The Problem of Party Government* (1526), Beer's *Modern British Politics: A Study of Parties and Pressure Groups* (1886), and McKenzie's *British Political Parties* (1923). Also important are Bulmer-Thomas's *The Growth of the British Party System* (1889), Finer's *The Changing British Party System, 1945–1979* (1905), and Rush's *The Selection of Parliamentary Candidates* (1936). In the area of representation, there are Humphreys's early *Proportional Representation: A Study in Methods of Elections* (1761), Ross's scholarly *Parliamentary Representation* (1860), and Pulzer's more recent *Political Representation and Elections in Britain* (1856).

There are a variety of studies on the Members of Parliament. Two useful works on Members of the House of Commons: the first, an older but still valuable reference work, is Escott's *Gentlemen of the House of Commons* (2112). The second is a recent socioeconomic study by Mellors, titled

The British MP (2017). Among the numerous studies of Backbenchers, there are several books that merit inclusion. These are Finer's and Berrington's *Backbench Opinion in the House of Commons, 1955–59* (2044), Leonard's and Herman's *The Backbencher and Parliament* (2052), and Richard's *Honourable Members: A Study of the British Backbencher* (2060) and *The Backbencher* (2059). In the last few years, several works on women in Parliament have been published. One of the books included in the bibliography is Vallance's *Women in the House: A Study of Women Members of Parliament* (2507).

The previously cited work by Williams, *The Clerical Organization of the House of Commons* (865), should again be mentioned for information on the support and housing of Parliament. Marsden's *The Officers of the Commons, 1363–1978* (2157) is another study on the Clerk of the House. Two surveys on information services and facilities are Baker's and Rush's *The Member of Parliament and His Information* (2183) and Rush's and Shaw's *The House of Commons: Services and Facilities* (2208).

In compiling this bibliography we had to establish limits. Three topics excluded from the bibliography were studies on the constitution, cabinet, and prime minister. In each case we felt that the amount of material was so large that each category could account for a substantial bibliography in itself. While we included some materials on those topics, especially when they covered the Parliament in detail as well, as a rule they are limited in number. The reader can gain knowledge of those areas by consulting any of the following standard works:

Constitution

Bagehot, Walter. *The English Constitution.*

Dicey, A.V. *An Introduction to the Study of Law of the Constitution.*

Keir, David L. *Constitutional History of Modern Britain Since 1485.*

Maitland, Frederic W. *Constitutional History of England.*

May, Thomas E. *Constitutional History of England.*

Phillips, O. Hood. *Constitutional Law of Great Britain and the Commonwealth.*

Wade, E.C.S., and Phillips, G.G. *Constitutional Law.*

Cabinet

Headey, Bruce W. *British Cabinet Ministers.*

Herman, Valentine, and Alt, James E. *Cabinet Studies: A Reader.*

Jennings, William I. *Cabinet Government.*

Mackintosh, John P. *The British Cabinet.*

Prime Minister

Benemy, Frank. *The Elected Monarch.*

Carter, Byrum. *The Office of Prime Minister.*

King, Anthony. *The Prime Minister: A Reader.*

Mackintosh, John. *British Prime Ministers.*

At the end of the bibliography there is an addendum that contains materials published during the last year and a half, plus British theses completed since 1950. Following the addendum, there is a complete author index and extensive subject index. While the entries are not annotated, the table of contents and subject index can be used to locate information. The table of contents indicates the overall organization of the bibliography and facilitates access to major topics. The subject index can be used to locate materials on major topics and subtopics appearing throughout the bibliography, as well as specific individuals, places, events, and subjects. When an item refers to a specific date or time period, we have included the dates in parentheses immediately following an item number in the subject index.

Though this bibliography is by no means definitive, we hope that it will prove useful to those interested in Parliament. We also hope that this bibliography will promote more intensive research and attention to aspects of parliamentary studies that have not been fully treated in the existing literature.

The Parliament
of Great Britain:
A Bibliography

Reference Works

Political Handbooks and Bibliographies

1. Anderson, Ian G., ed. *Councils, Committees and Boards: A Handbook of Advisory, Consultative, Executive and Similar Bodies in British Public Life.* Beckenham: CBD Research, 1977. 402 pp.
2. Barker, Anthony. "Parlimentary Studies, 1961–65: A Bibliography and Comment." *Political Quarterly* 36 (July 1965): 347–359.
3. Boardman, Robert. *Britain and the International Systems, 1945–1973: A Guide to the Literature.* Halifax: Center for Foreign Policy Studies, Dalhousie University, 1974. 159 pp.
4. Chrimes, S.B., and Roots, I.A. *English Constitutional History: A Select Bibliography.* London: Routledge and Paul, 1958. 38 pp.
5. Cobb, Henry S. *A Handlist of Articles in Periodicals and Other Serial Publications Relating to the History of Parliament.* London: House of Lords Record Office, 1973. 82 pp.
6. Cook, Chris. *Sources in British Political History, 1900–1951.* London: Macmillan, 1975. 5 vols.
7. Hailsham, Quintin M. *Parliament, A Reader's Guide.* London: Cambridge University Press, 1948. 15 pp.
8. Hyland, Henry Stanley. *King and Parliament; a Selected List of Books.* London: Cambridge University Press, 1951. 32 pp.
9. Inter-Parliamentary Union. *Parliaments of the World: A Reference Compendium.* London: Macmillan, 1976. 985 pp.
10. Inter-Parliamentary Union. *World-Wide Bibliography on Parliaments.* Geneva: Inter-Parliamentary Union, 1978. 440 pp.
11. Leeds, Christopher A. *Guide to British Government.* 3d ed. Swanage: Croxten Press, 1978. 172 pp.
12. Palmer, John. *Goverment and Parliament in Britain: A Bibliography.* 2d ed. London: Hansard Society, 1964. 51 pp.
13. Seymour-Ure, Colin. "Bibliography on British Central Government and Politics." In *English Constitution,* edited by. W. Bagehot, pp. 311–353. London: Watts, 1964.
14. Wilding, Norman W., and Laundy, Philip. *An Encyclopedia of Parliament.* 4th rev. ed. London: Cassell, 1972. 931 pp.

15. Willson, Francis M.G. *The Organization of British Central Government 1914–1964*. 2d ed. London: Allen and Unwin, 1968. 521 pp.

Indexes to Documents

16. *Cumulative Index to the Annual Catalogues of HMSO Publications, 1922–1972*. Arlington, Va.: Carrollton Press, 1978. 2 vols.
17. Great Britain. Stationary Office. *Government Publications: Catalogue*. 1923–   .
18. *The Sales Catalogues of British Government Publications 1836–1921*. Dobbs Ferry, N.Y.: Oceana Publications, 1977. 4 vols.

Guides to Documents

19. Bond, Maurice F. *Guide to the Records of Parliament*. London: H.M.S.O., 1971. 352 pp.
20. Brooke, John. *General Index to Reports from Committees of the House of Commons, 1715–1801*. Bishops Stort Ford: Chadwyck-Healy, 1973.
21. Cherns, J.J. *Official Publishing: An Overview*. Oxford: Pergamon Press, 1979. 527 pp.
22. Cornelius, I.V. *British Government Publications: An Introductory Guide*. Stirling: Stirling University Library, 1973. 24 pp.
23. Cromwell, Valerie; O'Leary, Cornelius; Bryan, Keith Lucas; and Wheare, Kenneth C. *Aspects of Government in Nineteenth-Century Britain*. Dublin: Irish University Press, 1978. 134 pp.
24. Erickson, Edgar L. "The Sessional Papers." *Library Journal* 78 (January 1953):13–17.
25. Erickson, Edgar L. "The Sessional Papers: An Epilogue to an Epilogue." *Library Journal* 88 (June 1963):2208–2209.
26. Erickson, Edgar L. "The Sessional Papers: Last Phase." *College and Research Libraries* 21 (September 1960):343–358.
27. Ford, G. *Select List of Reports and Other Papers in the Journals of the House of Commons 1688–1800*. Nendeln: KTO Press, 1976. 120 pp.
28. Ford, G., and Ford, Percy. *Breviate of Parliamentary Papers 1900–1916*. Oxford: Blackwell, 1957. 470 pp.
29. Ford, G., and Ford, Percy. *Breviate of Parliamentary Papers 1917–1939*. Oxford: Blackwell, 1951. 571 pp.
30. Ford, G., and Ford, Percy. *Breviate of Parliamentary Papers 1940–1954*. Oxford: Blackwell, 1961. 515 pp.

31. Ford, G., and Ford, Percy. *A Guide to Parliamentary Papers; What They Are: How to Find Them: How to Use Them.* 3d ed. Shannon: Irish University Press, 1972. 87 pp.
32. Ford, G., and Ford, Percy. *Select List of British Parliamentary Papers 1833-1899.* Oxford: Blackwell, 1953. 165 pp.
33. Ford, G., Ford, Percy, and Marshallsay, Diana. *Select List of British Parliamentary Papers 1955-1964.* Rev. ed. Shannon: Irish University Press, 1970. 117 pp.
34. Ford, Percy. *Ford List of British Parliamentary Papers, 1965-1974, Together with Specialist Commentaries.* Nendeln: KTO Press, 1979. 452 pp.
35. *Hansard's Catalog and Breviate of Parlimentary Papers, 1696-1834.* Oxford: Blackwell, 1953. 220 pp.
36. Holland, David. "British Official Publications." *Aslib Proceedings* 26 (July/August 1974):274-281.
37. Holland, David, and Edge, Susan. "British Government Publications." In *The Uses of Economic Literature,* edited by John Fletcher, pp. 75-88. Hamden, Conn.: Archon Books, 1971.
38. Hughes, Christopher J. *The British Statute Book.* London: Hutchinson's University Library, 1957. 168 pp.
39. Johansson, Eve. *Current British Government Publishing.* London: Association of Assistant Librarians, 1978. 64 pp.
40. Lewis, Peter R. *The Literature of the Social Sciences: An Introductory Survey and Guide.* London: Library Association, 1960. 222 pp.
41. Marshallsay, D.M. "Exploiting the Official Publications of the United Kingdom." In *Uses of Social Sciences Literature,* edited by N. Roberts, pp. 261-285. Boston: Butterworth, 1973.
42. Marshallsay, D.M., Smith, J.H. *Ford List of Parliamentary Papers, 1965-1974.* Nendeln: KTO Press, 1978. 452 pp.
43. Morgan, A. Mary. *British Publications: An Index to Chairmen and Authors, 1941-1946.* London: Library Association, 1969. 198 pp.
44. Morgan, A. Mary, and Stephen, Lorna R., comps. *British Government Publications, An Index to Chairmen, 1967-1971.* London: Library Association, Reference, Special and Information Section, 1976. 40 pp.
45. Moys, Elizabeth M., ed. *Manual of Law Librarianship: The Use and Organization of Legal Literature.* Boulder, Colo.: Westview Press, 1976. 733 pp.
46. Olle, James G. *An Introduction to British Government Publication.* 2d ed. London: Association of Assistant Librarians, 1973. 175 pp.

47. O'Neill, T.P. *British Parliamentary Papers: A Monograph on Blue Books.* Shannon: Irish University Press, 1968. 31 pp.
48. Pemberton, John E. *British Official Publications.* 2d ed. New York: Pergamon Press, 1973. 328 pp.
49. Richard, Stephen. "The Publications of British National Para-Governmental Organizations." *Government Publications Review* 5 (1978):399–408.
50. Rodgers, Frank, and Phelps, Rose B. *A Guide to Parliamentary Papers, #82.* Urbana: University of Illinois Graduate School of Library Science, 1967. 35 pp.
51. Rogers, Frank. *Serial Publications in the British Parliamentary Papers, 1900–1968: A Bibliography.* Chicago: American Library Association, 1971. 146 pp.
52. Smith, Barbara E. "British Official Publications—I. Scope and Substance." *Government Publications Review* 4 (1977):201–208.
53. Smith, Barbara E. "British Official Publications—II. Publication and Distribution." *Government Publications Review* 5 (1978): 1–12.
54. Smith, Barbara E. "British Official Publications—III. Accessibility and Use." *Government Publications Review* 6 (1979):11–18.
55. Stavely, Ronald, and Piggott, Mary. *Government Information and the Research Worker.* 2d ed. London: The Library Association, 1965. 267 pp.
56. Temperly, Harold W.V., and Penson, Lillian M. *A Century of Diplomatic Blue Books, 1814–1914.* Cambridge: Cambridge University Press, 1938. 600 pp.
57. Vogel, Robert. *A Breviate of British Diplomatic Blue Books: 1919–1939.* Montreal: McGill University Press, 1963. 474 pp.

Election Statistics

58. Bloomfield, Valerie. *Commonwealth Elections, 1945–1970: A Bibliography.* London: Mansell Information Publishing, 1976. 306 pp.
59. Craig, F.W.S., comp. *Boundaries of Parliamentary Constituencies, 1885–1972.* Chichester: Political Reference Publications, 1972. 212 pp.
60. Craig, F.W.S., comp. *British Electoral Facts, 1832–1980.* 4th ed. Chichester: Parliamentary Research Services, 1981. 201 pp.
61. Craig, F.W.S., comp. *British General Election Manifestos 1900–1974.* Rev. and enl. ed. London: Macmillan, 1975. 484 pp.
62. Craig, F.W.S. *British Parliamentary Election Results, 1832–1885.* London: Macmillan, 1977. 692 pp.

63. Craig, F.W.S. *British Parliamentary Election Results, 1885–1918.* London: Macmillan, 1974. 698 pp.
64. Craig, F.W.S. *British Parliamentary Election Results, 1918–1949.* Rev. ed. London: Macmillan, 1977. 785 pp.
65. Craig, F.W.S., comp. *British Parliamentary Election Results, 1950–1970.* Chichester: Political Reference Publications, 1971. 780 pp.
66. Craig, F.W.S., comp. *Minor Parties at British Parlimentary Elections, 1885–1974.* London: Macmillan, 1975. 147 pp.
67. Hand, Geoffrey; Georgel, Jacques; and Sasse, Christopher. *European Electoral Systems Handbook.* London: Butterworth, 1979. 252 pp.
68. Kinnear, Michael. *The British Voter; an Atlas and Survey Since 1885.* 2d ed. London: Batsford, 1981. 173 pp.
69. Mackie, Thomas T., and Rose, Richard. *The International Almanac of Electoral History.* London: Macmillan, 1974. 434 pp.
70. Rokkan, Stein, ed. *International Guide to Electoral Statistics: Vol. 1: National Elections in Western Europe.* The Hague: Mouton, 1969. 346 pp.
71. Rose, Richard, ed. *Electoral Behavior: A Comparative Handbook.* New York: Free Press, 1974. 753 pp.

Statistical Sources

72. Buston, N.K., and Mackay, D.I. *British Employment Statistics: A Guide to Sources and Methods.* Oxford: Basil Blackwell, 1977.
73. Comford, A.F., and Loveless, C. *Guide to Government Data: A Survey of Unpublished Social Science Material in Libraries of Government Departments in London.* London: Macmillan, 1974. 404 pp.
74. *Directory of Research Resources in the United Kingdom for Business, Industry and Public Affairs.* London: Library Associates, 1970. 62 pp.
75. Edwards, Bernhard. *Sources of Social Statistics.* London: Heinemann, 1970. 276 pp.
76. Halsey, A.H., ed. *Trends in British Society Since 1900: A Guide to the Changing Structure of Britain.* London: Macmillan, 1972. 578 pp.
77. Harvey, Joan M. *Sources of Statistics.* 2d ed., rev. and enl. London: C. Bingley, 1971. 126 pp.
78. Holland. D.C.L., and Edge, Susan. "British Government Publications." In *The Use of Economic Literature,* edited by John Fletcher, pp. 75–88. Hamden, Conn.: Archon Books, 1971.
79. Kendall, Maurice G., ed. *The Sources and Nature of the Statistics*

of the United Kingdom. London: Oliver & Boyd, 1952–1957. 2 vols.

80. Lawton, Richard, ed. *The Census and Social Structure: An Interpretative Guide to Nineteenth Century—Censuses for England and Wales.* London: Frank Cass, 1978. 330 pp.

81. Lee, Clive H. *British Regional Employment Statistics, 1841–1971.* Cambridge: Cambridge University Press, 1979. 200 pp.

82. Maltby, Arthur. *Economics and Commerce: The Sources of Information and Their Organization.* London: Glive Bingley, 1968. 239 pp.

83. Maunder, W.F., ed. *Reviews of United Kingdom Statistical Sources.* London: Heinemann, 1974–1976. 9 vols.

84. Mitchell, Brian R. *Abstract of British Historical Statistics.* Cambridge: Cambridge University Press, 1962. 513 pp.

85. Mitchell, Brian R. *European Historical Statistics 1750–1975.* 2d rev. ed. New York: Macmillan, 1980. 868 pp.

86. Palmer, Stanley H. *Economic Arithmetic: A Guide to the Statistical Sources of English Commerce, Industry and Finance, 1700–1850.* New York: Garland Publishing, 1977. 207 pp.

87. Pickett, Kathleen G. *Sources of Official Data.* London: Longmans, 1974. 158 pp.

88. Sergeant, Graham. *A Statistical Sourcebook for Sociologists.* London: Macmillan, 1972. 142 pp.

89. Sillitoe, Alan F. *Britain in Figures: A Handbook of Social Statistics.* 2d ed. Harmondsworth: Penguin, 1973. 187 pp.

90. Westfall, Gloria. "British Statistical Information." *Government Publications Review* 3 (1976):123–132.

Biographical Directories

91. Baylen, Joseph O., and Gossman, Norman J., eds. *Biographical Dictionary of Modern British Radicals.* Hassocks, England: Harvester Press, 1979– .

92. *The Business Background of MPs.* London: Parliamentary Profiles, 1958– .

93. *Dictionary of Labour Biography.* London: Macmillan, 1972– .

94. *Dictionary of National Biography.* London: Oxford University Press, 1885–1960. 73 vols.

95. *Directory of the Current Governments of the United Kingdom and the Nations of the Commonwealth.* Dallas: Political Research, 1979– .

96. Roth, Andrew, and Kerbey, Janice. *The MPs' Chart.* London: Parliamentary Profiles, 1965– .

97. Shipley, Peter. *Directory of Pressure Groups and Representative Associations.* 2d ed. New York: Bowker, 1979. 123 pp.
98. Stenton, Michael. *Who's Who of British Members of Parliament: A Biographical Dictionary of the House of Commons Based on Annual Volumes of Dod's Parliamentary Companion and Other Sources.* Atlantic Highlands, N.J.: Humanities Press, 1976– .
99. *Who's Who in History.* Oxford: Blackwell, 1960–1974. 5 vols.

Dictionaries

100. Abraham, L.A., and Hawtry, S.C. *A Parliamentary Dictionary.* 3d ed. London: Butterworth, 1970. 248 pp.
101. Brendon, John A., ed. *A Dictionary of British History.* London: E. Arnold, 1937. 603 pp.
102. Cowic, Leonard W. *A Dictionary of British Social History.* London: Bell, 1973. 326 pp.
103. Golding, Louis. *Dictionary of Local Government in England and Wales.* London: English Universities Press, 1962. 446 pp.
104. Huggett, Frank E. *A Dictionary of British History 1815–1973.* Oxford: Blackwell, 1974. 297 pp.
105. Richardson, John. *The Local Historian's Encyclopedia.* New Barnet: Historical Publications, 1975. 312 pp.
106. Steinberg, S.H., and Evans, I.H., eds. *Steinberg's Dictionary of British History.* 2d ed. London: E. Arnold, 1970. 421 pp.

Social and Economic Bibliographies

107. Ashford, Douglas E.; Katzenstein, Peter J.; and Pempel, T.J. *Comparative Public Policy: A Cross National Bibliography.* Beverly Hills, Calif.: Sage, 1978. 272 pp.
108. Bain, G.S., and Woolven, G.B. *A Bibliography of British Industrial Relations.* Cambridge: Cambridge University Press, 1979. 665 pp.
109. Blackstone, Tessa. *Social Policy and Administration in Britain: A Bibliography.* London: F. Pinter, 1975, 130 pp.
110. Brittain, J. Michael, and Roberts, Stephen A. *Inventory of Information Resources in the Social Sciences.* Farnborough: Saxon House, 1975. 239 pp.
111. Chaloner, W.J., and Richardson, R.C. *British Economic and Social History.* Manchester: Manchester University Press, 1976. 129 pp.
112. Cherns, Albert. *Using the Social Sciences.* London: Routledge and Kegan Paul, 1979. 502 pp.

113. Hamilton, F.E. Ian. *Regional Economic Analysis in Britain and the Commonwealth; a Bibliographic Guide.* London: Weidenfeld and Nicolson, 1969. 410 pp.

114. Higgs, Henry. *Bibliography of Economics 1751–1775.* New York: Macmillan, 1935. 743 pp.

115. Westergaard, John H. *Modern British Society: A Bibliography.* 2d ed. London: F. Pinter, 1977. 131 pp.

116. Williams, Judith B. *A Guide to the Printed Materials for English Social and Economic History, 1750–1850.* New York: Columbia University Press, 1926. 2 vols.

Historical Bibliographies

117. Bell, S. Peter. *Dissertations on British History, 1815–1914; An Index to British and American Theses.* Metuchen, N.J.: Scarecrow Press, 1974. 232 pp.

118. Brown, Lucy M., and Christie, Ian Ralph, eds. *Bibliography of British History 1789–1851.* London: Oxford University Press, 1977. 759 pp.

119. Bruce. A.P.C. *An Annotated Bibliography of the British Army, 1660–1914.* New York: Garland Publishing, 1975. 255 pp.

120. Conference on British Studies. *Anglo-Norman England, 1066–1154.* London: Cambridge University Press, 1969. 83 pp.

121. Conference on British Studies. *Late-Medieval England, 1377–1485.* Cambridge: Cambridge University Press, 1976. 143 pp.

122. Conference on British Studies. *Modern England, 1901–1970.* Cambridge: Cambridge University Press, 1976. 109 pp.

123. Conference on British Studies. *Restoration England, 1660–1689.* Cambridge: Cambridge University Press, 1971. 114 pp.

124. Conference of British Studies. *Tudor England, 1485–1603.* London: Cambridge University Press, 1968. 115 pp.

125. Conference on British Studies. *Victorian England, 1837–1901.* Cambridge: Cambridge University Press, 1970. 100 pp.

126. Davies, Godfrey. *Bibliography of British History: Stuart Period, 1603–1714.* 2d ed. Oxford: Clarendon Press, 1977. 734 pp.

127. Graves, Edgar B. *A Bibliography of English History to 1485.* Oxford: Clarendon Press, 1975. 1103 pp.

128. Gross, Charles. *A Bibliography of British Municipal History Including Gilds and Parliamentary Representation.* 2d ed. Leicester: Leicester University Press, 1966. 461 pp.

129. Hanham, Harold J., ed. *Bibliography of British History 1851–1914.* London: Oxford University Press, 1976. 1606 pp.

130. Harrison, J.F.C., and Thompson, D. *Bibliography of the Chartist Movement, 1837–1976.* Brighton, Sussex: Harvester Press, 1978. 214 pp.

131. Higham, Robin, ed. *A Guide to the Sources of British Military History.* Berkeley: University of California Press, 1978. 630 pp.

132. Johnson, Robert C. "Parliamentary Diaries of the Early Stuart Period." *Institute of Historical Research Bulletin* 44 (November 1971):293–300.

133. Kanner, Barbara. *The Women of England from Anglo-Saxon Times to the Present: Interpretive Bibliographic Essays.* Hamden, Conn.: Archon Books, 1979. 429 pp.

134. Madden, Lionel. *How to Find Out About the Victorian Period: A Guide to Sources of Information.* New York: Pergamon Press, 1970. 173 pp.

135. Mowat, Charles L. *Great Britain Since 1914.* Ithaca, N.Y.: Cornell University Press, 1971. 224 pp.

136. Nicholls, David. *Nineteenth Century Britain, 1815–1914.* Hamden, Conn.: Archon Books, 1978. 170 pp.

137. Pargellis, Stanley, and Medley, D.J. *Bibliography of British History: The Eighteenth Century, 1714–1789.* Oxford: Clarendon Press, 1951. 642 pp.

138. Read, Conyers. *Bibliography of British History: Tudor Period 1485–1603.* 2d ed. Oxford: Clarendon Press, 1959. 467 pp.

139. Ritchenson, Charles R., and Hargrave, O.T. *Current Research in British Studies: By American and Canadian Scholars.* Dallas: Southern Methodist University Press, 1969. 2 vols.

140. Snape, Wilfrid H. *How to Find Out About Local Government.* Oxford: Pergamon Press, 1969. 173 pp.

141. Ward, A.W., and Gooch, G.P., eds. *The Cambridge History of British Foreign Policy, 1783–1919.* Cambridge: Cambridge University Press, 1922–1923. 3 vols.

Historical Handbooks

142. Butler, David, and Sloman, Anne. *British Political Facts 1900–1975* 4th ed. London: Macmillan, 1975. 432 pp.

143. Cook, Chris, and Brendon, Keith. *British Historical Facts, 1830–1900.* London: Macmillan, 1975. 279 pp.

144. Cook, Chris, and Paxton, John. *Commonwealth Political Facts.* New York: Facts on File, 1978. 293 pp.

145. Powell, Ken, and Cook, Chris. *English Historical Facts: 1485–1603* Totowa, N.J.: Roman and Littlefield, 1977. 228 pp.

Public Opinion

146. Gallup, George H. *The Gallup International Public Opinion Polls;
     Great Britain 1937–1975,* New York: Random House, 1976. 2 vols.
147. *NOP Political Bulletin.* London: National Opinion Polls, 1963–1975.
148. *Political Social Economic Review.* London: NOP Market Research,
     1975–   .

Atlases

149. Cook, Chris, and Stevenson, John. *The Longman Atlas of Modern
     British History: A Visual Guide to British Society and Politics,
     1700–1900.* London: Longman, 1978. 208 pp.
150. Gilbert, Martin. *British History Atlas.* New York: Macmillan, 1971.
     118 pp.
151. *Oxford Atlas of Britain and Northern Ireland.* Oxford: Clarendon
     Press, 1963. 200 pp.
152. Readers' Digest Association. *Complete Atlas of the British Isles.*
     London: Readers' Digest, 1965. 229 pp.

Indexes

153. *Annual Bibliography of British and Irish History.* Atlantic High-
     lands, N.J.: Humanities Press, 1975–   .
154. *British Humanities Index.* 1962–   .
155. *Humanities Index.* 1974–   .
156. *International Political Science Abstracts.* 1951–   .
157. Royal Historical Society. *Writings on British History, 1901–1933.*
     5 vols. 1968–1970. Continued by *Writings on British History,
     1934–   .*
158. *Social Sciences Index.* 1974–   .
159. *United States Political Science Documents.* 1975–   .

Parliament

Origins and Development of Parliament

General Studies on Parliament

160. Aikin, C. "British Bureaucracy and the Origins of Parliamentary Policy." *American Political Science Review* 33 (February/April 1939):26–46, 219–233.

161. Allen, Agnes. *The Story of Our Parliament.* London: Faber and Faber, 1952. 192 pp.

162. Bailey, Sidney D. *British Parliamentary Democracy.* London: Harrap, 1971. 248 pp.

163. Bailey, Sidney D. *Parliamentary Government: A British Council Study Booklet.* 2d ed. London: The British Council, 1958. 39 pp.

164. Bassett, R. " British Parliamentary Government To-Day." *Political Quarterly* 23 (October 1952):380–389.

165. Bateman, Charles D. *Your Parliament.* Oxford: Pergamon Press 1968. 168 pp.

166. Battley, John. *A Visit to the Houses of Parliament.* 2d. ed. Westminster: Westminster City Publishing, 1949. 171 pp.

167. Beloff, Max. "Parliament in Britain: Changing System." *United Asia* 22 (March/April 1970): 75–78.

168. Benstead, C.R. *Mother of Parliaments: A Profound Study of A Cherished Institution.* London: Muller, 1948. 147 pp.

169. Boardman, Harry. *The Glory of Parliament.* Edited by Francis Boyd. London: Allen and Unwin, 1960. 208 pp.

170. Bodet, Gerald P., comp. *Early English Parliaments: High Courts, Royal Councils, or Representative Assemblies.* Boston: Heath, 1968. 107 pp.

171. Brocklebank-Fowler, Christopher. "Parliament at Westminster— Image and Reality." *Parliamentarian* 55 (January 1974):13–16.

172. Brown, W.J. *Everybody's Guide to Parliament.* 2d ed. London: Allen and Unwin, 1946. 199 pp.

173. Butt, Ronald. *The Power of Parliament.* 2d ed. London: Constable, 1969. 500 pp.

174. Cain, Thomas. *Pageant of Parliament.* London: University of London Press, 1948. 160 pp.

175. Cam, Helen M. "Parliamentary Writs de Expensis of 1258; with Latin Text." *English Historical Review* 46 (October 1931):630–632.

176. Catlin, George E.G. "Septicentenarian Parliament." *Political Studies* 14 (June 1966):191–199.

177. Cocks, Bernard. *The Parliament at Westminster.* London: Arnold, 1948. 192 pp.

178. Cox, Geoffrey. *Parliament.* London: News Chronicle, 1951. 40 pp.

179. Cox, H. "Decay of Parliament." *English Review* 48 (January 1929): 20–26.

180. Crick, Bernard R. "Parliament in the British Political System." In *Legislatures in Development Perspective,* edited by Allan Kornberg and Lloyd D. Musolf, pp. 33–54. Durham, N.C.: Duke University Press, 1970.

181. Crick, Bernard R., and Jenkinson, Sally. *Parliament and These People.* London: H. Hamilton, 1966. 128 pp.

182. "The Decline of Parliament." *Political Quarterly* 34 (July/September 1963):233–239.

183. De la Cour, P. "Parliamentary Threat to Freedom." *Law Society's Gazette* 64 (September/December 1967): 496, 557, 620, 670.

184. Dunnico, Herbert. *Mother of Parliaments.* London: Macdonald, 1951. 80 pp.

185. Eden, Guy. *The Parliament Book.* 2d ed. London: Staples Press, 1953. 162 pp.

186. Elsynge, Henry. *The Manner of Holding Parliaments in England.* Shannon: Irish University Press, 1971. 293 pp.

187. Fellowes, Edward. "The History of Parliament." *Parliamentary Affairs* 17 (Autumn 1964): 450–452.

188. Ford, Edgar John William. *700 Years of Parliament: Over 500 Entertaining and Instructive Questions with Answers.* Ifracomb: Stockwell, 1965. 147 pp.

189. Fox, F. *Parliamentary Government: A Failure?* London: S. Paul, 1928. 129 pp.

190. Fryde, E.B., and Miller, Edward, eds. *Historical Studies of the English Parliament.* Cambridge: Cambridge University Press, 1970. 2 vols.

191. Gneist, Rudolf von. *The English Parliament in Its Transformation Through a Thousand Years.* London: H. Grevel, 1886. 380 pp.

192. Gordon, Strathearn. *Our Parliament.* Rev. and enl. ed. London: Cassell, 1964. 261 pp.

193. Granada Television Network. *The State of the Nation-Parliament:*

A *Granada Television Enquiry Into the Working of Parliament.*
London: Granada Television, 1973. 272 pp.
194. Hailsham, Quintin M. *The Purpose of Parliament.* London: Blandford Press, 1946. 198 pp.
195. Hall, H.D. "The Community of the Parliaments of the British Commonwealth." *American Political Science Review* 36 (December
1942):1128–1135.
196. Hansard Society for Parliamentary Government. *Lords and Commons: How Parliament Began and How It Works.* London: The
Hansard Society, 1954. 24 pp.
197. Hansard Society for Parliamentary Government. *Parliament Through
Seven Centuries: Reading and Its M.P.s.* London: Cassell, 1962.
126 pp.
198. Hansard Society for Parliamentary Government. *A Visit to Parliament.* London: The Hansard Society, 1960. 11 pp.
199. Hanson, Albert Henry. "The Purpose of Parliament." *Parliamentary Affairs* 17 (Summer 1964):279–295.
200. Hardie, Frank M., and Pollard, Robert S.W. *Lords and Commons.*
London: Fabian Publications, 1948. 37 pp.
201. Heath, Edward. *Parliament and People.* London: Conservative
Political Centre, 1960. 31 pp.
202. Hemingford, Dennis Herbert H. *What Parliament Is and Does,
Being an Introduction to Parliamentary Government in the
United Kingdom.* 2d ed. Cambridge: Cambridge University
Press, 1948. 117 pp.
203. Herbert, Alan P. *The Point of Parliament.* 2d ed. London: Methuen,
1947. 111 pp.
204. Hill, Andrew, and Whichelow, Anthony. *What's Wrong with Parliament?* Harmondsworth: Penguin Books, 1964. 102 pp.
205. Hodgson, Patricia. *Parliament in Close-Up.* London: Bow Publications, 1972. 17 pp.
206. Hodson, H.L. "Parliament at Work." *British Magazine* 1 (May
1946):24–26.
207. Hollis, Christopher. *Can Parliament Survive?* London: Hollis and
Carter, 1949. 148 pp.
208. Hollis, Christopher. "The Function of Parliament." *Twentieth Century* 162 (October 1957):309–315.
209. Hollis, Christopher. *Has Parliament a Future?* London: Liberal
Publication Department, 1960. 13 pp.
210. Howarth, Patrick. *Questions in the House: The History of a Unique
British Institution.* London: Lane, 1956. 220 pp.
211. Humphreys, Mary Eleanor Beggs. *The Story of Parliament.* London:
Allen and Unwin, 1962. 35 pp.

212. Hyland, Henry Stanley. *Curiosities from Parliament.* London: A. Wingate, 1955. 211 pp.
213. Ilbert, Courtney P. *Parliament: Its History, Constitution and Practice.* 3d ed. London: Oxford University Press, 1956. 230 pp.
214. Illingsworth, Frank. *British Parliament.* London: Robinson, Skelton, 1949. 249 pp.
215. Jenkins, Wilfrid John. *Her Majesty's Government.* Exeter: Wheaton, 1967. 137 pp.
216. Jennings, William Ivor. *Parliament.* 2d ed. Cambridge: Cambridge University Press, 1957. 574 pp.
217. Jewell, R.E.C. "Government and Parliament." *The Solicitor* 27 (September 1960):267–270.
218. Keeton, George W. *The Passing of Parliament.* 2d ed. London: Benn, 1954. 218 pp.
219. King, Anthony Stephen. *Westminster and Beyond; Based on the B.B.C. Radio Series 'Talking Politics.'* London: Macmillan, 1973. 175 pp.
220. Laski, Harold J. *Parliamentary Government in England.* London: Allen and Unwin, 1938. 383 pp.
221. Liversidge, Douglas. *Parliament: the Story of the Mother of Parliaments.* London: F. Watts, 1977. 96 pp.
222. Lloyd, Trevor Owen. *The Growth of Parliamentary Democracy in Britain.* Adelaide: Rigby, 1973. 99 pp.
223. MacDonagh, Michael. *The Pageant of Parliament.* London: T.F. Unwin, 1921. 2 vols.
224. MacDonald, James R. *Parliament and Democracy.* London: National Labor Press, 1920. 75 pp.
225. MacDonald, James R. *Parliament and Revolution.* New York: Scott and Seltzer, 1920. 180 pp.
226. Mackenzie, Kenneth R. *The English Parliament.* Harmondsworth: Penguin Books, 1963. 208 pp.
227. Mackintosh, John P. "The British Parliament." In *European Parliament. Symposium on European Integration and the Future of Parliaments in Europe, Luxembourg, 1974,* pp. 156–168. Luxembourg: European Parliament, 1975.
228. Mackintosh, John P. "How Much Time Left for Parliamentary Democracy?" *Encounter* 43 (August 1974):48–52.
229. Mackintosh, John P. *People and Parliament.* Farnborough, Eng.: Saxon House, 1978. 214 pp.
230. March, Roman Robert. "An Empirical Test of M. Ostrogorski's Theory of Political Evolution in a British Parliamentary System." Ph.D. dissertation, Indiana University, 1968. 217 pp.
231. Margach, James C. *How Parliament Works.* London: Tom Stacey, 1972. 143 pp.

232. McKenna, J.W. "Myth of Parliamentary Sovereignty in Late-Medieval England." *English Historical Review* 94 (July 1979):481–506.

233. Menhennet, David and Palmer, John. *Parliament in Perspective.* London: Bodley, Head, 1967. 156 pp.

234. Miller, Harris N. "Future Research on Parliament." In *New Trends in British Politics: Issues for Research,* edited by Dennis Kavanagh and Richard Rose, pp. 123–139. Beverly Hills, Calif.: Sage, 1977.

235. Mitchell, Harry, and Birt, Phyllis. *Who Does What in Parliament, 1975.* London: Westminster Bookstall, 1976. 96 pp.

236. Morrison, Herbert Stanley. "British Parliamentary Democracy." *Parliamentary Affairs* 2 (Autumn 1949):349–360.

237. Morrison, Herbert Stanley. *Government and Parliament: A Survey from the Inside.* 3d ed. London: Oxford University Press, 1964. 384 pp.

238. Morrison, Herbert Stanley, et al. *Parliamentary Government in Britain: A Symposium.* London: Hansard Society, 1949. 105 pp.

239. Mount, F. "Anglo-Saxon Political Values; a Crisis of Confidence." *Round Table* 253 (January 1974):95–108.

240. Norris, Herbert W. *One From Seven Hundred: A Year in the Life of Parliament.* Oxford: Pergamon Press, 1966. 131 pp.

241. O'Hagan, Lord. "Purpose of Parliament." *Contemporary Review* 230 (April 1977):175–180.

242. Pendrill, C. "Old Parliament Nicknames." *National Review* 124 (June 1945):509–512.

243. Pollard, Albert Frederick. *The Evolution of Parliament.* 2d ed. London: Longmans, Green, 1926. 459 pp.

244. Pollard, Albert Frederick. "The Growth of an Imperial Parliament." In his *The Commonwealth at War,* pp. 149–177. London: Longmans, Green, 1917.

245. Pollock, J.K. "Position of the British Parliament." *American Political Science Review* 25 (April 1931):683–689.

246. Powell, John Enoch. *Great Parliamentary Occasions.* London: H. Jenkins, 1960. 125 pp.

247. Pryce, Roy. *How to Visit the British.* London: The Hansard Society, 1956. 12 pp.

248. Raison, Timothy. *Power and Parliament.* Oxford: Basil Blackwell, 1979. 122 pp.

249. Rasmussen, Jorgen Scott. "Problems of Democratic Development in Britain: An American View." *Political Quarterly* 35 (October 1964).386–396.

250. Richards, Peter G. *Parliament and Conscience.* London: Allen and Unwin, 1970. 229 pp.

251. Richards, Peter G. *The Study of Parliament.* Southampton: University of Southampton, 1972. 14 pp.
252. Ridley, F.F. "Introductions to British Government." *Parliamentary Affairs* 21 (Spring 1968):178–181.
253. Rooke, Patrick J. *Parliament.* London: Wayland Ltd., 1970. 128 pp.
254. Roskell, John S. "Perspective in English Parliamentary History." *Bulletin of the John Rylands Library* 46 (1963–1964):448–475.
255. Rush, Michael. *Parliament and the Public.* London: Longman, 1976. 140 pp.
256. Schwann, Duncan. *The Spirit of Parliament.* London: A. Rivers, 1908. 201 pp.
257. Shell, Donald R. "Parliamentary Developments." *Parliamentary Affairs* 32 (Summer 1979):243–247.
258. Shrapnel, Norman. *Parliament.* London: Oxford University Press, 1966. 33 pp.
259. Sidebotham, Herbert. "Future of Parliamentary Government." In his *Pillars of the State,* pp. 245–256. London: Nisbet, 1921.
260. Skottowe, Britiffe Constable. *A Short History of Parliament.* London: S. Sonnenschein, 1892. 345 pp.
261. Smalley, George W. "Notes of Parliament." In his *London Letters and Some Others,* pp. 161–256. London: Macmillan, 1890.
262. Smith, G.B. *History of the English Parliament: With an Account of the Parliaments of Scotland and Ireland.* London: Ward, Locke, 1882. 2 vols.
263. Snowman, Daniel. *The Machinery of Government.* London: Liberal Publication Department, 1966. 52 pp.
264. Stewart, Michael. "Power of Parliament." *Contemporary Review* 220 (April 1972):174–178.
265. Todd, Alpheus. *Parliamentary Government in England: Its Origin, Development and Practical Operation.* New ed. London: S. Low, Marston, 1892. 2 vols.
266. Wedgwood, Josiah C. "History of Parliament and of Public Opinion." *Political Quarterly* 5 (October 1934):506–516.
267. Williams, W.T. "The British Parliament and Its Influence." *Inter-Parliamentary Bulletin* 55 (1975):86–91, 89–95.
268. Wright, A., and Smith, P. *Parliament Past and Present: A Popular and Picturesque Account of a Thousand Years in the Palace of Westminster.* London: Hutchinson, 1902. 592 pp.
269. Wymer, Norman. *Behind the Scenes in Parliament.* London: Phoenix House, 1966. 95 pp.
270. Young, Roland A. *The British Parliament.* Evanston, Ill.: Northwestern University Press, 1962. 259 pp.

History of Parliament: Origins to 1600

271. Bayley, C.C. "Campaign of 1375 and the Good Parliament." *English Historical Review* 55 (July 1940):370–383.
272. Bryant, W.N. "Some Earlier Examples of Intercommuning in Parliament, 1340–1348." *English Historical Review* 65 (January 1970):54–58.
273. Cam, Helen M. "From Witness of the Shire to Full Parliament." *Royal Historical Society Transactions* 26 (1944):13–35.
274. Clarke, Maude V. *Medieval Representation and Consent: A Study of Early Parliaments in England and Ireland, with Special Reference to the Modus Tenendi Parliamentum.* London: Longmans, Green, 1936. 408 pp.
275. Coit, William Baer. "The English Parliaments and the English Towns, 1388–1399." Ph.D. dissertation, University of California at Berkeley, 1971. 265 pp.
276. Cooper, J.P. "Supplication Against the Ordinaries Reconsidered." *English Historical Review* 72 (October 1957):616–641.
277. Craig, Robert. *A History of Oratory in Parliament, 1213 to 1913.* London: Heath, Cranton and Ouseley, 1913. 329 pp.
278. Cuttino, G.P. "Mediaeval Parliament Reinterpreted." *Speculum* 41 (October 1966):681–687.
279. Dunham, W.H. "Notes from the Parliament at Winchester, 1449." *Speculum* 17 (July 1942):402–415.
280. Edwards, John Goronwy. *Historians and the Medieval English Parliament.* Glasgow: University of Glasgow, 1960. 52 pp.
281. Edwards, John Goronwy. *The Second Century of the English Parliament.* Oxford: Clarendon Press, 1979. 90 pp.
282. Elton, Geoffrey R. "Commons' Supplication of 1532: Parliamentary Manoeuvres in the Reign of Henry VIII." *English Historical Review* 66 (October 1951):507–534.
283. Elton, Geoffrey R. "Parliament in the Sixteenth Century: Functions and Fortunes." *Historical Journal* 22 (June 1979):255–278.
284. Elton, Geoffrey R. "Rolls of Parliament, 1449–1547." *Historical Journal* 22 (March 1979):1–29.
285. Gilkes, Rosslyn K. *The Tudor Parliament.* London: University of London, 1969. 192 pp.
286. Haskins, George Lee. "Petitions of Representatives in the Parliaments of Edward I." *English Historical Review* 53 (January 1938):1–20.
287. Haskins, George Lee. *The Statute of York and the Interest of the Commons.* Westport, Conn.: Greenwood Press, 1977, c. 1935. 129 pp.

288. Holmes, George A. *The Good Parliament.* Oxford: Clarendon Press, 1975. 206 pp.
289. Jenkinson, C. Hilary. "First Parliament of Edward I." *English Historical Review* 25 (April 1910):231–242.
290. Jenkinson, C. Hilary. "First Parliament of Edward I." *English Historical Review* 58 (October 1943):462–463.
291. Jolliffe, J.E.A. "Some Factors in the Beginnings of Parliament." *Royal Historical Society Transactions* 22 (1940):101–139.
292. Kennedy, W.P.M. "Some Notes on Henry VIII's Parliaments." *American Catholic Quarterly* 41 (October 1916):623–630.
293. Lapsley, Gaillard Thomas. "Archbishop Stratford and the Parliamentary Crisis of 1341." *English Historical Review* 30 (January/April 1915):6–18, 193–215.
294. Lapsley, Gaillard Thomas. "Commons and the Statute of York." *English Historical Review* 28 (January 1913): 118–124.
295. Lapsley, Gaillard Thomas. "Interpretation of the Statute of York." *English Historical Review* 56 (January/July 1941):22–51, 411–446.
296. Lapsley, Gaillard Thomas. "Knights of the Shire in the Parliaments of Edward II." *English Historical Review* 34 (January/April 1919):25–42, 152–171.
297. Lapsley, Gaillard Thomas. "Parliamentary Title of Henry IV." *English Historical Review* 49 (July/October 1934): 423–429, 577–606.
298. Lapsley, Gaillard Thomas. "Richard II's Last Parliament; Rejoinder." *English Historical Review* 53 (January 1938):53–78.
299. Latham, R.C. "Payment of Parliamentary Wages—the Last Phase (in the sixteenth and seventeenth centuries)." *English Historical Review* 66 (January 1951):27–50.
300. Lawson, J. "A Study of the Parliamentary Burgesses During the First Half of the Fifteenth Century, Based on the Returns of London, York, Norwich, Bristol and Southampton Between 1413 and 1437." Master's thesis, University of Manchester, 1936.
301. Lehmberg, Stanford E. "Parliamentary Attainder in the Reign of Henry VIII." *Historical Journal* 18 (December 1975):675–702.
302. Lehmberg, Stanford E. *The Later Parliaments of Henry VIII, 1536-1547.* Cambridge: Cambridge University Press, 1977. 379 pp.
303. Lehmberg, Stanford E. *The Reformation Parliament 1529-1536.* Cambridge: Cambridge University Press, 1970. 282 pp.
304. Mackenzie, Kenneth R. "Simon de Montfort and the Origins of Parliament." *Month* 34 (August 1965):76–83.
305. McCall, J.P., and Rudisill, G. "Parliament of 1386 and Chaucer's Trojan Parliament." *Journal of English and Germanic Philology* 58 (April 1959):276–288.

306. McFarlane, K.B. "Parliament and Bastard Feudalism." *Royal Historical Society Transactions* 26 (1944): 53–79.
307. McKisack, May. "Parliament in the Reign of Richard II." B. Litt., Oxford University, 1924.
308. Marriott, John Arthur Ransome. "Parliament in the Fifteenth Century." *Quarterly Review* 272 (April 1939):189–205.
309. Miller, Edward. *The Origins of Parliament.* London: Routledge and Kegan Paul, 1960. 24 pp.
310. Miller, Helen. "London and Parliament in the Reign of Henry VIII." *Bulletin of Institute Historical Research* 35 (November 1962): 128–149.
311. Morris, W.A. "Date of the Modus Tenendi Parliamentum." *English Historical Review* 49 (July 1934):407–422.
312. Myers, A.R. "A Parliamentary Debate of 1449." *Institute of Historical Research Bulletin* 51 (May 1978) 78–11.
313. Myers, A.R. "Parliamentary Debate of the Mid-Fifteenth Century." *John Rylands Library Bulletin* 22 (October 1938):388–404.
314. Myers, A.R. "Parliamentary Petitions in the Fifteenth Century." *English Historical Review* 52 (July/October 1937):385–404, 590–613.
315. Palmer, J.J.N. "Parliament of 1385 and the Constitutional Crisis of 1386." *Speculum* 46 (July 1971):477–490.
316. Pollard, Albert Frederick. "Authorship and Value of the Anonimalle Chronicle." *English Historical Review* 53 (October 1938): 577–605.
317. Poole, R.L. "Mad Parliament, 1258." *English Historical Review* 40 (July 1925):402.
318. Reel, Jerome Vincent. "The Parliament of 1316." Ph.D. dissertation, Emory University, 1967. 2 vols.
319. Reich, Aloyse Marie. "The Parliamentary Abbots to 1470: A Study in English Constitutional History." In *California Publications in History,* v. 17, no. 4., pp. 265–401. Berkeley: University of California Press, 1941.
320. Richardson, Henry Gerald. "Origins of Parliament." *Historical Society Transactions* 11 (1928):137–183.
321. Richardson, Henry Gerald. *Parliaments and the Great Councils in Medieval England.* London: Stevens, 1961. 49 pp.
322. Richardson, Henry Gerald. "Richard II's Last Parliament." *English Historical Review* 52 (January 1937):39–47.
323. Richardson, Henry Gerald, and Sayles, George O. "Earliest Known Official Use of the Term Parliament." *English Historical Review* 82 (October 1967):747–749.
324. Richardson, Henry Gerald, and Sayles, George O. "Parliament of

Carlisle, 1307—Some New Documents; with Text." *English Historical Review* 53 (July 1938):425–437.

325. Sayles, George O. *The Kings Parliament of England.* New York: Norton, 1974. 164 pp.

326. Smith, Philbrook Wilder. "A Study of the Lists of Military and Parliamentary Summons in the Reign of Edward I: the Families of Lists and Their Significance." Ph.D. dissertation, University of Iowa, 1967. 2 vols.

327. Spufford, Peter. *Origins of the English Parliament.* London: Longmans, 1967. 221 pp.

328. Stock, Leo Francis. "British Parliament in Early Colonial Administration, 1542–1625." Ph.D. dissertation, Catholic University, 1920.

329. Styran, Roberta McAfee. "The Parliament of 1406: A Quest for Good Governance." Ph.D. dissertation, University of Toronto, 1971.

330. Templeman, G. "The History of Parliament to 1400 in the Light of Modern Research." *University of Birmingham Historical Journal* 1 (1947–1948):202–231.

331. Thompson, Faith. *A Short History of Parliament, 1295–1642.* Minneapolis: University of Minnesota Press, 1953. 280 pp.

332. Treharne, R.F. "Nature of Parliament in the Reign of Henry III." *English Historical Review* 74 (October 1959):590–610.

333. Tuck, J.A. "Cambridge Parliament, 1388." *English Historical Review* 84 (April 1969): 225–243.

334. Wedgwood, Josiah C. *History of Parliament, 1439–1509.* London: H.M.S.O., 1936–1938. 2 vols.

335. Wilkinson, B. "Deposition of Richard II and the Accession of Henry IV." *English Historical Review* 54 (April 1939): 215–239.

History of Parliament: 1600s

336. Abbott, W.C. "The Pensionary or Long Parliament of Charles II." B.Litt., Oxford University, 1897.

337. Anderson, C.B. "Ministerial Responsibility in the 1620s." *Journal of Modern History* 34 (December 1962):381–389.

338. Antler, Steven D. "Quantitative Analysis of the Long Parliament." *Past and Present* 56 (August 1972):154–157.

339. Aylmer, G.E. "Americans and Seventeenth-Century Parliamentmen; Review Article." *History* 52 (October 1967) 287–292.

340. Beddow, J.F.H. "The History of the Fourth Parliament of William III." B. Litt., Oxford University, 1913.

341. Bidwell, William Bradford. "The Committees and Legislation of the Rump Parliament, 1648-1653: A Quantitative Study." Ph.D. dissertation, University of Rochester, 1977. 631 pp.

342. Brett, S.R. "Long Parliament: Historical Background of English Democracy." *Quarterly Review* 275 (July 1940):107-117.

343. Brown, L.F. "Religious Factors in the Convention Parliament of Charles II." *English Historical Review* 22 (January 1907):51-63.

344. Brunton, Douglas, and Pennington, D.H. *Members of the Long Parliament.* London: Allen and Unwin, 1954. 256 pp.

345. Carlson, Leland Henry. "A History of the Presbyterian Party From Pride's Purge to the Dissolution of the Long Parliament." Ph.D. dissertation, University of Chicago, 1940. 206 pp.

346. Cherry, George L. "Role of the Convention Parliament (1688-1689) in Parliamentary Supremacy." *Journal of the History of Ideas* 17 (June 1956):390-406.

347. Christianson, Paul. "From Expectation to Militance: Reformers and Babylon in the First Two Years of the Long Parliament." *Journal of Ecclesiastical History* 24 (July 1973):225-244.

348. Christianson, Paul. "Peers, the People, and Parliamentary Management in the First Six Months of the Long Parliament." *Journal of Modern History* 49 (December 1977):575-599.

349. Cope, Esther Sidney. "Parliament and Proclamations, 1604-1629." Ph.D. dissertation, Bryn Mawr College, 1969.

350. Crawford, P. "Savile Affair." *English Historical Review* 90 (January 1975):76-93.

351. Farnell, J.E. "Aristocracy and Leadership of Parliament in the English Civil Wars." *Journal of Modern History* 44 (March 1972):79-86.

352. Franell, J.E. "Usurpation of Honest London Householders: Barebone's Parliament." *English Historical Review* 82 (January 1967):24-46.

353. Flemion, Jess Stoddart. "Dissolution of Parliament in 1626: a Revaluation." *English Historical Review* 87 (October 1972):784-790.

354. Frear, Mary Reno. "The Personnel of the Commons in the Long Parliament." Ph.D. dissertation, Yale University, 1933. 496 pp.

355. Glow, Lotte. "The Committee-men in the Long Parliament, August 1642-December 1643." *Historical Journal* 8 (1965):1-15.

356. Goldwater, Ellen Davis. "Two Cromwellian Parliaments: Politics, Patronage and Procedure." Ph.D. dissertation, City University of New York, 1973. 456 pp.

357. Greenleaf, W.H. "Filmer's Patriarchal History." *Historical Journal* 9 (1966):157-177.

358. Hanft, Sheldon. "Some Aspects of Puritan Opposition in the First

Parliament of James I (Volumes I and II)." Ph.D. dissertation, New York University, 1969. 2 vols.

359. Helms, Mary Elizabeth. "The Convention Parliament of 1660." Ph.D. dissertation, Bryn Mawr College, 1963. 404 pp.

360. Henning, Basil D. "The Representation of Wiltshire in the Long Parliament of Charles II." Ph.D. dissertation, Yale University, 1937. 165 pp.

361. Hexter, J.H. "Power Struggle, Parliament and Liberty in Early Stuart England." *Journal of Modern History* 50 (March 1978): 1-50.

362. Hollis, Daniel Webster. "The Sale of the Crown Estate, 1640-1660: A Study of the Parliamentary Surveys." Ph.D. dissertation, Vanderbilt University, 1972. 253 pp.

363. Horwitz, Henry. "Parliament and the Glorious Revolution." *Institute of Historical Research Bulletin* 47 (May 1974):36-52.

364. Huntingdon, Henry Hastings. *The Hastings Journal of the Parliament of 1621.* London: Offices of the Royal Historical Society, 1953. 46 pp.

365. Jones, J.R. "Clegate Case." *English Historical Review* 90 (April 1975):262-286.

366. Keeler, Mary F. *The Long Parliament; 1640-1641: A Biographical Study of Its Members.* Philadelphia: American Philosophical Society, 1954. 410 pp.

367. Kershaw, R.N. "Elections for the Long Parliament, 1640." *English Historical Review* 38 (October 1923):496-508.

368. Kishlansky, M.A. "Army and the Levellers: the Roads to Putney." *Historical Journal* 22 (December 1979):795-824.

369. Kishlansky, M.A. "Emergence of Adversary Politics in the Long Parliament." *Journal of Modern History* 49 (December 1977): 617-640.

370. Lacey, Douglas Raymond. *Dissent and Parliamentary Politics in England, 1661-1689: A Study in the Perpetuation and Tempering of Parliamentarianism.* New Brunswick, N.J.: Rutgers University Press, 1969. 520 pp.

371. Lees, R.M. "Parliament and the Proposal for a Council of Trade, 1695-1696; with Text of Correspondence." *English Historical Review* 54 (January 1939):38-66.

372. Liu, Tai. "The Calling of the Barebones Parliament Reconsidered." *Journal of Ecclesiastical History* 22 (July 1971):223-236.

373. M'Arthur, E.A. "Women Petitioners and the Long Parliament." *English Historical Review* 24 (October 1909):698-709.

374. MacCormack, John Ronald. "The Long Parliament House of Commons, 1643-1648." Ph.D. dissertation, University of Toronto, 1961.

375. MacCormack, John Ronald. *Revolutionary Politics in the Long Parliament.* Cambridge, Mass.: Harvard University Press, 1973. 365 pp.
376. Mackintosh, A. *From Gladstone to Lloyd George: Parliament in Peace and War.* London: Hodder and Stoughton, 1921. 333 pp.
377. Magee, B. "First Parliament of Queen Elizabeth." *Dublin Review* 200 (January 1937):60–78.
378. Mensing, Raymond Clarke. "Attitudes on the Religious Toleration as Expressed in English Parliamentary Debates, 1660–1719." Ph.D. dissertation, Emory University, 1970. 237 pp.
379. Moir, Thomas L. *The Addled Parliament of 1614.* Oxford: Clarendon Press, 1958. 212 pp.
380. Mulligan, L. "Property and Parliamentary Politics in the English Civil War, 1642-6." *Historical Studies* 16 (1975):341–361.
381. Needels, Martin Davey. "The Revolution Secured Anglo-Scottish Negotiations from the Pacification of Berks until the Scottish Parliament of 1641." Ph.D dissertation, University of Nebraska, 1973. 312 pp.
382. O'Leary, Cornelius. "The Wedgwood Benn Case and the Doctrine of Wilful Perversity." *Political Studies* 13 (February 1965):65–78.
383. Olson, Alison G. "William Penn, Parliament, and Proprietary Government." *William and Mary Quarterly* 18 (April 1961):176–195.
384. Omond, John Stuart. *Parliament and the Army, 1642-1904.* Cambridge: Cambridge University Press, 1933. 187 pp.
385. Palmer, R.L. *English Social History in the Making.* London: Nicholson and Watson, 1934. 243 pp.
386. Pearl, Valerie, "Oliver St. John and the Middle Group in the Long Parliament: August 1643–May 1644." *English Historical Review* 81 (July 1966):490–519.
387. Pinckney, Paul Jan. "A Cromwellian Parliament: the Elections and Personnel of 1656." Ph.D. dissertation, Vanderbilt University, 1962. 380 pp.
388. Roberts, Clayton. "Constitutional Significance of the Financial Settlement of 1690." *Historical Journal* 20 (March 1977):59–76.
389. Roberts, Clayton. "Growth of Ministerial Responsibility to Parliament in Later Stuart England." *Journal of Modern History* 28 (September 1956):215–233.
390. Roberts, Clayton. "Privy Council Schemes and Ministerial Responsibility in Later Stuart England." *American Historical Review* 64 (April 1959):564–582.
391. Roberts, Clayton, and Duncan, Owen. "Parliamentary Undertaking of 1614." *English Historical Review* 93 (July 1978):481–498.
392. Rowe, V.A. "Influence of the Earls of Pembroke, on Parliamentary

Elections, 1625–41." *English Historical Review* 50 (April 1935): 242–256.

393. Rueger, Z. "Gerson, the Conciliar Movement and the Right of Resistance (1642–1644)." *Journal of the History of Ideas* 25 (October 1964):467–486.

394. Russell, Conrad S.R. "Parliamentary History in Perspective, 1604–1629." *History* 61 (February 1976):1–27.

395. Schofield, R.S. "Quantitative Analysis of the Long Parliament." *Past and Present* 68 (August 1975):124–130.

396. Schwoerer, Lois G. "A Journal of the Convention at Westminster Begun the 22 of January 1688/9." *Institute of Historical Research Bulletin* 49 (November 1976):242–263.

397. Sharpe, Kevin, ed. *Faction and Parliament: Essays on Early Stuart History.* Oxford: Clarendon Press, 1978. 292 pp.

398. Shrimp, Robert Everett. "The Parliament of 1625." Ph.D. dissertation, Ohio State University, 1970. 236 pp.

399. Simpson, A. *The Convention Parliament, 1688-9.* D. Phil., Oxford University, 1939, 417pp.

400. Smith, S.R. "Apprentices' Parliament of 1647." *History Today* 22 (August 1972):576–582.

401. Snow, Vernon F. "Parliamentary Reapportionment Proposals in the Puritan Revolution." *English Historical Review* 74 (July 1959): 409–442.

402. Spalding, J.C. "Sermons Before Parliament (1640–1649) As a Public Puritan Diary." *Church History* 36 (March 1967):24–35.

403. Taft, Barbara. "Voting Lists of the Council of Officers, December 1648." *Institute of Historical Research Bulletin* 52 (November 1979):138–154.

404. Thompson, Christopher. "The Origins of the Politics of the Parliamentary Middle Group, 1625–1629." *Royal Historical Society Transactions* 22 (1972):71–86.

405. Tyacke, Nicholas. "Wroth, Cecil and the Parliamentary Session of 1604." *Institute of Historical Research Bulletin* 50 (May 1977): 120–125.

406. Wallace, Willard Mosher. "Sir Edwin Sandys and the First Parliament of James I." Ph.D. dissertation, University of Pennsylvania, 1940. 114 pp.

407. White, Stephen Daniel. "Observations on Early Stuart Parliamentary History." *Journal of British Studies* 18 (Spring 1979):160–170.

408. Whitworth, E.C. "The Parliamentary Franchise in the English Boroughs in the Stuart Period." Master's thesis, University of London, 1926.

409. Williams, C.M. "Extremist Politics in the Long Parliament, 1642–1643." *Historical Studies* 15 (October 1971):136–150.

410. Willson, David Harris. *The Privy Councillors in the House of Commons, 1604–1629.* Minneapolis: University of Minnesota Press, 1940, 332 pp.
411. Woolrych, Austin. "The Calling of Barebone's Parliament." *English Historical Review* 80 (July 1965):492–513.
412. Worden, Blair. "The Bill for a New Representative: the Dissolution of the Long Parliament, April 1653." *English Historical Review* 86 (July 1971):473–496.
413. Worden, Blair. *The Rump Parliament, 1648–1653.* Cambridge: Cambridge University Press, 1974. 427 pp.
414. Zaller, Robert Michael. *The Parliament of 1621: A Study in Constitutional Conflict.* Berkeley: University of California Press, 1971. 242 pp.

History of Parliament: 1700s

415. Bailey, R.C.J.F. "The Parliamentary History of Reading Between 1750 and 1850." Master's thesis, University of Reading, 1944.
416. Cone, C.B. "Parliamenteering and Racing." *The Historian* 37 (May 1975):407–420.
417. Dickinson, H.T. "Eighteenth-Century Debate on the Glorious Revolution." *History* 61 (February 1976):28–45.
418. Dickinson, H.T. "The Eighteenth-Century Debate on the Sovereignty of Parliament." *Royal Historical Society Transactions* 26 (1976):189–210.
419. Downs, Murray Scott. "King, Ministers, and Parliament, 1774–1784." Ph.D. dissertation, Duke University, 1959. 579 pp.
420. Horwitz, Henry. *Parliament, Policy and Politics in the Reign of William III.* Manchester: Manchester University Press, 1977. 385 pp.
421. Kelly, Paul. "British Parliamentary Politics, 1784–1786. *Historical Journal* 17 (December 1974):733–753.
422. McMains, Howard Franklin. "The Parliamentary Opposition to Sir Robert Walpole, 1727–1731." Ph.D. dissertation, Indiana University, 1970. 249 pp.
423. Marini, Alfred J. "Parliament and the Marine Regiments, 1739." *Mariner's Mirror* 62 (February 1976):55–65.
424. Perry, Thomas Whipple. "The Jewish Naturalization Act of 1753: A Study in Parliamentary Politics and Public Opinion in Eighteenth-Century England." Ph.D. dissertation, Harvard University, 1957. 320 pp.
425. Smith, Henry Stooks. *The Parliaments of England, from 1715 to*

1847. 2d ed. Chichester: Political Reference Publications, 1973. 772 pp.

426. Snyder, Henry L. "A New Parliament List for 1711." *Institute for Historical Research Bulletin* 50 (November 1977):185-193.

427. Stubbs, William. "Parliament Under Henry VIII." In his *Seventeen Lectures on the Study of Medieval and Modern History,* pp. 305-304. Oxford: Clarendon Press, 1887.

428. Underdown, P.T. "The Parliamentary History of the City of Bristol, 1750-1790." Master's thesis, University of Bristol, 1948.

History of Parliament: 1800s

429. Aydelotte, William O. "The Business Interests of the Gentry in the Parliament of 1841-47." In *The Making of Victorian England,* edited by G. Kitson Clark, pp. 290-305. London: Methuen, 1962.

430. Bailey, R.C.J.F. "The Parliamentary Representation of Reading During the Eighteenth and Nineteenth Centuries." Master's thesis, University of Reading, 1944.

431. Behrman, Cynthia F. "The Parliament Crisis of 1873: A Comment on the Victorian Constitution." *Parliamentary Affairs* 23 (Spring 1970):184-196.

432. Dickinson, G.L. *Development of Parliament During the Nineteenth Century.* London: Longmans, 1895. 183 pp.

433. Dowse, Robert E. "The Left Wing Opposition During the First Two Labour Governments." *Parliamentary Affairs* 14 (Spring 1961): 229-243.

434. Duncan, Robert Samuel. "British Parliamentary Radicalism, 1886-1895: The Origins and Impact of the Newcastle Program." Ph.D. dissertation, Ohio State University, 1974. 320 pp.

435. Emden, Cecil S., "The Mandate in the Nineteenth Century." *Parliamentary Affairs* 11 (Summer 1958):260-272.

436. Fitzgerald, B. "First Victoria Parliament; with Story of Disraeli's Maiden Speech." *Saturday Review* 152 (December 1931):807-808.

437. Gibson, Edward Hiram. "The Public Health Agitation in England 1838-1848; A Newspaper and Parliamentary History." Ph.D. dissertation, University of North Carolina at Chapel Hill, 1956. 396 pp.

438. Gordon, Barry J. *Political Economy in Parliament, 1819-1823.* New York: Barnes and Noble, 1977. 246 pp.

439. Graham, A.H. "The Parliamentary Candidate Society, 1831." In

Essays Presented to Michael Roberts, edited by John Bossey and
   Peter Jupp, pp. 104–116. Belfast: Blackstaff Press, 1976.
440. Groves, R. "Marx and the Labour Parliament of 1854." *Labour
   Monthly* 12 (March 1930):172–176.
441. Johson, Dorothy C. "Public Opinion and Parliament Since 1832."
   B.Litt., Oxford University, 1922.
442. Lamb, W.K. "British Labour and Parliament, 1867–1893." Ph.D.
   dissertation, London School of Economics and Political Science,
   1934. 682 pp.
443. Lebeau, Sandra Smith. "Pride and Prejudice: the 1867 Parliaments'
   Image of the English Working Classes." Ph.D. dissertation,
   University of Pittsburgh, 1971.
444. Lucy, Henry W. *A Diary of the Home Rule Parliament.* London:
   Cassell, 1896. 488 pp.
445. Lucy, Henry W. *A Diary of the Salisbury Parliament, 1886–92.*
   London: Cassell, 1892. 530 pp.
446. Manley, Jeanne Frances. "Disraeli's Tory Democracy: A Parliamentary Study." Ph.D. dissertation, St. Louis University, 1968.
   307 pp.
447. Martin, Ged. "Empire Federalism and Imperial Parliamentary
   Union, 1820–1870." *Historical Journal* 16 (March 1973):65–92.
448. Newbould, Ian D.C. "The Politics of the Cabinets of Grey and Melbourne and Ministerial Relations With the House of Commons,
   1830–41." Ph.D. dissertation, University of Manchester, 1971.
449. Newbould, Ian D.C. "William IV and the Dismissal of the Whigs,
   1834." *Canadian Journal of History* 11 (December 1976):311–
   330.
450. Nicholls, Robert Lyle. "The Prescriptive Guardian: Parliament and
   Public Morality, 1830–1880." Ph.D. dissertation, University of
   Maryland, 1970. 313 pp.
451. Wexler, Victor G. "David Hume's Discovery of a New Scene of Historical Thought." *Eighteenth-Century Studies* 10 (Winter 1976–
   1977):185–202.
452. Williams, Lance. "Parliamentary General Enclosure from 1790
   Through the General Act of 1845." Ph.D. dissertation, University of Georgia, 1970. 263 pp.
453. Willis, Richard Eugene. "The Politics of Parliament, 1800–1806."
   Ph.D. dissertation, Stanford University, 1969. 370 pp.
454. Woodall, Robert. "Orsini and the Fall of Palmerston." *History
   Today* 26 (October 1976):636–643.
455. Zimmer, L.B. "The Politics of John Stuart Mill and the Second Reform Bill of 1867 Evaluated Against the Background of His
   Political and Moral Philosophy." Ph.D. dissertation, New York
   University, 1970. 2 vols.

History of Parliament: 1900s

456. Chester, Daniel N. "The British Parliament, 1939–66." *Parliamentary Affairs* 19 (Autumn 1966):417–445.
457. Fellowes, Edward. "Changes in Parliamentary Life, 1918–1961." *Political Quarterly* 36 (July 1965):256–265.
458. Jones, Constance McCulloch. "Crisis of Parliamentary Liberalism: Extremism in Britain in the 1930's." Ph.D. dissertation, Duke University, 1974. 258 pp.
459. Lucy, Henry W. *The Balfourian Parliament, 1900–1905.* London: Hodder and Stoughton, 1906. 439 pp.
460. McCreedy, H.H. "The Revolt of the Unionist Free Traders." *Parliamentary Affairs* 16 (Spring 1963):188–206.
461. Punnett, R.M. "The Structure of the Macmillan Government 1957–63." *Quarterly Review* 302 (January 1964):12–23.
462. Richardson, J.J., and Jordan, A.G. *Governing Under Pressure: The Policy Process in a Post-Parliamentary Democracy.* Oxford: Martin Robertson, 1979. 212 pp.
463. Siriex, P.H. "The Deviations of the Parliamentary System of the United Kingdom Since 1911." B. Litt., Oxford University, 1934.
464. White, Gavin. "That Hectic Night: the Prayer Book Debate, 1927–1928." *Theology* 77 (December 1974):639–646.

Comparative Studies

465. Anderson, Bruce L. "Legislative Reform and the Political System: A Survey of British and American Proposals." *South Carolina Journal of Political Science* 4 (1972):88–111.
466. Bottomley, Arthur. "Relationship Between the British Parliament and the European Parliament." *Journal of Parliamentary Information* 21 (1975):553–555.
467. Bradshaw, Kenneth, and Pring, David. *Parliament and Congress.* New ed. London: Quartet, 1981. 500 pp.
468. Campion, Gilbert Francis Montrion, and Lidderdale, D.W.S. *European Parliamentary Procedure.* London: Allen and Unwin, 1953. 270 pp.
469. Chauhan, D.N.S., and Chopra, S.L. "Socio-economic Background of the Legislators in Great Britain, India and the USA." *Journal of Constitutional and Parlimentary Studies* 3 (1969):120–125.
470. Frankland, E. Gene. "Cross-National Determinants of Parliamentary Career Advancement: Britain and West Germany." Ph.D. dissertation, University of Iowa, 1973. 195 pp.

471. Frankland, E. Gene. "Parliamentary Career Achievement in Britain and West Germany: A Comparative Analysis." *Legislative Studies Quarterly* 2 (May 1977):137–154.

472. Galloway, George B. *Congress and Parliament: Their Organization and Operation in the U.S. and the U.K.* Washington: National Planning Association, 1955. 105 pp.

473. Greenwood, Lord. "MPs and MEPs at Westminster." *Parliamentarian* 60 (October 1979):216–218.

474. King, Anthony Stephen. "Modes of Executive-Legislative Relations: Great Britain, France and West Germany." *Legislative Studies Quarterly* 1 (February 1976):11–36.

475. Laing, L.H. "The Transplantation of the British Parliament." *Parliamentary Affairs* 11 (Autumn 1958):405–423.

476. Lazar, H. "British Populism: the Labour Party and the Common Market Parliamentary Debate." *Political Science Quarterly* 91 (Summer 1976):259–277.

477. Lewis, Stuart. "Corrupt Practices in British Parliamentary and American Congressional Elections." Ph.D. dissertation, American University, 1923.

478. Ling, B. "Parliaments and the Peace Treaty: A Comparative Study of the Reactions of the British and French Parliaments to the Treaty of Peace of 1919." Ph.D. dissertation, London School of Economics and Political Science, 1938.

479. Lodge, Juliet. "Members of the House of Commons and the European Parliament." *Parliamentarian* 59 (October 1978):239–246.

480. Low, A.M. "Legislative Procedure in Two Anglo-Saxon Countries." *American Political Science Review* 8 (February 1914): 148–154.

481. Mapor, J.R. "Payment of the Deputies to the French National Assemblies, 1484–1627." *Journal of Modern History* 27 (September 1955):217–229.

482. Markesinis, B. *The Theory and Practice of Dissolution of Parliament: A Comparative Study with Special Reference to the United Kingdom and Greek Experience.* Cambridge: Cambridge University Press, 1972. 283 pp.

483. Needler, M. "On the Dangers of Copying from the British." *Political Science Quarterly* 77 (September 1962):379–396.

484. Russett, Bruce M. "International Communication and Legislative Behavior: the Senate and the House of Commons." In *Comparative Legislative Systems: A Reader in Theory and Research,* edited by Herbert Hirsch and M. Donald Hancock, pp. 140–159. New York: Free Press, 1971.

485. Shakdher, S.L. *The Commonwealth Parliaments.* New Delhi: Government of India Press, 1975. 249 pp.

486. Shakdher, S.L. *Comparative Study of Financial Procedure in Parliament in U.K. and India*. New Delhi: Government of India Press, 1968. 14 pp.

487. Shakdher, S.L. *Two Estimates Committees (U.K. and India)*. New Delhi: Government of India Press, 1959. 43 pp.

488. Shakdher, S.L. "Two Systems of Financial Procedure in Parliament (U.K. and India)." *Parliamentary Affairs* 6 (Summer 1953): 288–298.

489. Shaw, Malcolm. "Parliament and Congress." *Parliamentarian* 50 (April 1969):83–91.

490. Stamps, N.L. "Comparative Study of Legislative Investigations: England, France, and Weimar Germany." *Journal of Politics* 14 (November 1952):592–615.

491. Stephens, David. "The Private Member of Parliament Under the British, French and US Congressional Systems of Government." *Constitutional and Parliamentary Information* 105 (1976):1–28.

492. Wahlke, John C. "Policy Demands and System Support: The Role of the Represented." In *Modern Parliaments, Change or Decline?*, edited by Gerhard Loewenberg, pp. 141–171. Chicago: Aldine-Atherton, 1971.

493. "Westminster and the European Community—Documents and Information." *Parliamentarian* 55 (January 1974):62–65.

494. Wheater, Stanley B. "Parliamentary Rhetoric: the American Congress and the House of Commons Compared." *Parliamentary Affairs* 28 (Winter 1974–1975):8–21.

Sovereignty

495. Dike, Chijioke. "The Case Against Parliamentary Sovereignty." *Public Law* (Autumn 1976):283–297.

496. Fazal, M.A. "Entrenched Rights and Parliamentary Sovereignty." *Public Law* (Winter 1974):295–315.

497. Gilmour, D.R. "Sovereignty of Parliament and the European Commission of Human Rights." *Public Law* 1 (Spring 1968):62–73.

498. Gray, H.R. "Sovereignty of the Imperial Parliament." *Modern Law Review* 23 (November 1960):647–652.

499. Hollis, Christopher. *Parliament and Its Sovereignty*. London: Hollis and Carter, 1973. 189 pp.

500. Hsieh, Chia-Chin. "The Development of the British Parliamentary Supremacy in the Age of the War of American Independence—A Study in Political Change." Ph.D. dissertation, University of Missouri, 1971. 199 pp.

501. Lampson, E.T. "Some New Light on Growth of Parliamentary Sovereignty; Wimbish Versus Taillebois." *American Political Science Review* 35 (October 1941):952–960.

502. Laski, Harold J. *Reflections on the Constitution: The House of Commons, the Cabinet and the Civil Service.* New York: Viking Press, 1951. 220 pp.

503. Marshall, Geoffrey. "Parliament and the Constitution." *Political Quarterly* 36 (July–September 1965):266–276.

504. Marshall, Geoffrey. "What is Parliament? The Changing Concept of Parliamentary Sovereignty." *Political Studies* 2 (October 1954):193–209.

505. Mitchell, John David Bawden. "Sovereignty of Parliament: Yet Again." *Law Quarterly Review* 79 (April 1963):196–223.

506. Mitchell, John David Bawden. "The Sovereignty or Supremacy of Parliament." In *Constitutional Law*, pp. 63–91. Edinburgh: Green, 1968.

507. Rawlinson, Peter. "Dissolution in the United Kingdom." *Parliamentarian* 58 (January 1977):1–4.

508. Scott, F.R. "Redistribution of Imperial Sovereignty." *Royal Society of Canada, Proceedings and Transactions* 44 (1950):27–34.

509. Van Themoat, H. ver Loren. "Equality of Status of the Dominions and the Sovereignty of the British Parliament." *Journal of Comparative Legislation* 15 (February 1933):47–53.

510. Wang, Chi-Kao. *Dissolution of the British Parliament, 1832–1931.* New York: Columbia University Press, 1934. 174 pp.

511. Winterton, George. "The British Grundnorm: Parliamentary Supremacy Re-Examined." *Law Quarterly Review* 92 (October 1976):591–617.

Legislative Process

Legislative Procedure

512. Andrews, William G. "Some Thoughts on the Power of Dissolution." *Parliamentary Affairs* 13 (Summer 1960):286–296.

513. Barlas, R.D. "Question Hour in the British Parliament." *Constitutional and Parliamentary Information* 65 (1966):21–27.

514. Barratt, Robin. "Statute Law: New System Needed." *Parliamentarian* 56 (January 1975):21–25.

515. Boisvert, H.V. "A Legislative Tool for Supervision of Administrative Agencies: the Laying System." *Fordham Law Review* 25 (Winter 1956–57):638–671.

516. Bridge, J.W. "Judicial Review of Private Legislation in the United Kingdom." *Juridical Review* 18 (August 1973):135–147.

517. Burton, Ivor F., and Drewry, Gavin. "Public Legislation: A Survey of the Session 1968/69." *Parliamentary Affairs* 23 (Spring 1970): 154–183.

518. Burton, Ivor F., and Drewry, Gavin. "Public Legislation: A Survey of the Session 1969/70." *Parliamentary Affairs* 23 (Spring 1970): 307–344.

519. Burtin, Ivor F., and Drewry, Gavin. "Public Legislation: A Survey of the Session 1970/71." *Parliamentary Affairs* 25 (Spring 1972): 123–162.

520. Burton, Ivor F., and Drewry, Gavin. "Public Legislation: A Survey of the Session 1971/72." *Parliamentary Affairs* 26 (Spring 1973): 145–185.

521. Burton, Ivor F., and Drewry, Gavin. "Public Legislation: A Survey of the Session 1972/73." *Parliamentary Affairs* 27 (Spring 1974): 120–158.

522. Burton, Ivor F., and Drewry, Gavin. "Public Legislation 1973/74 and a Parliament in Retrospect." *Parliamentary Affairs* 28 (Spring 1975):125–153.

523. Burton, Ivor F., and Drewry, Gavin. "Public Legislation: A Survey of the Session 1974." *Parliamentary Affairs* 29 (Spring 1976): 155–189.

524. Burton, Ivor F., and Drewry, Gavin. "Public Legislation: A Survey of the Session 1974/75." *Parliamentary Affairs* 30 (Spring 1977): 161–192.

525. Butler, R.A. "The Birth of a Bill." *Parliamentary Affairs* 2 (Summer 1949):210–217.

526. Campbell, Enid. "Expulsion of Members of Parliament." *University of Toronto Law Journal* 21 (1971):15–43.

527. Carr, Cecil Thomas. *Concerning English Administrative Law.* London: Oxford University Press, 1941. 189 pp.

528. Chorley, Robert Samuel Theodore. "Bringing the Legislative Process into Contempt." *Public Law* (Spring 1968):52–61.

529. Clough, Owen. "House of Commons: Guillotine and Business Committees." *The Table* 18 (1949):141–149.

530. Clough, Owen. "The Parliament Bill, 1947–48." *The Table* 17 (1948):136–180.

531. Craig, J.T. "The Working of the Statutory Instruments Act, 1946." *Public Administration (London)* 39 (Summer 1961):181–191.

532. Crick, Bernard R. "The Life Peerages Act." *Parliamentary Affairs* 11 (Autumn 1958):455–465.

533. Ditchfield, G.M. "Debates on the Test and Corporation Acts, 1787–

90: The Evidence of the Division Lists." *Institute of Historical Research Bulletin* 50 (May 1977):69-81.

534. Ditchfield, G.M. "Parliamentary Struggle over the Repeal of the Test and Corporation Acts, 1787-1790." *English Historical Review* 89 (July 1974):551-577.

535. Drewry, Gavin. "Reform of the Legislative Process: Some Neglected Questions." *Parliamentary Affairs* 25 (Autumn 1972): 286-302.

536. Drewry, Gavin, and Morgan, Jenny. "Law Lords as Legislators." *Parliamentary Affairs* 22 (Summer 1969):226-239.

537. Dryer, V.L. "Impeachment and the Sommers Case: A Crown Memorandum." *University of British Columbia Law Review* 1 (March 1960):264-276.

538. Ecclestone, G.S. "Expiring Laws." *Parliamentarian* 50 (July 1969): 239-241.

539. Forbes, Anthony Henry. "Faith and True Allegiance—the Law and the Internal Security of England, 1559-1714: A Study of the Evolution of the Parliamentary Legislation and the Problem of Its Local Administration and Enforcement." Ph.D. dissertation, University of California at Los Angeles, 1960. 417 pp.

540. Garran, A. "Significance of the Form of Acts of Parliament." *Australian Law Journal* 29 (March 1956):630-634.

541. Gray, H.L. *The Influence of the Commons on Early Legislation: A Study of the Fourteenth and Fifteenth Centuries.* Cambridge, Mass.: Harvard University Press, 1932. 423 pp.

542. Griffith, John A.G. *The Legislation Process in the House of Commons.* New Delhi: Institute of Constitutional and Parliamentary Studies, 1972. 31 pp.

543. Griffith, John A.G. *Parliamentary Scrutiny of Government Bills.* London: Allen and Unwin, 1974. 285 pp.

544. Griffith, John A.G. "Place of Parliament in the Legislative Process." *Modern Law Review* 14 (July/October 1951):279-296, 425-436.

545. Hanumanthappa, T.C. "Rule of Sub-Judice." *Journal of Parliamentary Information* 22 (1976):619-638.

546. Harris, J.P. "Legislative Control of Administration: Some Comparisons of American and European Practice." *Western Political Quarterly* 10 (June 1957):465-467.

547. Henderson, W. Craig. "Procedure on Hybrid Bills." *Parliamentary Affairs* 2 (Spring 1969):148-155.

548. Herbert, Alan P. *The Ayes Have It: The Story of the Marriage Bill.* London: Methuen, 1937. 238 pp.

549. Herman, Valentine. "What Governments Say and What Govern-

ments Do: An Analysis of Post-War Queen's Speeches." *Parliamentary Affairs* 28 (Winter 1974/1975):22–30.

550. Holland, D.C.L. "Abolition of Rule in Ashby V. White and Other Changes in the Parliamentary Franchise." *The Solicitor* 18 (April 1951):81–82, 87.

551. Hornby, R. "Case for a Stronger Parliament: Improving the Effectiveness of the Legislature." *Round Table* 269 (January 1978): 20–24.

552. Hutton, N. "Mechanics of Law Reform." *Modern Law Review* 24 (January 1961):18–31.

553. Ivanoff, Julia Scaife. "A Study of the Bills Before the House of Commons, 1621–1629." Ph.D. dissertation, Mississippi State University, 1964. 161 pp.

554. Jeger, L.M. "Politics of the Non-Political." *Political Quarterly* 30 (October 1959):367–378.

555. Jennings, William Ivor. *The Law and the Constitution.* 5th ed. London: University of London Press, 1967. 354 pp.

556. Jones, W.H.M. "Parliament Bill, 1947: Agreed Statement on Conclusion of Party Leaders, February-April, 1948." *Modern Law Review* 11 (July 1948):332–335.

557. King, Horace Maybray. *Parliament and Freedom.* Rev. ed. London: J. Murray, 1966. 144 pp.

558. Korah, Valentine. "Counter-Inflation Legislation: Whither Parliamentary Sovereignty?" *Law Quarterly Review* 92 (January 1976):42–61.

559. Lambert, Sheila. *Bills and Acts: Legislative Procedure in Eighteenth-Century England.* Cambridge: Cambridge University Press, 1971. 246 pp.

560. Machin, G.I.T. "Resistance to Repeal of the Test and Corporation Acts, 1828." *Historical Journal* 22 (March 1979):115–139.

561. Marshall, Geoffrey. "The British Parliamentary Commissioner for Administration." *The Annals of the American Academy of Political and Social Science* 377 (May 1968):87–96.

562. Marshall, Geoffrey. "Parliamentary Supremacy in and the Language of Constitutional Limitation." *Juridical Review* 67 (April 1955): 62–78.

563. Marshall, H.H. "The Preparation of Legislation in the United Kingdom." *International and Comparative Law Quarterly* 24 (1975): 572–576.

564. Mitchell, John David Bawden "Administrative Law and Parliamentary Control." *Political Quarterly* 38 (October 1967):360–374.

565. Mitchell, John David Bawden. "Legislative Business." In *Constitutional Law,* pp. 139–152. Edinburgh: Green, 1968.

566. "Parliament and Legislation, by Some Members of the Study of Parliament Group." *Parliamentary Affairs* 22 (Summer 1969): 210–215.

567. "Parliament and Ultra Vires." *Law Quarterly Review* 72 (January 1956):29–31.

568. Parry, C. "Legislatures and Secrecy." *Harvard Law Review* 67 (March 1954):737–785.

569. Perceval, R.W. "The Origin and Essence of Hybrid Bills." *Parliamentary Affairs* 2 (1949):139–147.

570. Pethick-Lawrence, Lord. "Legislative and Deliberative Functions." *Parliamentary Affairs* 7 (Winter 1953/1954):68–76.

571. Popofsky, Linda Seltzer. "Habeas Corpus and Liberty of the Subject; Legal Arguments for the Petition of Right in the Parliament of 1628." *Historian* 41 (February 1979):257–275.

572. Rayner, D. "Forms and Machinery of the Commune Petition in the Fourteenth Century." *English Historical Review* 56 (April/October 1941):198–233; 549–570.

573. Rees, Peter. "Clarity in the Preparation of Legislation." *Parliamentarian* 56 (October 1975):232–233.

574. Reznick, S. "Early History of the Parliamentary Declaration of Treason." *English Historical Review* 42 (October 1927):497–513.

575. Robinton, M.R. "Lynskey Tribunal: the British Method of Dealing with Political Corruption." *Political Science Quarterly* 68 (March 1953):109–124.

576. Romer, Kinsley Gird. "Parliament and the Death Penalty During the Age of Reform." Ph.D. disseration, University of Georgia, 1970. 227 pp.

577. Rose, Hannan. "The Immigration Act 1971: A Case Study in the Work of Parliament." *Parliamentary Affairs* 26 (Winter 1972/1973):69–91.

578. Rose, J.R. "Westminster and European Communities Legislation," *The Table* 42 (1974):73–80.

579. Snyder, Henry L. "The Defeat of the Occasional Conformity Bill and the Tack: A Study in the Techniques of Parliamentary Management in the Reign of Queen Anne." *Institute of Historical Research Bulletin* 41 (November 1968):172–192.

580. Thornton, G.C. *Legislative Drafting.* 2d ed. London: Butterworth, 1979. 350 pp.

581. Waite, P.B. "The Struggle of Prerogative and Common Law in the Reign of James I." *Canadian Journal of Economics and Political Science* 25 (May 1959):144–152.

582. Walkland, S.A. *The Legislative Process in Great Britain.* New York: Praeger, 1968. 109 pp.

583. Whitelaw, William. "Over-Legislation." *Parliamentarian* 59 (April 1978):88–89.
584. Wolffe, B.P. "Acts of Resumption in the Lancastrian Parliaments, 1399–1456." *English Historical Review* 73 (October 1958):583–613.
585. Woodall, Robert. "Jewish Relief Act, 1858." *History Today* 25 (June 1975):410–417.
586. Yardley, D.C.M. "British Constitution and the Rule of Law." *Jahrbuch des Oeffentlichen Rechts* 13 (1964):129–138.

Delegated Legislation

587. Allen, Carleton Kemp. *Law and Orders: An Inquiry into the Nature and Scope of Delegated Legislation and Executive Powers in English Law.* New ed. London: Stevens, 1956. 482 pp.
588. Byrne, Paul. "Parliamentary Control of Delegated Legislation." *Parliamentary Affairs* 29 (Autumn 1976):366–377.
589. Carr, Cecil Thomas. *Delegated Legislation: Three Lectures.* Cambridge: Cambridge University Press, 1921. 72 pp.
590. Carr, Cecil Thomas. "Parliamentary Control of Delegated Legislation." *Public Law* (Autumn 1956):200–217.
591. Chen, Chin-Mai. *Parliamentary Opinion of Delegated Legislation.* New York: Columbia University Press, 1933. 149 pp.
592. Christie, Ian Ralph. "Parliamentary Control of Delegated Legislation." *Journal of Comparative Legislation* 26 (November 1944): 62–63.
593. Grey, J.E. "Delegated Legislation in the United Kingdom Parliament—the Work of the Brooke Committee, 1971/72–1972/73." *The Table* 42 (1974):47–60.
594. Griffith, John A.G. "Delegated Legislation—Some Recent Developments." *Modern Law Review* 12 (July 1949):297–318.
595. Hewitt, D.J. "Delegated Legislative Power and the Problem of Control." *New Zealand Law Journal* 27 (February 1951):41–43.
596. Keeton, George W. "Delegated Legislation and Its Control in England." *South African Law Journal* 69 (February 1952):33–52.
597. Kersell, John E. *Parliamentary Supervision of Delegated Legislation: The United Kingdom, Australia, New Zealand and Canada.* London: Stevens, 1960. 178 pp.
598. Kersell, John E. "Upper Chamber Scrutiny of Delegated Legislation: Great Britain and Australia." *Public Law* (Spring 1959):46–60.
599. Lanham, D.J. "Delegated Legislation and Publication." *Modern Review* 37 (September 1974):510–543.
600. McKay, W.R. "Delegated Legislation: The Scrutiny Committees at Westminster." *The Table* 33 (1976):79–89.

601. Northey, J.F. "Sub-Delegated Legislation and *delegatus non protest delegare."* Res Judicatae 6 (February 1954):294–303.
602. Speed, Robert. "Parliamentary Scrutiny of Delegated Legislation." *Parliamentarian* 59 (October 1978):266–271.
603. Wheare, Kenneth C. "Controlling Delegated Legislation: A British Experiment." *Journal of Politics* 11 (November 1949):748–768.

Private Bills and Private Member Bills

604. Bromhead, Peter A. *Private Members' Bills in the British Parliament.* London: Routledge and Paul, 1956. 216 pp.
605. Clifford, Frederick. *A History of Private Bill Legislation.* London: Butterworth, 1885–1887. 2 vols.
606. Davies, E. "Role of Private Members' Bills." *Political Quarterly* 28 (January 1957):32–39.
607. Norton, Philip. "Private Legislation and the Influence of the Backbench M.P." *Parliamentary Affairs* 30 (Autumn 1977):356–362.
608. "Parliamentary Agent: the Promotion of Private Bills." *Law Society's Gazette* 55 (February 1958):67.
609. Ryle, Michael. "Private Members' Bills." *Political Quarterly* 37 (October 1966):385–393.
610. Speir, Rupert. "The Promotion of a Private Member's Bill—Its Problems and Pitfalls." *Parliamentary Affairs* 12 (Winter 1958-1959):83–88.
611. Williams, Orlo C. *The Historical Development of Private Bill Procedure and Standing Orders in the House of Commons.* London: H.M.S.O., 1948–1949. 2 vols.
612. Yardley, D.C.M. "The Work and Status of the Parliamentary Agent." *Parliamentary Affairs* 18 (Spring 1965):162–166.

Budgetary Practices

613. Allen, F.G. "House of Commons Expenditure Committee." *Constitutional and Parliamentary Information* 99 (1974):96–108.
614. Allison, Lincoln, and Benyon, John. "Public Planning of Private Development: Report of the Expenditure Committee on Planning Procedures." *Public Administration* 56 (Spring 1978):73–85.
615. Britain, Herbert. *The British Budgetary System.* London: Allen and Unwin, 1959. 320 pp.
616. Bryne, Paul. "Expenditure Committee: A Preliminary Assessment." *Parliamentary Affairs* 27 (Summer 1974):273–286.
617. Chubb, Basil. *The Control of Public Expenditures: Financial Com-*

mittees of the House of Commons. Oxford: Clarendon Press, 1952. 291 pp.

618. Chubb, Basil. "Parliamentary Control of the Public Accounts, I-II." *Parliamentary Affairs* 3 (Summer 1950):344–351, 450–457.

619. Chubb, Basil. "The Powers of Inquisition Into and Control Over Public Finance Exercised by the House of Commons, More Especially by Its Committees." D. Phil., Oxford University, 1950.

620. Chubb, Basil. "The Select Committee on Estimates, 1946–48." *Parliamentary Affairs* 2 (Summer 1949):284–291.

621. Clarke, R. "Parliament and Public Expenditure." *Political Quarterly* 44 (April 1974):137–153.

622. Cocks, Bernhard. "Control by the Commons of Overseas Expenditure." *Parliamentary Affairs* 9 (Winter 1955–1956):88–95.

623. Davenport, E.H. *Parliament and the Taxpayer.* London: Skeffington and Sons, 1918. 256 pp.

624. Davies, Lyn. "Planning in Parliament: the Eighth Report from the Commons Expenditure Committee: An Opportunity for Self-Appraisal?" *Planner* 64 (September 1978):146–147.

625. d'Avigdor-Goldsmid, Henry. "The House of Commons Expenditure Committee." *Parliamentarian* 54 (October 1973):205–208.

626. Du Cann, Edward. *Parliament and the Purse Strings: How to Bring Public Expenditure Under Parliamentary Control.* London: London Conservative Political Center, 1977. 24 pp.

627. Du Cann, Edward. "Some Reflections Upon the Control of Public Expenditure in the United Kingdom." *Parliamentarian* 57 (July 1976):151–158.

628. Einzig, Paul. *Control of the Purse; Progress and Decline of Parliament's Financial Control.* London: Secker and Warburg, 1959. 344 pp.

629. Fellowes, Edward. "Control of Expenditure by the Commons." *Parliamentary Affairs* 21 (Winter 1967/1968):16–18.

630. Fellowes, Edward. "Parliament and the Executive: Financial Control of the House of Commons." *Journal of the Parliaments of the Commonwealth* 43 (July 1962):223–231.

631. Gladden, E.N. "The Estimates Committee Looks at the Civil Service." *Parliamentary Affairs* 19 (Spring 1966):233–240.

632. Gray, Andrew. "The Civil Service and Parliament: Eleventh Report of the Expenditure Committee, 1976–1977." *Parliamentary Affairs* 32 (Winter 1979):37–55.

633. Harris, J.P. "Legislative Control of Expenditure: the Public Accounts Committee of the British House of Commons." *Canadian Public Administration* 2 (September 1959):113–131.

634. Harriss, G.L. "Thomas Cromwell's New Principle of Taxation." *English Historical Review* 93 (October 1978):721–738.

635. Hyder, Masood. "Parliament and Defense Affairs: the Defense Sub-Committee of the Expenditure Committee." *Public Administration* 55 (Spring 1977):59–78.

636. Jay, Peter. "Public Expenditure and Administration." *Political Quarterly* 41 (April/June 1970):195–206.

637. Jewell, R.E.C. "Parliamentary Procedure and the Control of Expenditure." *The Solicitor* 27 (May 1960):138–141.

638. Johnson, Nevil. "The Expenditure Committee on the Civil Service." *Public Administration* 56 (Spring 1978):1–12.

639. Johnson, Nevil. *Parliament and Administration: The Estimates Committee, 1945–1965.* London: Allen and Unwin, 1966. 186 pp.

640. Kennon, Andrew. "Recent Work of the General Sub-Committee of the Expenditure Committee." *Parliamentary Affairs* 33 (Spring 1980):159–165.

641. Millar, David. "Parliamentary Control of Taxation in Britain." In *The Power of the Purse,* edited by David Coombes, pp. 198–214. London: Allen and Unwin, 1976.

642. Molinier, Joel. "Parliament's Financial Powers: A Comparison Between France and Britain." In *The Power of the Purse,* edited by David Coombes, pp. 163–178. London: Allen and Unwin, 1976.

643. Owen, David. "Parliamentary Control of Defence Budgeting." In *Brassey's Annual* (1973):48–59.

644. Perceval, R.W. "The Commons Grant, the Lords Assent." *Parliamentary Affairs* 5 (Autumn 1952):469–479.

645. Pringle, James Ward. "The Committee for Compounding with Delinquents, 1643–1654: A Study of Parliamentary Finance During the English Civil Wars." Ph.D. dissertation, University of Illinois at Urbana-Champaign, 1961. 282 pp.

646. Reid, Gordon. *The Politics of Financial Control: The Role of the House of Commons.* London: Hutchinson, 1966. 176 pp.

647. Robinson, Ann. *Parliament and Public Spending: the Expenditure Committee of the House of Commons, 1970–76.* London: Heinemann Educational, 1978. 184 pp.

648. Ryle, Michael. "Parliamentary Control of Expenditure and Taxation." *Political Quarterly* 38 (October 1967):435–446.

649. Shakdher, S.L. "Two Estimates Committees." *Indian Journal of Public Administration* 5 (October/December 1959):388–404.

650. Silkin, Arthur. "The Expenditure Committee: A New Development?" *Public Administration* 53 (Spring 1975):45–66.

651. Tribe, F. "Parliamentary Control of Public Expenditure." *Public Administration (London)* 32 (Winter 1954):363–381.

652. Williams, David W. "Taxing Statutes are Taxing Statutes: The Interpretation of Revenue Legislation." *Modern Law Review* 41 (July 1978):404–422.

Rules and Practices

653. Arnstein, Walter L. "Bradlaugh Case: A Reappraisal." *Journal of the History of Ideas* 18 (April 1957):254–269.
654. Arnstein, Walter L. *The Bradlaugh Case: A Study in Late Victorian Opinion and Politics.* Oxford: Clarendon Press, 1965. 348 pp.
655. Bossom, Alfred. *Our House: An Introduction to Parliamentary Procedure.* London: Barrie, 1948. 238 pp.
656. Bradshaw, Kenneth. "Parliamentary Questions." *Parliamentary Affairs* 7 (Summer 1954):317–326.
657. Bromhead, Peter A. "The Ten Minutes Rule." *Parliamentary Affairs* 8 (Autumn 1955):492–502.
658. Bunburg, H. "Proposed Changes in British Parliamentary Procedure." *American Political Science Review* 40 (August 1946): 740–748.
659. Carr, Cecil Thomas. "Parliamentary Supervision in Britain." *New York University Law Review* 30 (May 1955):1045–1056.
660. Chapman, Donald. "The Select Committee on Procedure at Westminister." *Parliamentarian* 51 (April 1970):139–144.
661. Chapman, Richard A. "The Significance of Parliamentary Procedure." *Parliamentary Affairs* 16 (Spring 1963):179–187.
662. Chester, Daniel N., and Bowring, Nona. *Questions in Parliament.* Oxford: Clarendon Press, 1962. 335 pp.
663. Cocks, Bernard. "Book of the House." *Times Literary Supplement* 3878 (July 1976):842.
664. Day, W.L. "British Parliament and State Legislatures." *State Government* 48 (Summer 1975):160–163.
665. Elliott, W., and Walker, G. "Delaying Power: Two Views." *Parliamentary Affairs* 7 (Winter 1953/1954):121–128.
666. Elsynge, Henry. *The Method of Passing Bills in Parliament.* London: Printed by F.L. for M. Gilliflower, 1685. 33 pp.
667. Forsey, Eugene A. "Parliament's Power to Advise." *Canadian Journal of Economics and Political Science* 29 (May 1963):203–210.
668. Hanson, Albert Henry, and Wiseman, Herbert B. *Parliament at Work: A Case-Book of Parliamentary Procedure.* London: Stevens, 1962. 358 pp.
669. Hayden, R. "Changes in British Parliamentary Procedure." *American Political Science Review* 14 (August 1920):471–477.

670. Hayter, P.D.G. "Pecuniary Penalties and Procedure." *The Table* 34 (1965):31–39.
671. Hughes, Edward. "The Changes in Parliamentary Procedure, 1880–1882." In *Essays Presented to Sir Lewis Namier,* edited by R. Pares and A.J.P. Taylor, pp. 289–319. London: Macmillan, 1956.
672. Johnson, Donald McIntosh. *A Doctor in Parliament.* London: C. Johnson, 1958. 288 pp.
673. Johnson, Nevil. "Parliamentary Questions and the Conduct of Administration." *Public Administration* 39 (Summer 1961):131–148.
674. Jones, G.W. "A Forgotten Night Discovered." *Parliamentary Affairs* 19 (Summer 1966):363–372.
675. Jones, G.W. "The Prime Minister and Parliamentary Questions." *Parliamentary Affairs* 26 (Summer 1973):260–273.
676. Judge, David. "Backbench Specialization— A Study in Parliamentary Questions." *Parliamentary Affairs* 27 (Spring 1974):171–186.
677. Kaberry, Donald. "On Long Speeches." *Parliamentarian* 56 (April 1975):91–95.
678. Kersell, John E. "Parliamentary Ventilation of Grievances." *Public Law* (Summer 1959):152–168.
679. Kimber, Richard H.; Richardson, J.J.; Brookes, S.K.; and Jordan, A.G. "Parliamentary Questions and the Allocation of Departmental Responsibilities." *Parliamentary Affairs* 27 (Summer 1974):287–293.
680. Lascelles, F.W. "Procedure and the Standing Orders." *Parliamentary Affairs* 7 (Winter 1953–1954):88–95.
681. Lehmberg, Stanford E. "Early Tudor Parliamentary Procedure: Provisos in the Legislation of the Reformation Parliament." *English Historical Reviews* 85 (January 1970):1–11.
682. Maxwell-Hylsop, Robin. "Aspects of Hybridity." *Parliamentarian* 57 (October 1976):287–289.
683. May, Thomas Erskine. *Treaties on the Law, Privileges, Proceedings and Usage of Parliament.* 19th ed. Edited by David Lidderdale. London: Butterworth, 1976. 1139 pp.
684. Millar, David. "The Process of Legislation: Second Report from the Procedure Committee, 1970–71." *The Table* 40 (1971):73–78.
685. Milman, A. "Parliamentary Procedure Versus Obstruction." *Quarterly Review* 178 (April 1894):486–503.
686. Mond, A. "Remedies for Parliamentary Deadlock." *English Review* 5 (May 1910):354–363.
687. Myers, A.R. "Some Observations on the Procedure of the Commons in Dealing with Bills in the Lancastrian Period." *University of Toronto Law Journal* 3 (1939):51–73.

688. Palmer, John. "Allocation of Time: The Guillotine and Voluntary Timetabling." *Parliamentary Affairs* 23 (Summer 1970):232–247.

689. Parker, John. "The Battle for the Legitimacy Act 1959." *Political Quarterly* 43 (July/September 1972):308–316.

690. Perceval, R.W. "Orders of the Day." *The Table* 36 (1967):34–40.

691. Randall, J.G. "Frequency and Duration of Parliaments." *American Political Science Review* 10 (November 1916):654–682.

692. Renton, D. "Legislative Habits of the British Parliament." *The John Marshall Journal of Practice and Procedure* 10 (Spring 1977): 437–446.

693. Riddell, W.R. "Delegation of Powers of Parliament." *Canadian Bar Record* 4 (September 1926):429–431.

694. Riddell, W.R. "Delegation of Powers of Parliament." *Canadian Bar Review* 7 (March 1929):179–181.

695. Snow, Vernon F. *Parliament in Elizabethan England: John Hooker's Order and Usage.* New Haven, Conn.: Yale University Press, 1977. 221 pp.

696. Sparks, J.A. "Some Aspects of British Parliamentary Procedure." *Pakistan Horizon* 7 (June 1954):61–68.

697. Strateman, Catherine. "The Liverpool Tractate, an Eighteenth Century Manual on the Procedure of the House of Commons, edited with an Introduction." Ph.D. dissertation, Columbia University, 1938. 105 pp.

698. Swinhoe, K. "Lines of Division Among Members of Parliament Over Procedural Reform of the House of Commons." *Political Studies* 18 (September 1970):400–402.

699. Webster, T.L. "Parliamentary Procedure and Oversea Assemblies." *Empire Review* 38 (October 1923):1095–1107.

700. Wheeler, Gerald John. *The Practice of Private Bills, with the Standing Orders of the House of Lords and House of Commons, and Rules as to Provisional Orders.* London: Shaw and Sons, 1900. 531 pp.

701. Wiseman, Herbert V. "Supply and Ways and Means: Procedural Changes in 1966." *Parliamentary Affairs* 21 (Winter 1967/1968): 10–15.

702. Wolf-Phillips, Leslie. "Parliamentary Divisions and Proxy Voting." *Parliamentary Affairs* 18 (Autumn 1965):416–421.

Privileges

703. Bridge, C. "Churchill, Hoare, Derby and Committee of Privileges, April to June 1934." *Historical Journal* 22 (March 1979):215–227.

704. Cocks, Bernard. "Privilege and the Official Secrets Acts." *Parliamentarian* 51 (July 1970):170–174.

705. Hirst, D. "Elections and the Privileges of the House of Commons in the Early Seventeenth Century: Confrontation or Compromise?" *Historical Journal* 18 (December 1975):851–862.

706. Keeton, George W. "Question of Privilege." *The Solicitor* 25 (August 1958):209–213.

707. Keith, A.B. "Parliamentary Privilege and the Official Secrets Acts." *Judicial Review* 51 (September 1939):260–269.

708. Kilmuir, David Maxwell Fyfe. *The Law of Parliamentary Privilege.* London: Athlone Press, 1959. 22 pp.

709. Kingdon, John W. "Models of Legislative Voting." *Journal of Politics* 39 (August 1977):563–596.

710. Levy, H.P. "Parliamentary Privilege and the Freedom of the Press." *Australian Quarterly* 28 (June 1956):52–61.

711. Marshall, Geoffrey. "Parliamentary Privilege in 1957." *Parliamentary Affairs* 11 (Spring 1958):211–219.

712. Marshall, Geoffrey. "Privilege and 'Proceedings in Parliament.'" *Parliamentary Affairs* 11 (Autumn 1958):396–404.

713. Mummery, David R. "The Privilege of Freedom of Speech in Parliament." *Law Quarterly Review* 94 (April 1978):276–290.

714. Neale, John E. "The Commons' Privilege of Free Speech in Parliament." In *Tudor Studies,* edited by R.W. Seton-Watson, pp. 257–286. London: Longmans, Green, 1924.

715. "Parliamentary Privilege, the Sandys Case." *Modern Law Review* 2 (September/December 1938):163–165, 231–232.

716. Perceval, R.W. "Publication Versus Privilege: A Cautionary Tale." *The Table* 33 (1964):17–24.

717. Phillips, O. Hood. "Parliamentary Privilege: Allighan and Walkden Cases." *Modern Law Review* 11 (April 1948):214–217.

718. Phillips, O. Hood. "Parlimentary Privilege—the Case of Mr. W.J. Brown." *Modern Law Review* 10 (October 1947):420–424.

719. "Power and Privilege." *Justice of the Peace* 122 (July 1958): 473, 489.

720. Robinton, M.R. "Parliamentary Privilege and Political Morality in Britain, 1939–1957." *Political Science Quarterly* 73 (June 1958): 179–205.

721. Sarkar, R.C.S. "Privileges of Press and Parliament." *Journal of Constitutional and Parliamentary Studies* 1 (January/March 1967):42–58.

722. Seymour-Ure, Colin. "The Misuse of the Question of Privilege in the 1964–5 Session of Parliament." *Parliamentary Affairs* 18 (Autumn 1965):380–388.

723. Seymour-Ure, Colin. "Parliamentary Privilege and Broadcasting." *Parliamentary Affairs* 16 (Autumn 1963):411–418.
724. Seymour-Ure, Colin. "Proposed Reforms of Parliamentary Privilege: An Assessment in the Light of Recent Cases." *Parliamentary Affairs* 23 (Summer 1970):221–231.
725. Silkin, S.C. "The Select Committee on Parliamentary Privilege in the U.K." *Parlamentarian* 51 (January 1970):1–10.
726. Smith, S.A., de. "Parliamentary Privilege and the Bill of Rights." *Modern Law Review* 21 (September 1958):465–483.
727. Stricklin, Thomas Edgar. "The Privilege of Freedom From Arrest and Molestation in the House of Commons, 1604–1629." Ph.D. dissertation, Mississippi University, 1968. 199 pp.
728. Thompson, D. "Letters to Ministers and Parliamentary Privilege." *Public Law* (Spring 1959):10–22.
729. Wittke, Carl. *The History of English Parliamentary Privilege.* Columbus: Ohio State University Press, 1921. 212 pp.
730. Yardley, D.C.M. "The House of Commons and Its Privileges Since the Strauss Affairs." *Parliamentary Affairs* 15 (Autumn 1962): 500–510.
731. Zellick, Graham, "Bribery of Members of Parliament and the Criminal Law." *Public Law* (Spring 1979):31–58.
732. Zellick, Graham. "When is a Bribe Not a Bribe? Answer: When It is Paid to an MP." *Contemporary Review* 230 (March 1977):127–130.

House of Commons

General Studies of the House of Commons

733. Baker, Arthur. *The House is Sitting.* London: Blandford Press, 1958. 264 pp.
734. Barclay, H.M. "Accommodation for the House of Commons." *The Table* 32 (1963):69–72.
735. Barker, Anthony. "Parliament and Patience." *Political Studies* 15 (February 1967):74–81.
736. Belloc, J.H.P. *The House of Commons and Monarchy.* London: Allen and Unwin, 1920. 188 pp.
737. Bourne, R.C. "Parliament and the National Finances." *English Review* 42 (March 1926):319–325.
738. Bromhead, Peter A. "The Guillotine in the House of Commons." *Parliamentary Affairs* 11 (Autumn 1958):443–454.

739. Campion, Gilbert Francis Montriou. *Parliament: A Survey*. London: Allen and Unwin, 1952. 296 pp.
740. Chamberlin, Austen. "House of Commons." *Empire Review* 39 (April 1924):363–372.
741. Christoph, James B. "Study of Voting Behavior in the British House of Commons." *Western Political Quarterly* 11 (June 1958):310–318.
742. Craik, G.L. "The House of Commons." In *London*, edited by Charles Knight, pp. 65–96. London: Henry G. Bohn, 1851.
743. Crowe, Edward W. "Cross-Voting in the British House of Commons: 1945–1974." *Journal of Politics* 42 (May 1980):487–510.
744. Doig, Alan. "Self Discipline and the House of Commons: The Poulson Affairs in a Parliamentary Perspective." *Parliamentary Affairs* 32 (Summer 1979):248–267.
745. Dowse, Robert E. "The M.P. and His Surgery." *Political Studies* 11 (October 1963):333–341.
746. Dowse, Robert E., and Smith, Trevor A. "Party Discipline in the House of Commons." *Parliamentary Affairs* 16 (Spring 1963): 159–164.
747. Edelman, Maurice. "Uproar in the House." *Parliamentarian* 52 (July 1971):187–190.
748. Francome, C. "Abortion: Why the Issue Has Not Disappeared." *Political Quarterly* 49 (April 1978):217–222.
749. Gallacher, W. "Fight for Unity in Parliament." *Labour Monthly* 18 (February 1936):82–86.
750. Giddings, Philip. "Parliament, Boards and Autonomy: the Case of Agricultural Marketing Boards." *Public Administration* 53 (Winter 1975):383–401.
751. Hockin, Thomas A. "The Roles of the Loyal Opposition in Britain's House of Commons: Three Historical Paradigms." *Parliamentary Affairs* 25 (Winter 1971/1972):50–68.
752. Houghton, Douglas. "Making M.P.s Accountable." *Political Quarterly* 43 (October/December 1972):375–379.
753. James, Robert R. *An Introduction to the House of Commons*. London: Collins, 1966. 160 pp.
754. Jennings, William Ivor. "Technique of Opposition." *Political Quarterly* 6 (April 1935):208–221.
755. Laurence, W.B. "Finance and the Commons." *Quarterly Review* 257 (October 1931):300–314.
756. Lindsay, Martin. *The House of Commons*. London: Collins, 1947. 48 pp.
757. Liversidge, Douglas. *The House of Commons*. London: F. Watts, 1974. 96 pp.

758. Lloyd, G.R. "The House of Commons System." *Statist* 132 (October 1938):431–432.

759. Low, S. "The Decline of the House of Commons." *Nineteenth Century* 37 (April 1895):567–578.

760. Lucy, Henry W. *Men and Manner in Parliament*. London: T.F. Unwin, 1919. 259 pp.

761. Milman, A. "The House of Commons and the Obstructive Party." *Quarterly Review* 145 (January 1878):231–257.

762. Millett, J.H. "Role of an Interest Group Leader in the House of Commons." *Western Political Quarterly* 9 (December 1956): 915–926.

763. Moon, Jhang Shick. "The British Two-Party System: A Study of Voting Cohesion and Patterns in the British House of Commons." Ph.D. dissertation, Tulane University, 1964. 261 pp.

764. Nicolson, Nigel. *People and Parliament*. London: Weidenfeld and Nicolson, 1958. 191 pp.

765. Norton, Philip. "Government Defeats in the House of Commons: Myth and Reality." *Public Law* (Winter 1978):360–378.

766. Norton, Philip. "Government Defeats in the House of Commons: Three Restraints Overcome." *Parliamentarian* 59 (October 1978):231–238.

767. Norton, Philip. "Party Organization in the House of Commons." *Parliamentary Affairs* 31 (Autumn 1978):406–423.

768. Palgrave, R.F.D. *The House of Commons*. London: Macmillan, 1869. 196 pp.

769. Patterson, Samuel C. "The British House of Commons as a Focus for Political Research." *British Journal of Political Science* 3 (July 1973):363–381.

770. Patterson, Samuel C. *Review Article: The British House of Commons as a Focus for Political Research*. Beverly Hills, Calif.: Sage Publications, 1973. 18 pp.

771. Richardson, J.J., and Kimber, Richard H. "The Role of the All-Party Committees in the House of Commons." *Parliamentary Affairs* 25 (Autumn 1972):339–349.

772. Schuyler, Robert L. "Decline of the House of Commons." *Columbia University Quarterly* 21 (October 1919):310–318.

773. Schwartz, John E. "Exploring a New Role in Policy Making: The British House of Commons in the 1970's." *American Political Science Review* 74 (March 1980):23–37.

774. Scism, Thomas Edgar. "Behavior in the House of Commons: The Relationship Between Demographic, Ecological and Political Factors and the Activity of the Parliamentary Labour Party." Ph.D. dissertation, University of North Carolina at Chapel Hill, 1969. 256 pp.

775. Study of Parliament Group. *The Commons in Transition.* London: Fontana, 1970. 285 pp.

776. Taylor, Eric S. *The House of Commons at Work.* 9th ed. London: Macmillan, 1979. 190 pp.

777. Thorne, Peter F. *Official Dress Work in the House of Commons.* London: H.M.S.O., 1960. 11 pp.

778. Tyler, Moses C. "The House of Commons." In his *Glimpses of England,* pp. 92–121. New York: G.P. Putnam's Sons, 1898.

779. Urbach, Philip. *The House of Commons: A Programmed Text.* London: Longmans, 1966. 160 pp.

780. Walcott, E. "An M.P.'s Work." *National Review* 129 (October 1947):313–315.

781. Walkland, S.A., ed. *The House of Commons in the Twentieth Century: Essays by Members of the Study of Parliament Group.* Oxford: Clarendon Press, 1979. 649 pp.

782. White, William. *The Inner Life of the House of Commons.* London: T.F. Unwin, 1897. 2 vols.

783. Wilkin, F.J. "The Work of the House of Commons Fees Office." *The Table* 46 (1978):56–60.

784. Wyatt, Woodrow. *Turn Again, Westminster.* London: Andre Deutsch, 1973. 259 pp.

Functions and Duties

785. Barker, Anthony. "Disqualification From the House—the 'Reverse' System." *Parliamentary Affairs* 12 (Summer/Autumn 1959): 469–474.

786. Barker, Anthony. "The Most Important and Venerable Function: A Study of Commons Supply Procedure." *Political Studies* 13 (February 1965):45–64.

787. Boulton, C.J. "Recent Developments in House of Commons Procedure." *Parliamentary Affairs* 23 (Winter 1969/1970):61–71.

788. Brasher, Norman Henry. "The House of Commons: Some Procedural Problems." In his *Studies in British Government,* 2d ed., pp. 90–108. London: Macmillan, 1971.

789. Bromhead, Peter A. "The Commons and Supply." *Parliamentary Affairs* 12 (Summer/Autumn 1959):337–348.

790. Bromhead, Peter A. "Free Votes in the House of Commons." *Durham University Journal* (June 1953):104–113.

791. Burn, W.L. "Property Qualifications in the House of Commons." *Parliamentary Affairs* 2 (Summer 1949):274–283.

792. Campion, Gilbert Francis, Montriou. *An Introduction to the Procedure of the House of Commons.* 3d ed. London: Macmillan, 1958. 350 pp.

793. Doughty, C. "House of Commons Disqualification." *Public Law* 1957 (Winter 1957):340–353.

794. Edwards, John Goronwy. "The Emergence of Majority Rule in the Procedure of the House of Commons." *Royal Historical Society Transactions* 15 (1965):165–187.

795. Fellowes, Edward. "Practice and Procedure in the House of Commons 1919–61." *Journal of the Parliaments of the Commonwealth* 43 (April 1962):105–114.

796. Foster, Elizabeth Read. "Speaking in the House of Commons." *Institute of Historical Research Bulletin* 43 (May 1970):35–55.

797. Greenleaf, W.H. "Urgency Motions in the Commons." *Public Law* (Autumn 1960):270–284.

798. Hatsell, John. *Precedents of Proceedings in the House of Commons.* Shannon: Irish University Press, 1971–1972. 5 vols.

799. Herman, Valentine. Adjournment Debates in the House of Commons." *Parliamentary Affairs* 26 (Winter 1972/1973):92–104.

800. Hulme, Harold. "Winning of Freedom of Speech by the House of Commons." *American Historical Review* 61 (July 1956):825–853.

801. Judge, David. "Public Petitions and the House of Commons." *Parliamentary Affairs* 31 (Autumn 1978):391–405.

802. Kemp, Betty. "Resignation From the House of Commons." *Parliamentary Affairs* 6 (Spring 1953):211–215.

803. Lees-Smith, Hastings Bertrand. "The Time-Table of the House of Commons." *Economica* 4 (June 1924):140–162.

804. Lidderdale, D.W.S. "Power of the House of Commons to Discipline Its Members." *Parliamentarian* 56 (July 1975):212–214.

805. McCulloch, Robert Winslow. "Parliamentary Control: Question Hour in the English House of Commons." Ph.D. dissertation, University of Michigan, 1934. 296 pp.

806. McCulloch, Robert Winslow. "Question Time in the British House of Commons." *American Political Science Review* 27 (December 1933):971–977.

807. Mackintosh, John P. "The House of Commons and Taxation." *Political Quarterly* 42 (January 1971):75–86.

808. Millett, J.H. "Notes on Functional Representation in the House of Commons." *Social Science Quarterly* 40 (September 1959):113–124.

809. Perceval, R.W. "On the Origins of Divisions: A Speculation." *Parliamentary Affairs* 4 (Spring 1951):216–223.

810. Read, Elizabeth. "The Procedures of the House of Commons Against Patents and Monopolies, 1621–1624." Ph.D. dissertation, Yale University, 1938. 214 pp.

811. Redlich, Joseph. *The Procedure of the House of Commons: A Study*

of Its History and Present Form. London: A. Constable, 1908. 311 pp.

812. Williams, Orlo C. "The Historical Development of Private Bill Procedure and Standing Orders in the House of Commons." B.C.L. & D.C.L., Oxford, 1946. 2 vols.

813. Williams, Orlo C. "Introduction to the Procedure of the House of Commons, by G. Campion. Review." *National Review* 128 (June 1947):488–494.

History of the House of Commons: Origins to 1600

814. Bayne, C.G. "First House of Commons of Queen Elizabeth," *English Historical Review* 23 (July/October 1908):455–476, 643–682.

815. Brown, A.L. "The Commons and the Council in the Reign of Henry IV." *English Historical Review* 79 (January 1964):1–30.

816. Bryant, W.N. "Commons' Immunity From Arrest: The Earliest Known Case (1340)." *Institute of Historical Research Bulletin* 43 (November 1970):214–215.

817. Edwards, John Goronwy. *The Commons in Medieval English Parliaments.* London: University of London Press, 1958. 44 pp.

818. Harriss, G.L. "The Commons' Petitions of 1340." *English Historical Review* 78 (October 1963):625–654.

819. Kent, Joan. "Attitudes of Members of the House of Commons to the Regulation of 'Personal Conduct' in the Late Elizabethan and Early Stuart England." *Institute of Historical Research Bulletin* 46 (May 1973):41–71.

820. Levett, A.E. "Summons to a Great Council, 1213." *English Historical Review* 31 (January 1916):85–90.

821. Morris, W.A. "Beginnings of the House of Commons." *Pacific Historical Review* 2 (June 1933):141–157.

822. Neale, John E. *Elizabeth I and Her Parliaments, 1559–1581.* London: Cape, 1953. 434 pp.

823. Neale, John E. *The Elizabethan House of Commons.* London: Fontana/Cape, 1976, c. 1949. 444 pp.

824. Niles, Philip Harcourt. "Parliament and Society in 1376: The Role of the Commons and the Background of the Membership." Ph.D. dissertation, University of Toronto, 1969. 353 pp.

825. Pasquet, D. *An Essay on the Origins of the House of Commons.* Cambridge: Cambridge University Press, 1925. 248 pp.

826. Rayner, D. "Aspects of the History of the Commons in the Fourteenth Century." Ph.D. dissertation, University of Manchester, 1934.

827. Richardson, Henry Gerald. "Commons and Medieval Politics." *Royal Historical Society Transactions* 28 (1946):21–45.
828. Roskell, John S. *The Commons and Their Speakers in English Parliaments, 1376–1523*. New York: Barnes and Noble, 1965. 390 pp.
829. Roskell, John S. *The Commons in the Parliament of 1422: English Society and Parliamentary Representation Under the Lancastrians*. Manchester: Manchester University Press, 1954. 266 pp.
830. Roskell, John S. "The Personnel of the House of Commons in 1422." D. Phil., Oxford University, 1941.

History of the House of Commons: 1600s

831. Amspoker, Gertrude Joanne. "The Development of Procedure in the House of Commons in the Early Stuart Period (1603–1629)." Ph.D. dissertation, University of Minnesota, 1959. 328 pp.
832. Barrows, Floyd Dell. "The House of Commons of 1685: A Study of the Membership and Politics of the Only Parliament of King James II." Ph.D. dissertation, University of California at Los Angeles, 1967. 234 pp.
833. Croessmann, Allen Ward. "Critics of the Crown: Leadership in the House of Commons During the Early Parliaments of Charles I, 1625–1629." Ph.D. dissertation, Harvard University, 1976. 466 pp.
834. Croft, Pauline. "Free Trade and the House of Commons, 1605–6." *Economic History Review* 28 (February 1975):17–27.
835. Cruikshanks, Eveline G.; Ferris, John; and Hayton, David. "The House of Commons Vote on the Transfer of the Crown, 5 February 1689." *Institute of Historical Research Bulletin* 52 (May 1979):37–47.
836. DeVilliers, E. "Parliamentary Boroughs Restored by the House of Commons, 1621–41." *English Historical Review* 67 (April 1952): 175–202.
837. Hirst, D. "Unanimity in the Commons, Aristocratic Intrigues, and the Origins of the English Civil War." *Journal of Modern History* 50 (March 1978):51–71.
838. Hulme, Harold. "Sheriff as a Member of the House of Commons From Elizabeth to Cromwell." *Journal of Modern History* 1 (September 1929):361–377.
839. Hulme, Harold. "A Study of the Personnel of the House of Commons Between 1604 and 1629, Taken from the Source Material of Eighteen English Countries." Ph.D. dissertation, Cornell University, 1925. 5 pp.

840. Kenny, R.W. "Parliamentary Influence of Charles Howard, Earl of Nottingham, 1536–1624." *Journal of Modern History* 39 (September 1967):215–232.

841. Kershaw, R.N. "The Composition, Organization, and Character of the House of Commons, 1640–1653." B. Litt., Oxford University, 1923.

842. McIlwain, Charles Howard. "The House of Commons in 1621." In *Constitutionalism and the Changing World,* pp. 183–195. Cambridge: Cambridge University Press, 1939.

843. Maclear, J.F. "Influence of the Puritan Clergy on the House of Commons: 1625–1629." *Church History* 14 (December 1945): 272–289.

844. Marcham, Frederick George. "Sir Edwin Sandys, and the Growth of Opposition in the House of Commons, 1604–1610." Ph.D. dissertation, Cornell University, 1927, 167 pp.

845. Mitchell, William M. *The Rise of the Revolutionary Party in the English House of Commons, 1603–1629.* New York: Columbia University Press, 1957. 209 pp.

846. Moore, T.K., and Horowitz, Henry. "Who Runs the House? Aspects of Parliamentary Organization in the Later Seventeenth Century." *Journal of Modern History* 43 (June 1971):205–227.

847. Notestein, Wallace. *The House of Commons, 1604–1610.* New Haven Conn.: Yale University Press, 1971. 598 pp.

848. Nourse, G.B. "Richard Cromwell's House of Commons." *John Rylands University Library of Manchester Bulletin* 60 (Autumn 1977):95–113.

849. Townsend, William C. *History of the House of Commons, from the Convention Parliament of 1688-9, to the Passing of the Reform Bill, in 1832.* London: H. Colburn, 1843-1844. 2 vols.

850. Usher, R.G. "Institutional History of the House of Commons, 1547–1641." *Washington University State (Hum. Ser.)* 11 (April 1924):187–254.

851. Ward, Cedric Charles. "Disputed Elections to the House of Commons, 1604–1641." Ph.D. dissertation, University of Nebraska, 1974. 379 pp.

852. Willson, David Harris. *The Privy Councillors in the House of Commons, 1604–1629.* Minneapolis: University of Minnesota Press, 1940. 332 pp.

History of the House of Commons: 1700s

853. Brooke, John. *The House of Commons, 1754–1790: An Introductory Survey.* London: Oxford University Press, 1968. 312 pp.

854. Cox, M.D. "Mercantile Interests in the House of Commons, 1710–13." Master's thesis, University of Manchester, 1949.

855. Namier, Lewis B. "Circular Letters: An 18th Century Whip to Members of Parliament." *English Historical Review* 44 (October 1929):588–611.

856. Namier, Lewis B., and Brooke, John. *The House of Commons, 1754–1790.* New York: Oxford University Press, 1964. 3 vols.

857. Newman, A.N. "Proceedings in the House of Commons, 1721–2." *Bulletin of Institute of Historical Research* 36 (November 1963): 206–212.

858. Porritt, Edward, and Porritt, A.G. *The Unreformed House of Commons: Parliamentary Representation Before 1832.* Cambridge: Cambridge University Press, 1903. 3 vols.

859. Sainty, John Christopher. "The History of Parliament: the House of Commons, 1754–1790." *Parliamentary Affairs* 17 (Autumn 1964):453–457.

860. Sedgwick, Romney. *The House of Commons, 1715–1754: The History of Parliament.* London: Oxford University Press, 1970. 2 vols.

861. Tate, W.E. "Commons' Journals as Sources of Information Concerning the Eighteenth-Century Enclosure Movement." *Economic Journal* 54 (April 1944):75–95.

862. Thomas, Peter D.G. "Check List of M.P.'s Speaking in the House of Commons, 1768–1774." *Bulletin of Institute of Historical Research* 35 (November 1962):220–226.

863. Thomas, Peter D.G. *The House of Commons in the Eighteenth Century.* Oxford: Clarendon Press, 1971. 382 pp.

864. Walcott, Robert R. "The 'Family' and the House: the Churchills and the Management of Parliament, 1702–1708." Ph.D dissertation, Harvard University, 1938.

865. Williams, Orlo C. *The Clerical Organization of the House of Commons, 1661–1850.* Oxford: Clarendon Press, 1954. 366 pp.

History of the House of Commons: 1800s

866. Aspinall, Arthur. "Le Marchant's Reports of Debate in the House of Commons, 1833; Text with Introduction." *English Historical Review* 58 (January 1943):78–105.

867. Aspinall, Arthur. "The Old House of Commons and Its Members. I." *Parliamentary Affairs* 14 (Winter 1960–1961):13–15.

868. Aspinall, Arthur. "The Old House of Commons and Its Members, c. 1783–1832." *Parliamentary Affairs* 15 (Winter 1961–1962):15–38.

869. Aspinall, Arthur. "The Old House of Commons and Its Members (c. 1783–1832): Curiosities of Politics." *Parliamentary Affairs* 15 (Spring 1962):170–187.

870. Aspinall, Arthur. "The Old House of Commons and Its Members (c. 1783–1832)." *Parliamentary Affairs* 15 (Autumn 1962):424–449.

871. Aspinall, Arthur. "The Old House of Commons and Its Members (c. 1783–1832)." *Parliamentary Affairs* 15 (Summer 1962):284–293.

872. Aydelotte, William O. "The House of Commons in the 1840's." *History* 39 (October 1954):249–262.

873. Aydelotte, William O. "Voting Patterns in the British House of Commons in 1840's. *Comparative Studies in Society and History* 5 (January 1963):134–163.

874. Ball, Enid. "Glamorgan: A Study of the Concerns of the County and the Work of Its Members in the House of Commons From 1825 to 1835." Ph.D. dissertation, University of London, External Degree, 1965.

875. Berrington, Hugh B. "Partisanship and Dissidence in the Nineteenth-Century House of Commons." *Parliamentary Affairs* 21 (Autumn 1968):338–374.

876. Bylsma, John Robert. "Party Structure in the 1852–1857 House of Commons: A Scalogram Analysis." *Journal of Interdisciplinary History* 7 (Spring 1977):617–635.

877. Bylsma, John Robert. "Political Issues and Party Unity in the House of Commons, 1852–1857: A Scalogram Analysis." Ph.D. dissertation, University of Iowa, 1968. 234 pp.

878. Close, David H. "The Formation of a Two-Party Alignment in the House of Commons Between 1832–1841." *English Historical Review* 84 (April 1969):257–277.

879. Cromwell, Valerie. "The Losing of the Initiative by the House of Commons, 1780–1914." *Royal Historical Society Transactions* 18 (1968):1–23.

880. Durrans, P.J. "House of Commons and the British Empire 1868–1880." *Canadian Journal of History* 9 (April 1974):19–44.

881. Eckles, Robert B. "The Character and Management of the Parties in the House of Commons, 1847–1859." Ph.D. dissertation, Harvard University, 1938. 268 pp.

882. Fraser, P. "Growth of Ministerial Control in the Nineteenth-Century House of Commons." *English Historical Review* 75 (July 1960):444–463.

883. Fraser, P. "The Conduct of Public Business in the House of Commons, 1812–1827." Ph.D. dissertation, London, 1957.

884. Grey, Earl. "The House of Commons." *Nineteenth Century* 15 (1884):507–536.

885. Gwyn, William B. "Financial Aspects of a Parliamentary Career in Aristocratic and Democratic Britain: A Study of the Expenses of Membership in the House of Commons, With Special Reference to the 19th Century." Ph.D. dissertation, London School of Economics, 1956.

886. McGill, B. "Conflict of Interest: English Experience 1782–1914." *Western Political Quarterly* 12 (September 1959):808–827.

887. May, Thomas Erskine. *Erskine May's Private Journal, 1857–1882: Diary of a Great Parliamentarian.* Edited by David Holland and David Menhennet. London: H.M.S.O., 1972. 72 pp.

888. Muller, William Dale. *The Kept Men: The First Century of Trade Union Representation in the House of Commons, 1874–1975.* Hassocks, Eng.: Harvester Press, 1977. 283 pp.

889. O'Connor, T.P. *Gladstone's House of Commons.* London: Ward and Downey, 1885. 567 pp.

890. Porritt, Edward. "Amendments in House of Commons Procedure Since 1881." *American Political Science Review* 2 (November 1908):515–531.

891. Potter, M. "What Sealed Baldwin's Lips?" *Historian* 27 (November 1964):21–36.

892. Roberts, M. "Leadership of the Whig Party in the House of Commons, From 1807 to 1815." *English Historical Review* 50 (October 1935):620–638.

893. Thomas, John Alun. "An Enquiry Into the Change in the Character of the House of Commons, 1832–1901." Ph.D. dissertation, University of London, 1926.

894. Thomas, John Alun. *The House of Commons, 1832–1901: A Study of Its Economic and Functional Character.* Cardiff: University of Wales Press, 1939. 176 pp.

895. Whiteley, William Henry. "Social Composition of the House of Commons, 1868–1885." Ph.D. dissertation, Cornell University, 1960. 605 pp.

History of the House of Commons: 1900s

896. Buck, P.W. "Election Experience of Candidates for the House of Commons, 1918–1955." *Western Political Quarterly* 12 (June 1959):485–491.

897. Buck, P.W. "First Time Winners in the British House of Commons Since 1918." *American Political Science Review* 58 (September 1964):662–667.

898. Cohen, John, and Cooper, Peter. "The 1959 House of Commons." *Occupational Psychology* 35 (October 1961):181–212.

899. Holdsworth, W.S. "The Commons Debates, 1921." *Law Quarterly Review* 52 (October 1936):481–493.

900. Norton, Philip, ed. *Dissension in the House of Commons: Intra-Party Dissent in the House of Commons' Division Lobbies, 1945–1974.* London: Macmillan, 1975. 643 pp.

901. Norton, Philip. *Dissension in the House of Commons, 1974–1979.* Oxford: Clarendon Press, 1980. 524 pp.

902. Norton, Philip. "Intra-Party Dissent in the House of Commons: A Case Study: The Immigration Rules, 1972." *Parliamentary Affairs* 29 (Autumn 1976):404–420.

903. Norton, Philip. "Intra-Party Dissent in the House of Commons: The Parliament of 1974." *Parliamentarian* 58 (October 1977): 240–245.

904. Savoy, D. "Parliamentary Reminiscences, 1940–1955." *Contemporary Review* 192 (August/October 1957):76–80, 137–140, 196–200.

905. Shrapnel, Norman. *The Performers.* London: Constable, 1978. 213 pp.

906. Stone, H.W.J. "The Changing Scene: 25 Years of the House of Commons." *Empire Review* 62 (November 1935):286–292.

907. Study of Parliament Group. *The Commons in the Seventies.* 2d ed. London: Fontana Collins, 1977. 285 pp.

908. Thomas, John Alun. *The House of Commons, 1906–1911, An Analysis of Its Economics and Social Character.* Cardiff: University of Wales Press, 1958. 53 pp.

909. Walkland, S.A. "The House of Commons and the Estimates, 1960." *Parliamentary Affairs* 13 (Autumn 1960):477–488.

910. Wiggin, Jerry. "The Parliamentary Year." *Parliamentarian* 55 (January 1974):17–19.

911. Willson, F.M.G. "Some Career Patterns in British Politics: Whips in the House of Commons, 1906–1966." *Parliamentary Affairs* 24 (Winter 1970/1971):33–42.

912. Winterton, Edward. T. *Orders of the Day.* London: Cassell, 1953. 369 pp.

House of Lords

General Studies of the House of Lords

913. Bailey, Sidney D. *The Future of the House of Lords.* London: The Hansard Society, 1954. 180 pp.

914. Bailey, Sidney D., ed. *The House of Lords: A Symposium.* New York: Praeger, 1954. 180 pp.

915. Bailey, Sidney D. "Introduction to Special Issue on the Future of the House of Lords." *Parliamentary Affairs* 7 (Winter 1953/1954):7–15.

916. Brasher, Norman Henry. "The House of Lords." In his *Studies in British Government,* 2d ed., pp. 121–134. London: Macmillan, 1971.

917. Brasher, Norman Henry. *Studies in British Government.* 2d ed. London: Macmillan, 1971. 224 pp.

918. Bromhead, Peter A., and Shell, Donald R. "The Lords and Their House." *Parliamentary Affairs* 20 (Autumn 1967):337–349.

919. Campion, Gilbert Francis Montriou. "Second Chambers in Theory and Practice." *Parliamentary Affairs* 7 (Winter 1953/1954): 17–32.

920. Chorley, Robert Samuel Theodore. "The House of Lords Controversy." *Public Law (London)* 3 (Autumn 1958):216–235.

921. Chowdharay-Best, George. "Peeresses at the Opening of Parliament." *The Table* 41 (1972/1973):10–27.

922. Coe, Dennis. "Services for British MPs: Progress in the New Parliament." *Parliamentarian* 51 (January 1970):24–29.

923. Crick, Bernard R. "What Should the Lords be Doing?" *Political Quarterly* 34 (April 1963):174–184.

924. Drewry, Gavin, and Brock, Jenny. "Prelates in Parliament." *Parliamentary Affairs* 24 (Summer 1971):222–250.

925. Elwyn-Jones, Lord. "The House of Lords and the EEC." *Journal of Parliamentary Information* 21 (1975):689–698.

926. FitzAlan of Derwent. "The Problem of the House of Lords." *Empire Review* 48 (October 1928):227–231.

927. Furneaux, Rupert. *Tried by Their Peers.* London: Cassell, 1959. 202 pp.

928. Harrison, F. "Real Upper House." *English Review* 4 (March 1910): 695–705.

929. Hayes, Carlton. "Curbing of the Lords." In his *British Social Politics: Materials Illustrating Contemporary State Action for the Solution of Social Problems,* pp. 42–505. Boston: Ginn and Co., 1913.

930. Hazell, R. "Dangerous Law of Conspiracy." *Contemporary Review* 226 (January 1975):25–30.

931. Headlam, Cuthbert. "Conservatives and the House of Lords." *English Review* 42 (May 1926):591–597.

932. Headlam, Cuthbert. "Problem of the House of Lords." *Quarterly Review* 263 (October 1934):185–202.

933. Herbert, Alan P. "House of Lords." *National Review* 131 (October 1948):355–365.

934. Hinchingbrooke, Viscount, and King-Hall, Stephen. "Should Peers Be Paid? Two Views." *Parliamentary Affairs* 7 (Winter 1953/1954):129–135.

935. Kinnear, J.B. "Question of the House of Lords: Contemporary Opinions (report)." *Fortnightly* 180 (December 1953):402–408.

936. Labor Research Department. *The Lords Against the Unions.* London: The Labor Research Department, 1976. 28 pp.

937. Langbein, J.H. "Modern Jurisprudence in the House of Lords: The Passing of London Tramways." *Cornell Review* 53 (May 1968): 807–813.

938. Laski, Harold J. "The Problem of a Second Chamber." In his *Studies in Law and Politics,* pp. 104–124. London: Allen and Unwin, 1932.

939. Liversidge, Douglas. *The House of Lords.* London: F. Watts, 1976. 96 pp.

940. "Lords; Revival of an Old Controversy." *Round Table* 38 (December 1947):411–419.

941. Marriott, John Arthur Ransome. "The Case for the House of Lords." In *Unicameral Legislatures,* edited by E.C. Buehler, pp. 209–222. New York: Barnes and Noble, 1937.

942. Marriott, John Arthur Ransome. "The House of Lords: Analytical and Historical Sketch." In his *Second Chambers,* pp. 6–26. Oxford: Clarendon Press, 1910.

943. Massereene, John S. *The Lords.* London: Frewin, 1973. 287 pp.

944. Mond, A. "Parliament Act and After." *English Review* 9 (November 1911):656–665.

945. Page, A. "Then and Now; Weakened Power of the House of Lords, and Autocratic Tendency of the Executive Government." *National Review* 126 (February 1946):139–143.

946. Pearce, C. "Legal Expenses and the House of Lords." *English Review* 50 (June 1930):720–733.

947. Pike, Luke O. *A Constitutional History of the House of Lords.* London: Macmillan, 1894. 405 pp.

948. Punnett, R.M. "Labour and the Lords." *Contemporary Review* 206 (May 1965):254–256.

949. Punnett, R.M. "The 1964 Ministers of the Crown Act and Ministerial Representation in the House of Lords." *The Table* 33 (1964):69–80.

950. Roberts, G.B. *The Functions of an English Second Chamber.* London: Allen and Unwin, 1926. 254 pp.

951. Rogers, Alan. "Companions of the King." *History Today* 18 (November 1968):805–807.

952. Round, J.H. "The House of Lords and the Model Parliament." *English Historical Review* 30 (July 1915):385–397.

953. Rowse, A.L. "House of Lords and Legislation; a Historical Survey." *Political Quarterly* 4 (July 1933):385–402.

954. Rowse, A.L. *The Question of the House of Lords.* London: Hogarth Press, 1934. 64 pp.

955. Shepherd, Lord. "The House of Lords." *Parliamentarian* 53 (January 1972):1–7.

956. Skene, Norman Hay. *The British Peerage in Parliament.* Ilfra-Combe, Devon: A.H. Stockwell, 1962. 22 pp.

957. Spalding, Thomas A. *The House of Lords: A Retrospect and Forecast.* London: T.F. Unwin, 1894. 281 pp.

958. Stephens, David. "The House of Lords." *Constitutional and Parliamentary Information* 70 (1967):60–70.

959. Stewart, L. "Why a Strong Second Chamber is Needed." *English Review* 43 (August 1926):159–161.

960. "Symposium: The Future of the House of Lords." *Parliamentary Affairs* 7 (Winter 1953/1954):7–176.

961. Vernon-Harcourt, Leveson William. *His Grace the Steward and Trial of Peers.* London: Longmans, Green, 1907. 500 pp.

962. Vincent, John R. "The House of Lords." *Parliamentary Affairs* 19 (Autumn 1966):475–535.

963. Wagner, Anthony, and Sainty, John Christopher. "The Origins of the Introduction of Peers in the House of Lords." *Archaeologia* 101 (1967):119–150.

964. Wallace, Alfred R. "A Representative House of Lords." In his *Studies Scientific and Social,* vol. II, pp. 223–234. London: Macmillan, 1900.

965. Weare, Vincent. "The House of Lords—Prophecy and Fulfillment." *Parliamentary Affairs* 18 (Autumn 1965):422–433.

966. Weare, Vincent, "The Lords Spiritual." *Church Quarterly Review* 167 (April/June 1966):208–214.

967. Wedgwood Benn, Anthony Neil. *The Privy Council as a Second Chamber.* London: Fabian Society, 1957. 26 pp.

968. Windlesham, David James. *Politics in Practice.* London: J. Cape, 1975. 205 pp.

969. Winterton, George. "Is the House of Lords Immortal?" *Law Quarterly Review* 95 (July 1979):386–392.

970. York, Archbishop of. "The Lords Spiritual." *Parliamentary Affairs* 7 (Winter 1953/1954):96–101.

Functions and Duties

971. Burrows, H. "Powers of the House of Lords." *The Table* 20 (1951): 116–125.

972. Burrows, Henry. "Standing Orders of the House of Lords Relative to Private Bills, Etc." *The Table* 17 (1948):67–135.
973. Campbell, C. "House of Lords and Money Bills." *English Review* 45 (November 1927):515–516.
974. Catlin, George E.G. "House of Lords." *Contemporary Review* 193 (January 1958):5–8.
975. Gairdner, J. "The House of Lords: Its Functions." *The Antiquary* 9 (1884):149–156, 255–259.
976. Gibb, Andrew Dewar. *Law From Over the Border: A Short Account of a Strange Jurisdiction.* Edinburgh: W. Green, 1950. 137 pp.
977. Graham, E.D. "Private Legislation in the Light of the Local Government Act of 1972: House of Lords Procedures." *The Table* 47 (1979):109–121.
978. Hobson, J.A. "After the Destruction of the Veto." *English Review* 4 (December 1909):111–121.
979. Landau, J.E. "Precedents in the House of Lords." *Juridical Review* 63 (December 1951):222–233.
980. Marriott, John Arthur Ransome. "The Powers and Duties of the House of Lords." In his *Second Chambers,* pp. 47–88. Oxford: Clarendon Press, 1910.
981. Marsden, Philip Kitson. *In Peril Before Parliament.* London: Barrie and Rockcliff, 1965. 270 pp.
982. McFarlene, K.B. "Had Edward I a Policy Towards the Earls?" *History* 50 (June 1965):145–149.
983. Mirfield, P. "Can the House of Lords Lawfully Be Abolished?" *Law Quarterly Journal* 95 (January 1979):36–58.
984. Powell, John Enoch. "Proxy Voting in the House of Lords." *Parliamentary Affairs* 9 (Spring 1956):203–212.
985. Punnett, R.M. "The Sessional Time-Table of the House of Lords." *The Table* 32 (1963):107–115.
986. Utley, T.E. "Constitution or Tyranny? Proposed Bill to Reduce Power of House of Lords." *National Review* 130 (January 1948): 21–26.
987. Vincent, John R. "Legislation in the House of Lords: A Correction and Reconsideration (of Article in 19 Autumn 1966)." *Parliamentary Affairs* 20 (Spring 1967):178–180.
988. Williams, Ernest Edwin. *The House of Lords and Taxation.* London: P.S. King and Son, 1909. 24 pp.

History of the House of Lords: Origins to 1600

989. Davis, E.J. "Unpublished Manuscript of the Lords' Journals for April and May 1559." *English Historical Review* 28 (July 1913): 531–542.

990. Graves, M.A.R. "The Two Lords' Journals of 1542." *Institute of Historical Research Bulletin* 43 (November 1970):182–189.
991. Herr, Elmer Francis. "The House of Lords Under Charles II." Ph.D. dissertation, University of Wisconsin, 1957. 329 pp.
992. Perceval, R.W. "The Origin and Developments of the House of Lords." *Parliamentary Affairs* 7 (Winter 1953/1954):33–48.
993. Powell, John Enoch, and Wallis, Keith. *The House of Lords in the Middle Ages: A History of the English House of Lords to 1540.* London: Weidenfeld and Nicolson, 1968. 671 pp.
994. Sainty, John Christopher. *Officers of the House of Lords, 1485–1971; a List.* London: House of Lords Record Office, 1971. 22pp.
995. Sainty, John Christopher. "The Origin of the Leadership of the House of Lords." *Institute of Historical Research Bulletin* 47 (May 1974):53–73.
996. Turberville, Arthur S. "House of Lords Under Charles II." *English Historical Review* 44 (July 1929):400–417; 45 (January 1930): 58–77.
997. Weston, Corinne Comstock. *English Constitutional Theory and the House of Lords, 1556–1832.* New York: Columbia University Press, 1965. 304 pp.

History of the House of Lords: 1600s

998. Dawson, D.J. "The Political Activity and Influence of the House of Lords, 1603–1629." B. Litt., Oxford University, 1950.
999. Flemion, Jess Stoddart. "The Nature of Opposition in the House of Lords in the Early Seventeenth Century: A Reevaluation." *Albion* 8 (Spring 1976):17–34.
1000. Flemion, Jess Stoddart. "Slow Process, Due Process, and the High Court of Parliament: A Reinterpretation of the Revival of Judicature in the House of Lords in 1621." *Historical Journal* 17 (March 1974):3–16.
1001. Foster, Elizabeth Read. "House of Lords and Ordinances, 1641–1649." *American Journal of Legal History* 21 (April 1977):157–173.
1002. Hall, M.G. "House of Lords, Edward Randolph, and the Navigation Act of 1696." *William and Mary Quarterly* 14 (October 1957):494–515.
1003. Hart, M.C. "The Upper House During the Protectorates of Oliver and Richard Cromwell." Master's thesis, University of London, 1929.

1004. Horstman, Allen Henry. "Justice and Peers: The Judicial Activities of the Seventeenth-Century House of Lords." Ph.D. dissertation, University of California, Berkeley, 1977. 539 pp.

1005. Miller, Helen. "Attendance in the House of Lords During the Reign of Henry VIII." *Historical Journal* 10 (1967):325-351.

1006. Neale, John E. "The House of Lords Under Elizabeth." Master's thesis, University of Liverpool, 1915.

1007. Relf, F.H. "Debates in the House of Lords, 1628." *Royal Historical Society Transactions* 4 (1925):38-55.

1008. Russell, Conrad S.R. "The Authorship of the Bishop's Diary of the House of Lords in 1641." *Institute of Historical Research Bulletin* 41 (November 1968):229-236.

1009. Schoenfeld, Maxwell Philip. *The Restored House of Lords.* The Hague: Mouton, 1967. 244 pp.

1010. Strickland, Jessie Lovinda. "Constitutional Crisis and the House of Lords, 1621-1629." Ph.D. dissertation, University of California at Berkeley, 1966. 407 pp.

1011. Turberville, Arthur S. *The House of Lords in the Reign of William III.* Oxford: Clarendon Press, 1913. 264 pp.

1012. Vincent, William Allan. "Politics and the Restoration of the House of Lords: 1660-1685." Ph.D. dissertation, Yale University, 1974. 750 pp.

History of the House of Lords: 1700s

1013. Holdsworth, W.S. "The House of Lords, 1689-1783." *Law Quarterly Review* 45 (July-October 1929):307-342, 432-458.

1014. Jones, C. "Debates in the House of Lords on the Church in Danger, 1705, and on Dr. Sacheverell's Impeachment, 1710." *Historical Journal* 13 (September 1976):759-771.

1015. Large, David. "Decline of 'the Party of the Crown' and the Rise of Parties in the House of Lords, 1783-1837." *English Historical Review* 78 (October 1963):669-695.

1016. Lowe, William Curtis. "Politics in the House of Lords, 1760-1775." Ph.D. dissertation, Emory University, 1975. 1077 pp.

1017. McCahill, Michael Woods. *Order and Equipoise: the Peerage and the House of Lords, 1783-1806.* London: Royal Historical Society, 1978. 256 pp.

1018. Turberville, Arthur S. *The House of Lords in the 18th Century.* Oxford: Clarendon Press, 1927. 556 pp.

1019. Turner, R. "Peerage Bill of 1719." *English Historical Review* 28 (April 1913):243-259.

History of the House of Lords: 1800s

1020. Anderson, Olive. "Wensleydale Peerage Case and the Position of the House of Lords, in the Mid-Nineteenth Century." *English Historical Review* 82 (July 1967):486–502.

1021. Collieu, E.G. "The Radical Attitude Towards the Monarchy and the House of Lords, 1868–1885." B. Litt., Oxford University, 1936.

1022. Firth, Charles Harding. *The House of Lords During the Civil War.* New York: Longmans, Green, 1910. 309 pp.

1023. Fraser, Robert S. "The House of Lords in the First Parliament of Queen Victoria, 1837–1841." Ph.D. dissertation, Cornell University, 1967. 1352 pp.

1024. Heuston, R.F.V. "The Wensleydale Peerage Case: A Function of Further Comment." *English Historical Review* 83 (October 1968):777–782.

1025. Large, David. "The House of Lords and Ireland in the Age of Peel, 1832–1850." *Irish Historical Studies* 9 (September 1955):367–399.

1026. Large, David. "The House of Lords, 1832–47." B. Litt., University of Dublin, 1953.

1027. McCahill, Michael Woods. "The House of Lords in the Late Eighteenth Century, 1783–1801." Ph.D. dissertation, Harvard University, 1971. 482 pp.

1028. Macpherson, Norman. *The Appellate Jurisdiction of the House of Lords in Scotch Causes, Illustrated by the Litigation Relating to the Custody of the Marquis of Bute.* Edinburgh: T. and T. Clarke, 1861. 95 pp.

1029. Panteli, S. "House of Lords Since 1830." *Contemporary Review* 212 (April 1968):210–216.

1030. Sachab, A.L. "The Victorian House of Lords." Ph.D. dissertation, Cambridge University, 1924.

1031. Snow, Vernon F. "The Reluctant Surrender of an Absurd Privilege: Proctorial Representation in the House of Lords, 1810–1868." *Parliamentary Affairs* 29 (Winter 1976):60–78.

1032. Stevens, Robert B. *Law and Politics: The House of Lords As a Judicial Body, 1800–1976.* Chapel Hill: University of North Carolina Press, 1978. 701 pp.

1033. Turberville, Arthur S. "The House of Lords as a Court of Law, 1784–1837." *Law Quarterly Review* 52 (April 1936):189–219.

1034. Turberville, Arthur S. *The House of Lords in the Age of Reform 1784–1837; with an Epilogue on Aristocracy and the Advent of Democracy, 1837–1867.* London: Faber and Faber, 1958. 519 pp.

1035. Zaring, Philip Brewer. "In Defense of the Past: the House of Lords, 1860–1886." Ph.D. dissertation, Yale University, 1966. 375 pp.

History of the House of Lords: 1900s

1036. Bromhead, Peter A. *The House of Lords and Contemporary Politics, 1911–1957*. London: Routledge and Paul, 1958. 283 pp.
1037. Morgan, Janet P. *The House of Lords and the Labor Government, 1964–1970*. Oxford: Clarendon Press, 1975. 254 pp.
1038. Phillips, Gregory D. *The Diehards: Aristocratic Society and Politics in Edwardian England*. Cambridge, Mass.: Harvard University Press, 1979. 228 pp.
1039. Punnett, R.M. "House of Lords and Conservative Governments, 1951–64." *Political Studies* 13 (February 1965).83–88.
1040. Stephens, David. "The Procedure of the House of Lords in 1971." *The Table* 40 (1971):60–72.
1041. Weston, Corinne Comstock. "The Liberal Leadership and the Lords' Veto, 1907–1910." *Historical Journal* 11 (1968):508–537.

Organization of Parliament

General Studies on Committees

1042. Bennett, Anthea. "Advising the Cabinet: the Committee of Civil Research and the Economic Advisory Council: A Brief Comparison." *Public Administration* 56 (Spring 1978):51–71.
1043. Body, Richard. "Unofficial Committees in the House of Commons." *Parliamentary Affairs* 11 (Summer 1958):295–302.
1044. Borthwick, R.L. "An Early Experiment with Standing Committees in the House of Lords." *Parliamentary Affairs* 25 (Winter 1971/1972):80–86.
1045. Borthwick, R.L. "Public Bill Committees in the House of Lords." *Parliamentary Affairs* 26 (Autumn 1973):440–453.
1046. Borthwick, R.L. "The Welsh Grand Committee." *Parliamentary Affairs* 21 (Summer 1968):264–276.
1047. Boulton, C.J. "Committees in the British House of Commons." *Constitutional and Parliamentary Information* 68 (1966):192–196.
1048. Burns, J.H. "Scottish Committees of the House of Commons, 1948–59." *Political Studies* 8 (October 1960):272–296.
1049. Chien, Thomson, S. "Parliamentary Committees: A Study in Com-

parative Government." Ph.D. dissertation, Harvard University, 1924. 543 pp.

1050. Edwards, G.E. "The Scottish Grand Committee, 1958 to 1970." *Parliamentary Affairs* 25 (Autumn 1972):303–325.

1051. Edwards, John Goronwy. "Parliamentary Committee of 1398." *English Historical Review* 40 (July 1925):321–333.

1052. Glow, Lotte. "Committee of Safety." *English Historical Review* 80 (April 1965):289–313.

1053. Goldsworthy, David. "The Debate on a Parliamentary Committee for Colonial Affairs." *Parliamentary Affairs* 19 (Spring 1966): 191–207. 252 pp.

1054. Gordon, Strathearn, and Cocks, T.G.B. *A People's Conscience.* London: Constable, 1952.

1055. Hanson, Albert Henry. "Parliamentary Control of Nationalized Industries." *Parliamentary Affairs* 11 (Summer 1958):328–340.

1056. Hanson, Albert Henry, and Wiseman, Herbert V. "The Use of Committees by the House of Commons." *Public Law* 1959 (Autumn 1959):277–292.

1057. Herbert, Alan P. *Anything But Action? A Study of the Uses and Abuses of Committees of Inquiry.* London: Barrie and Rockcliff, 1960. 52 pp.

1058. Kennedy, A.R. "The Shorthand Writer to the Houses of Parliament." *The Table* 43 (1975):58–60.

1059. Lankester, R.S. "Specialist Committees in the House of Commons." *The Table* 38 (1969):64–79.

1060. Mackintosh, John P. *Specialist Committees in the House of Commons: Have They Failed?* Edinburgh: Department of Politics, University of Edinburgh, 1971. 75 pp.

1061. Mather, Jean. "The Parliamentary Committees and the Justices of the Peace, 1642–1661." *American Journal of Legal History* 23 (April 1979):120–143.

1062. Miller, Harris N. "The Influence of British Paliamentary Committees on European Communities Legislation." *Legislative Studies Quarterly* 2 (February 1977):45–75.

1063. Morgan, G. "All Party Committees in the House of Commons." *Parliamentary Affairs* 32 (Spring 1979):56–65.

1064. Morris, Alfred, ed. *The Growth of Parliamentary Scrutiny by Committee: A Symposium.* Oxford: Pergamon Press, 1970. 141 pp.

1065. Neave, Airey. *Control by Committee: The Reform of the Committee System of the House of Commons.* London: Conservative Political Center, 1968. 10 pp.

1066. Partington, Martin. "Parliamentary Committees: Recent Developments." *Parliamentary Affairs* 23 (Autumn 1970):366–379.

1067. Ryle, Michael. "Committees of the House of Commons." *Political Quarterly* 36 (July 1965):295–308.
1068. Study of Parliament Group. *Specialist Committees in the British Parliament: The Experience of a Decade.* London: PEP, 1976. 48 pp.
1069. Walkland, S.A. "Committees in the British House of Commons." in *Committees in Legislatures: A Comparative Analysis,* edited by John D. Lees and Malcolm Shaw, pp. 242–287. Durham, N.C.: Duke University Press, 1979.
1070. Wilcox. J.H. "Some Aspects of the Early History of Committees of the Whole House." *Parliamentary Affairs* 7 (Autumn 1954): 409–419.
1071. Zebel, S.H. "The Committee of the Whole in the Reign of James I." *American Political Science Review* 35 (October 1941):941– 952.

Standing Committees

1072. Borthwick, R.L. "When the Short Cut May be a Blind Alley: The Standing Committee on Regional Affairs." *Parliamentary Affairs* 31 (Spring 1978):201–209.
1073. Chowdharay-Best, George. "The History of Standing Committees." *Parliamentarian* 57 (October 1976):289–293.
1074. Higgins, Graham M. "The Chairmen's Panel." *Parliamentary Affairs* 8 (Autumn 1955):514–525.
1075. Higgins, Graham M. "The Origin and Development of the Standing Committees of the House of Commons, with Special Reference to Their Procedure, 1882–1951. D. Phil., Oxford University, 1953. 262 pp.
1076. Hughes, Christopher J. "The Early History of Standing Committees; 1832–1905. *Parliamentary Affairs* 2 (Autumn 1949):378–390.
1077. Kimber, Richard H., and Richardson, J.J. "Specialization and Parliamentary Standing Committees." *Political Studies* 16 (February 1968):97–101.
1078. Koester, C.B. "Standing Committees in the British House of Commons." *Parliamentarian* 49 (April 1968):64–72.
1079. Norton, Philip. "Dissent in Committee: Intra-Party Dissent in Commons' Standing Committees, 1959–74." *Parliamentarian* 57 (January 1976):15–25.
1080. Norton, Philip. "Standing Committees and the Composition of the House." *Parliamentarian* 57 (October 1976):293–295.

1081. Pring, David. "Standing Committees in the House of Commons."
       Parliamentary Affairs 11 (June 1958):303–317.
1082. Scott, D. "The Financial Bill of 1968 in Standing Committee." *The
       Table* 37 (1968):75–80.
1083. Shearer, J.G.S. "Standing Committees in the House of Commons."
       Parliamentary Affairs 3 (Autumn 1950):558–568.

Select Committees

1084. Allen, E.G. "Pub. and Deb." *Parliamentary Affairs* 5 (Autumn
       1952):356–363.
1085. Arora, R.S. "Parliamentary Scrutiny: The Select Committee De-
       vice." *Public Law* (Spring 1967):30–41.
1086. Barlas, R.D. "Protection of Select Committees Sitting Outside the
       Palace of Westminster." *The Table* 38 (1969):80–84.
1087. Beamish, D.R. "The House of Lords Select Committee on Practice
       and Procedure, 1976–1979." *The Table* 47 (1979):37–47.
1088. Bond, Maurice F. "Witnesses in Parliament: Some Historical
       Notes." *The Table* 40 (1970):15–37.
1089. Bottomley, Arthur. "Specialized Select Committee Procedure in
       U.K." *Journal of Parliamentary Information* 22 (1976):215–
       219.
1090. Boys-Carpenter, John. "Development of the Select Committee in the
       British Parliament." *Parliamentarian* 52 (April 1971):101–104.
1091. Coombes, David L. *The Member of Parliament and the Administra-
       tion: The Case of the Select Committee on Nationalized Indus-
       tries.* London: Allen and Unwin, 1966. 221 pp.
1092. Coombes, David L. "The Scrutiny of Ministers' Powers by the Select
       Committee on Nationalized Industries." *Public Law* (Spring
       1965):9–29.
1093. Davies, E. "Select Committee on Nationalized Industries." *Polit-
       ical Quarterly* 29 (October 1958):378–388.
1094. Donaldson, Frances. *The Marconi Scandal.* New York: Harcourt,
       Brace and World, 1962. 304 pp.
1095. Farmer, H.R.M. "The Select Committee on Procedure." *The Table*
       32 (1963):35–38.
1096. Flegmann, Vilma. "The Public Accounts Committee: A Successful
       Select Committee?" *Parliamentary Affairs* 33 (Spring 1980):
       166–172.
1097. Fluno, Robert Younger. "Parliamentary Control of the British
       Nationalized Industries." Ph.D. dissertation, University of Min-
       nesota, 1952. 209 pp.

1098. Griffith, John A.G. "Special Report from the Select Committee on the House of Commons Disqualification Bill (H.C. 349 of 1955–1956)." *Modern Law Review* 20 (January 1957):52–54.

1099. Iwi, Edward F. "Select Committee." *Modern Law Review* 8 (November 1945):240–243.

1100. Kolinsky, Martin. "Parliamentary Scrutiny of European Legislation." *Government and Opposition* 10 (Winter 1975):46–69.

1101. Lee, J.M. "Select Committees and the Constitution." *Political Quarterly* 21 (April 1970):182–194.

1102. Linstead, Hugh. "The Parliamentary and Scientific Committee." *Parliamentary Affairs* 9 (Autumn 1956):465–469.

1103. Myers, P. "The Select Committee on Scottish Affairs." *Parliamentary Affairs* 27 (Autumn 1974):359–370.

1104. "A New Report from the Nationalized Industries Committee." *Parliamentary Affairs* 13 (Winter 1959/1960):96–99.

1105. Palmer, Arthur. "The Select Committee on Science and Technology." *Parliamentarian* 50 (April 1969):102–105.

1106. Poole, K.P. "The Powers of Select Committees of the House of Commons to Send for Persons, Papers and Records." *Parliamentary Affairs* 32 (Summer 1979):268–278.

1107. Popham, G.T., and Greengrass, D. "The Role and Functions of the Select Committee on Agriculture." *Public Administration* 48 (Summer 1970):137–151.

1108. Proctor, W.A. "The House of Commons Select Committee on Procedure; 1970–1979." *The Table* 47 (1979):13–36.

1109. Scott, D. "The Select Committee on the Civil List (Sessions 1970–71 and 1971–72)." *The Table* 40 (1971):84–89.

1110. "Select Committees of the House of Commons, Westminster." *Parliamentarian* 52 (January 1971):78–82.

1111. Shackleton, Lord. "The Parliamentary and Scientific Committee." *Parliamentarian* 60 (July 1979):149–151.

1112. Shell, Donald R. "Specialist Select Committees." *Parliamentary Affairs* 23 (Autumn 1970):380–404.

1113. Simmons, R.H. "Role of the Select Committee on Nationalized Industry in Parliament." *Western Political Quarterly* 14 (September 1961):741–747.

1114. Strauss, George. "The Member's Financial Interests: Select Committee at Westminster." *Parliamentarian* 51 (April 1970):96–100.

1115. Taylor, Eric S. "The Select Committee on Parliamentary Privilege, 1966–67." *The Table* 37 (1968):16–25.

1116. Walkland, S.A. "Science and Parliament: the Origins and Influence of the Parliamentary and Scientific Committee." *Parliamen-*

tary Affairs 17 (Summer 1964):308–320; 17 (Autumn 1964): 389–402.

1117. Walkland, S.A. "Science and Parliament: The Role of the Select Committees of the House of Commons." *Parliamentary Affairs* 18 (Summer 1965):266–278.

1118. Walkland, S.A. "Unusual or Unexpected Use and the Select Committee on Statutory Instruments." *Parliamentary Affairs* 13 (Winter 1959/1960):61–69.

1119. Williams, Roger. "The Select Committee on Science and Technology: The First Round." *Public Administration* 46 (Autumn 1968):299–313.

1120. Wiseman, Herbert V., "Procedure: the House of Commons and the Select Committee." *Parliamentary Affairs* 13 (Spring 1960): 236–247.

The Speaker

1121. Alderman, R.K. "Contested Elections in the Constituency of Mr. Speaker." *Parliamentarian* 47 (April 1966):132–134.

1122. Alderman, R.K., and Cross, J.A. "The Choosing of Mr. Speaker." *Parliamentarian* 47 (January 1966):77–80.

1123. Bond, Maurice F. "The Manuscripts of Speaker Arthur Onslow." *Institute of Historical Research Bulletin* 45 (November 1972): 327–332.

1124. Cawthorne, Graham. *Mr. Speaker, Sir.* London: Cleaver-Hume Press, 1952. 164 pp.

1125. Cross, J.A. "Deputy Speakers and Party Politics." *Parliamentary Affairs* 18 (Autumn 1965):361–367.

1126. Dasent, Arthur Irwin. *The Speaker of the House of Commons From the Earliest Times to the Present Day . . . with A Portrait of Every Speaker Where One is Known to Exist.* London: John Lane, 1911. 455 pp.

1127. Fowler, Harold L. "Edward Seymour, Speaker of the House of Commons, 1673–1678." Ph.D. dissertation, Harvard University, 1934. 336 pp.

1128. Hitchner, D.G. "The Speaker of the House of Representatives." *Parliamentary Affairs* 13 (Spring 1960):185–197.

1129. King, Horace Maybray. "The Impartiality of the Speaker." *Parliamentarian* 47 (April 1966):125–131.

1130. Laundy, Philip. *The Office of Speaker.* London: Cassell, 1964. 508 pp.

1131. Laundy, Philip. "The Speaker of the House of Commons." *Parliamentary Affairs* 14 (Winter 1960/1961):72–79.

1132. Livingston, W.S. "The Security of Tenure of the Speaker of the House of Common." *Parliamentary Affairs* 11 (Autumn 1958): 484–504.

1133. Lloyd, Selwyn. *Mr. Speaker, Sir.* London: Cape, 1976. 192 pp.

1134. MacDonagh, Michael. *The Speaker of the House.* London: Methuen, 1914. 387 pp.

1135. Millar, David. "Election of a Speaker: First Report of the Procedure Committee, 1971–72." *The Table* (1972/1973):39–44.

1136. Milner, James. "The House of Commons From the Chair." *Parliamentary Affairs* 1 (Winter 1947):59–66.

1137. Perceval, R.W., and Hayter, P.D.G. "The Oath of Allegiance." *The Table* 33 (1964):85–90.

1138. Reid, Loren Dudley. "Charles James Fox: A Study of the Effectiveness of an Eighteenth Century Parliamentary Speaker." Ph.D. dissertation, University of Iowa, 1930. 181 pp.

1139. Rolf, David. "Origins of Mr. Speaker's Conference During the First World War." *History* 64 (February 1979):36–46.

1140. Roskell, John S. "The Medieval Speakers." *Parliamentary Affairs* 4 (1951):451–460.

1141. Roskell, John S. "Thomas Thorpe, Speaker in the Parliament of 1453–4." *Nottingham Mediaeval Studies* 7 (1963):79–105.

1142. Round, J.H. "John Doreward, Speaker, 1399, 1413." *English Historical Review* 29 (October 1914):717–719.

1143. Shakdher, S.L. *Election of the Speaker of the House of Commons.* New Delhi: Government of India Press, 1960. 12 pp.

1144. Sneden, Billy M. "The Westminster Convention and the Speaker." *Parliamentarian* 60 (July 1979):129–132.

1145. Speck, William A. "The Choice of a Speaker in 1705." *Bulletin of Institute of Historical Research* 37 (May 1964):20–46.

1146. Thomas, George. "The Speakership, House of Commons, Westminster." *Parliamentarian* 59 (January 1978):1–7.

1147. Tyler, J.E. "Lord North and the Speakership in 1780." *Parliamentary Affairs* 8 (Summer 1955):363–378.

1148. Wade, Donald William. *Behind the Speaker's Chair.* Leeds: Austicks Publications, 1978. 217 pp.

Whips

1149. Abel, D. "The Whip in History." *Parliamentary Affairs* 9 (Spring 1956):230–237.

1150. Gladstone, Viscount. "The Chief Whip in the British Parliament." *American Political Science Review* 21 (August 1927): 519–528.

1151. Glow, Lotte. "Political Affiliations in the House of Commons After Pym's Death." *Institute of Historical Research Bulletin* 38 (May 1965):48–70.
1152. Gower, G. Leveson. "Recollections of a Government Whip." *Cornhill* 70 (January 1931):55–64.
1153. Norton, Philip. "The Forgotten Whips: Whips in the House of the Lords." *Parliamentarian* 57 (April 1976):86–92.
1154. Searing, Donald D., and Game, C. "Horses for Courses: the Recruitment of Whips in the British House of Commons." *British Journal of Political Science* 7 (July 1977):361–385.

Ombudsman

1155. Cohen, Lionel H. "The Parliamentary Commissioner and the 'M.P. Filter.'" *Public Law* (Autumn 1972):204–214.
1156. Compton, E. "The British Ombudsman." *Administration (Dublin)* 18 (Summer 1970):129–148.
1157. Friedmann, Karl A. "The Public and the Ombudsman: Perceptions and Attitudes in Britain and in Alberta." *Canadian Journal of Political Science* 10 (September 1977):497–525.
1158. Gregory, Roy, and Alexander, A. "'Our Parliamentary Ombudsman'—Part I: Integration and Metamorphosis." *Public Administration (London)* 50 (Autumn 1972):313–331.
1159. Gregory, Roy, and Alexander, A. "'Our Parliamentary Ombudsman'—Part II: Development and the Problem of Identity." *Public Administration (London)* 51 (Spring 1973):41–59.
1160. Gregory, Roy, and Hutchesson, Peter. *The Parliamentary Ombudsman: A Study in the Control of Administrative Action.* London: Allen and Unwin, 1975. 683 pp.
1161. Gwyn, William B. "The British PCA: 'Ombudsman or Ombudsmouse.'" *Journal of Politics* 35 (February 1973):45–69.
1162. Jackson, Paul. "The Work of the Parliamentary Commissioner for Administration." *Public Law* (Spring 1971):39–50.
1163. Mitchell, J.D.B. "The Ombudsman Fallacy." *Public Law* (Spring 1962):24–33.
1164. "Ombudsman and Parliamentary Reform." *Political Quarterly* 37 (January 1966):1–7.
1165. Pedersen, I.M. "The Parliamentary Commissioner: A Danish View." *Public Law* (Spring 1962):15–23.
1166. Pugh, Idwal. "The Ombudsman: Jurisdiction, Powers and Practice." *Public Administration* 56 (Summer 1978):127–138.
1167. Schwartz, B. "The Parliamentary Commissioner and His Office:

The British Ombudsman in Operation." *New York University Law Review* 45 (November 1970):963–994.

1168. Smith, S.A. de. "Anglo-Saxon Ombudsman." *Political Quarterly* 33 (January/March 1962):9–19.

Pressures on Parliament

Crown

1169. Andervont, Carolyn Bancroft. "The Parliamentary Challenge to the Royal Prerogative, 1660–1685." Ph.D. dissertation, University of Wisconsin, 1957. 305 pp.

1170. Belloc, H. "Crown and the Breakdown of Parliament." *English Review* 58 (February 1934):145–152.

1171. Cruickshanks, Eveline G. "The Tories and the Succession of the Crown in the 1714 Parliament." *Institute of Historical Research Bulletin* 46 (November 1973):176–185.

1172. Foord, Archibald Smith. "The Development of the Parliamentary Opposition (Chapters in the History of 'His Majesty's Loyal Opposition')." Ph.D. dissertation, Yale University, 1942. 371 pp.

1173. Forsey, Eugene A. "The Royal Power and Dissolution of Parliament in the British Commonwealth." Ph.D. dissertation, McGill University, 1941. 316 pp.

1174. Forsey, Eugene A. "The Royal Prerogative of Dissolution of Parliament." *Canadian Political Science Association Papers and Proceedings* (1930):81–94.

1175. Gruenfelder, John K. "The Use of the Royal Prerogative in Summoning and Dissolving Parliament, 1603–1642." Ph.D. dissertation, University of Minnesota, 1964. 314 pp.

1176. Hardie, Frank M. "King and the Constitutional Crisis." *History Today* 20 (May 1970):338–347.

1177. Hayter, P.D.G. "Royal Assent: A New Form." *The Table* 36 (1967): 53–57.

1178. Heasman, D.J. "The Monarch, the Prime Minister and the Dissolution of Parliament." *Parliamentary Affairs* 14 (Winter 1960/1961):94–107.

1179. Moodie, Graeme C. "The Crown and Parliament." *Parliamentary Affairs* 10 (1957):256–264.

1180. Napier, A. "The Queen in Parliament." *Parliamentary Affairs* 7 (Winter 1953/1954):49–59.

1181. "Parliament and the Succession Question in 1562–3 and 1566." *English Historical Review* 36 (October 1921):497–520.
1182. Perceval, R.W. "Henry VIII and the Origin of Royal Assent by Commission." *Parliamentary Affairs* 3 (Summer 1950):307–315.
1183. Schaefer, Lawrence V. "The King's Prerogative to Dissolve Parliament and the Political Crisis of December 1783." Ph.D. dissertation, Fordham University, 1976. 324 pp.
1184. Teichman, Raymond Joseph. "King James I, Parliament and the Great Contract, 1603–1610." Ph.D. dissertation, Loyola University of Chicago, 1973. 284 pp.

Executive

1185. Albu, Austen. "The Member of Parliament, the Executive and Scientific Policy." *Minerva* 2 (Autumn 1963):1–20.
1186. Alderman, R.K., and Cross, J.A. "Prime Minister and the Decision to Dissolve." *Parliamentary Affairs* 28 (Autumn 1975):386–404.
1187. Blue, R.N., and Turner, J.E. "Parliament vs. the Executive." *Teaching Political Science* 2 (January 1975):172–200.
1188. Butler, David E. "Ministerial Responsibility in Australia and Britain." *Parliamentary Affairs* 26 (Autumn 1973):403–414.
1189. Chester, Daniel N. "Boards and Parliament." *Public Administration (London)* 36 (Spring 1958):87–92.
1190. Davies, E. "Ministerial Control and Parliamentary Responsibility of Nationalized Industries." *Political Quarterly* 21 (April 1950):150–159.
1191. Eaves, John. *Emergency Powers and the Parliamentary Watchdog: Parliament and the Executive in Great Britain, 1939–1951.* London: Hansard Society, 1957. 208 pp.
1192. Fellowes, Edward. "Parliament and the Executive." *Journal of the Parliaments of the Commonwealth* 43 (October 1962):336–346.
1193. Gavriloff, Gantcho G. "The British Prime Minister as Leader in Parliament, 1950–1953." Ph.D. dissertation, University of Missouri, 1971. 760 pp.
1194. Gladden, E.N. "Parliament and the Civil Service." *Parliamentary Affairs* 10 (Spring 1957):165–179.
1195. Gowan, I. "Ministers of the Crown and the House of Commons." *Public Administration* 30 (Summer 1952):159–162.
1196. Hampton, William. "Parliament and the Civil Service." *Parliamentary Affairs* 17 (Autumn 1964):430–438.
1197. Hanson, Albert Henry. *Parliament and Public Ownership.* London: Cassell, 1961. 248 pp.

1198. Jewell, R.E.C. "Ministry and Parliament." *The Solicitor* 26 (December 1959):297–299.
1199. Jones, G.W.; Smith, B.C.; and Wiseman, Herbert V. "Regionalism and Parliament." *Political Quarterly* 38 (October/December 1967):403–410.
1200. Jones, J.W. "The Prime Minister's Power." *Parliamentary Affairs* 18 (Spring 1965):167–185.
1201. Lee, J.M. "Parliament and the Re-organization of Central Government." *Parliamentary Affairs* 24 (Spring 1971):164–173.
1202. Mackintosh, John P. "The Prime Minister and the Cabinet." *Parliamentary Affairs* 21 (Winter 1967/1968):53–68.
1203. "Ministerial Statements and Explanations. Ministerial Consultations with Outside Bodies." *Modern Law Review* 7 (July 1944): 144–146.
1204. Mukherjee, Amitabha. *Oliver Cromwell and the English Parliament, 1653–1658.* Calcutta: Progressive Publishers, 1964. 92 pp.
1205. Punnett, R.M. "The Parliamentary and Personal Backgrounds of British Prime Ministers, 1812 to 1963." *Quarterly Review* 302 (July 1964):254–266.
1206. Punnett, R.M. "Prime Minister and the Dissolution of Parliament." *Contemporary Review* 208 (February 1966):77–82.
1207. Sainty, John Christopher. "The Evolution of the Parliamentary and Financial Secretaryships of the Treasury." *English Historical Review* 91 (July 1976):566–584.
1208. Walkland, S.A. "Parliament and the Economy in Britain: Some Reflections." *Parliamentary Affairs* 32 (Winter 1979):6–18.
1209. Williams, Thomas. "Parliament and the Executive." *Parliamentarian* 60 (April 1979):81–88.
1210. Willis, John M. *The Parliamentary Powers of English Government Departments.* Cambridge, Mass.: Harvard University Press, 1933. 214 pp.
1211. Willson, F.M.G. "The Parliamentary Charity Commissioner." *Parliamentary Affairs* 12 (Spring 1959):189–198.
1212. Wiseman, Herbert V., comp. *Parliament and the Executive: An Analysis with Readings.* London: Routledge and Kegan Paul, 1966. 271 pp.
1213. Yardley, D.C.M. "The Primacy of the Executive in England." *Parliamentary Affairs* 21 (Spring 1968):155–165.

Foreign Policy

1214. Ajibola, W.A. "The British Parliament and Foreign Policymaking: A Case Study of Britain's Policy Towards the Nigerian Civil

War." *Journal of Economic and Social Studies* 16 (March 1974): 129–147.

1215. Aligwekwe, Evalyn Cumblidge. "The Cyprus Question in the British House of Commons, 1954–1959." Ph.D. dissertation, Bryn Mawr College, 1960. 475 pp.

1216. Anderson, Clifford Bennett. "Parliament and Foreign Affairs, 1604–1629." Ph.D. dissertation, University of Minnesota, 1959. 424 pp.

1217. Anderson, Olive. "Cabinet Government and the Crimean War." *English Historical Review* 79 (July 1964):548–551.

1218. Bennett, Edward Earl. "Parliament and the Colonies to 1715." Ph.D. dissertation, University of Wisconsin, 1925. 195 pp.

1219. Chappell, M.G. "The Select Committee of 1861 on Colonial Military Expenditure and Its Antecedents." Master's thesis, University of London, Westfield College, 1934.

1220. Chase, E.P. "Parliamentary Control of Foreign Policy in Great Britain." *American Political Science Review* 25 (November 1931):861–880.

1221. Cocks, Bernard. "Parliament Goes Abroad." *Parliamentarian* 52 (January 1971):8–13.

1222. Coombes, David L. *Westminster to Brussels: The Significance for Parliament of Accession to the European Community.* London: Hansard Society and the Study of Parliament Group, 1973. 28 pp.

1223. Cumming-Bruce, C.H. "The United Kingdom Delegation to the European Parliament." *The Table* 43 (1975):67–70.

1224. Cumpston, M. "Some Early Indian Nationalists and Their Allies in the British Parliament, 1851–1906." *English Historical Review* 76 (April 1961):279–297.

1225. Dennis, John Harold. "Parliament and the West Indian Economy, 1841–1854." Ph.D. dissertation, University of Georgia, 1975. 207 pp.

1226. Dewey, A.G. "Parliamentary Control of External Relations in the British Dominions." *American Political Science Review* 25 (May 1931):285–310.

1227. Farley, Edith Chapman. "The Relationships of the Venetian Ambassadors in England with the Royal Family, Privy Council and Parliament, 1603–1629." Ph.D. dissertation, Mississippi State University, 1976. 447 pp.

1228. Finer, H. "The British Cabinet, the House of Commons and the War." *Political Science Quarterly* 56 (September 1944):321–360.

1229. Flournoy, Francis Rosebro. "Parliament and War: the Relation of the British Parliament to the Administration of Foreign Policy in Connection with the Initiation of War." Ph.D. dissertation, Columbia University, 1927. 282 pp.

1230. Garland, John Middleton, "Parliament, Foreign Policy and Supply: A Study of English Politics in the Mid 1620s." Ph.D. dissertation, University of Minnesota, 1977. 2 vols.

1231. Gibbs, G.C. "Parliament and Foreign Policy in the Age of Stanhope and Walpole." *English Historical Review* 77 (January 1962):18–37.

1232. Goldsworthy, David. "Parliamentary Questions on Colonial Affairs: A Retrospective Analysis." *Parliamentary Affairs* 23 (Spring 1970):141–153.

1233. Greaves, H.R.G. "Parliament in War-Time." *Political Quarterly* 12 (April 1941):202–213, 292–304, 419–430.

1234. Greaves, H.R.G. "Parliament in War-Time." *Political Quarterly* 13 (October 1942):78–90, 181–192, 311–320, 437–440.

1235. Greaves, H.R.G. "Parliament in War-Time." *Political Quarterly* 14 (April 1943):173–184.

1236. Jennings, William Ivor. "Parliament in War-Time." *Political Quarterly* 11 (April 1940 and January 1941):183–195, 232–247, 351–367; 53–65.

1237. Kenney, Marion L. "The Role of the House of Commons in British Foreign Policy During the 1935–1936, 1936–1937, and 1937–1938 Sessions of Parliament." Ph.D. dissertation, University of Pennsylvania, 1951. 449 pp.

1238. Lachs, P.S. "Advise and Consent: Parliament and Foreign Policy Under the Later Stuarts." *Albion* 7 (Spring 1975):41–54.

1239. Lambert, Sheila. "The Influence of Parliament Upon the Foreign Policy of the Gladstone Government, 1868–74." Master's thesis, University of London, Bedford College, 1949.

1240. Lidderdale, D.W.S. "The House of Commons, Europe and Devolution." *Journal of Parliamentary Information* 22 (1976):15–26.

1241. Ling, Chun Chi. "The British Parliament and Treaty Making." Ph.D. dissertation, University of Wisconsin, 1935. 233 pp.

1242. Mackenzie, Kenneth R. "Going Into Europe." *The Table* 41 (1972/1973):28–33.

1243. "Parliament in War." *Round Table* 127 (June 1942):358–363.

1244. Partin, William Thurman. "English Foreign Policy and the Parliamentary Opposition, 1674–1678." Ph.D. dissertation, Ohio State University, 1971. 201 pp.

1245. Pecker, G.F. "Parliament and the Affairs of the East India Company, 1765–1784." Master's thesis, University of Liverpool, 1910.

1246. Place, Overton Walter. "Parliamentary Debate in Great Britain

Regarding the War with France, 1793–1806.'' Ph.D dissertation, University of Kentucky, 1975. 302 pp.

1247. Powell, I.G. ''The Adhesion of the Royal Navy to Parliament at the Outbreak of the Civil War.'' Master's thesis, University of London, 1919.

1248. Rafuse, John Laurence. ''Egypt and the British Parliament, 1882–1918.'' Ph.D. dissertation, University of Notre Dame, 1972. 235 pp.

1249. Reid, D.S. ''Analysis of British Parliamentary Opinion on American Affairs at the Close of the War of Independence.'' *Journal of Modern History* 18 (September 1946):202–221.

1250. Richards, Peter G. *Parliament and Foreign Affairs.* London: Allen and Unwin, 1967. 191 pp.

1251. Roth, Andrew. *Can Parliament Decide—About Europe, or About Anything?* London: Macdonald, 1971. 229 pp.

1252. Ruigh, Robert Edgar. *The Parliament of 1624: Politics and Foreign Policy.* Cambridge, Mass.: Harvard University Press, 1971. 434 pp.

1253. Russell, Conrad S.R. ''Foreign Policy Debate in the House of Commons in 1621.'' *Historical Journal* 20 (June 1977):289–309.

1254. Rust, William Anthony. ''Defense and Parliamentary Inquiry in Great Britain: Problems of Secrecy, Structure, and Nationality.'' Ph. D. dissertation, Columbia University, 1970. 527 pp.

1255. Ryan, Michael, and Isaacson, Paul. ''Parliament and the European Communities.'' *Parliamentary Affairs* 28 (Spring 1975):199–215.

1256. Sainsbury, John Albert. ''The Pro-American Movement in London 1769–1782: Extra-Parliamentary Opposition to the Government's American Policy.'' Ph.D. dissertation, McGill University, 1975. 412 pp.

1257. Särlvik, Bo; Crewe, Ivor; Alt, James; and Fox, Anthony. ''Britain's Membership of the EEC: A Profile of Electoral Opinions in the Spring of 1974—with a Postscript on the Referendum.'' *European Journal of Political Research* 4 (March 1976):83–113.

1258. Shuman, Allida Lee. ''Parliament and War, 1624–1629.'' Ph.D. dissertation, Bryn Mawr College, 1972. 447 pp.

1259. Stevens, Anne. ''Problems of Parliamentary Control of European Community Policy.'' *Millennium* 5 (Winter 1976/1977):269–281.

1260. Stewart, Michael. ''British Parliament and Foreign Policy.'' *Parliamentarian* 52 (January 1971):1–7.

1261. Strang, L. ''Politicians and Professionals in Diplomacy.'' *Yearbook of World Affairs* 28 (1974):5–14.

1262. Taylor, John. ''British Membership of the European Communities: the Question of Parliamentary Sovereignty.'' *Government and Opposition* 10 (Summer 1975):278–293.

1263. Townsend, Grey Mannering. "British Reactions to the Belgian and Polish Revolutions of 1830: a Study of Diplomatic, Parliamentary, and Press Responses." Ph.D. dissertation, Tulane University, 1974. 455 pp.

1264. Turner, A.C. "The House of Commons and Foreign Policy Between the First and Second Reform Acts." B.Litt., Oxford University, 1948.

1265. Turner, E.R. "Parliament and Foreign Affairs, 1603-1760." *English Historical Review* 34 (April 1919):172-197.

1266. Viton, Albert. "British Parliament in Total War." *Virginia Quarterly Review* 21 (December 1944):19-39.

1267. Willy, T.G. "Defaming the American Indian in the Parliament of 1777." *Indian Historian* 10 (Summer 1977):3-8.

1268. Windreich, Elaine. "Parliamentary Control of British Foreign Policy in Relation to the Spanish Civil War." Ph.D. dissertation, University of California at Berkeley, 1947. 490 pp.

1269. Wollman, David Harris. "Parliament and Foreign Affairs, 1697-1714." Ph.D. dissertation, University of Wisconsin, 1970. 489 pp.

Judicial Appeal

1270. Allott, Philip. "The Courts and the Executive: Four House of Lords Decisions." *Cambridge Law Journal* 36 (November 1977): 255-283.

1271. Bellamy, J.G. "Appeal and Impeachment in the Good Parliament." *Institute of Historical Research Bulletin* 39 (May 1966):35-46.

1272. Blom-Cooper, Louis J., and Drewry, Gavin. *Final Appeal: A Study of the House of Lords and Its Judicial Capacity.* Oxford: Clarendon Press, 1972. 584 pp.

1273. Blom-Cooper, Louis J., and Drewry, Gavin R. "The House of Lords: Reflections on the Social Utility of Final Appellate Courts." *Modern Law Review* 32 (May 1969):262-275.

1274. Brazier, Rodney. "Overruling House of Lords Criminal Cases." *Criminal Law Review* (February 1973):98-104.

1275. Clark, Stanley M. "Gentlemen, Their Leaderships." *American Bar Association Journal* 62 (November 1976):1440-1444.

1276. Cross, Rupert. "Fourth Time Lucky: Similar Fact Evidence in the House of Lords." *Criminal Law Review* (February 1975):62-70.

1277. Cross, Rupert. "The Ratoi Recidendi and a Plurality of Speeches in the House of Lords." *Law Quarterly Review* 93 (July 1977):378-385.

1278. Devlin, Patrick. "Judges, Government and Politics." *Modern Law Review* 41 (September 1978):501–511.

1279. Drewry, Gavin. "Leapfrogging: and a Lords' Justices' Eye View of the Final Appeal." *Law Quarterly Review* 89 (April 1973): 260–281.

1280. Drewry, Gavin. "One Appeal Too Many? An Analysis of the Functions of the House of Lords as a Final Court of Appeal." *British Journal of Sociology* 19 (December 1968):445–452.

1281. Drewry, Gavin. "Parliament and Hanging: Further Episodes in an Undying Saga." *Parliamentary Affairs* 27 (Summer 1974): 251–261.

1282. Edwards, John Goronwy. "Justice in Early Parliaments." *Bulletin of the Institute for Historical Research* 27 (May 1954):35–53.

1283. Fletcher, A.J. "Petitioning and the Outbreak of the Civil War in Derbyshire." *Derbyshire Archaeological Journal* 93 (1973): 33–44.

1284. Fyfe, David Patrick Maxwell. "British Courts and Parliament: The Judiciary in the British Constitution." *American Bar Association Journal* 35 (May 1949):373–374.

1285. Goodman, V.M.R. "Appellate Jurisdiction of the House of Lords." *Parliamentary Affairs* 7 (Winter 1953/1954):77–87.

1286. "The House of Lords and Suspension of the Death Penalty." *Justice of the Peace* 112, 29 May 1948, pp. 334–335.

1287. Iwi, Edward F. "Lords of Appeal in Ordinary Peers or Commoners." *Law Journal* 102 (February 1952):103–104.

1288. Lee, J.M. "Parliament and the Appointment of Magistrates." *Parliamentary Affairs* 13 (Winter 1959/1960):85–94.

1289. Leys, C. "Petitioning in the Nineteenth and Twentieth Centuries." *Political Studies* 3 (February 1955):45–64.

1290. McGregor, Harvey. "In Defence of Lord Devlin." *Modern Law Review* 34 (September 1971):520–527.

1291. McIlwain, Charles Howard. "The High Court of Parliament and Its Supremacy." Ph.D. dissertation, Harvard University, 1911. 409 pp.

1292. McIlwain, Charles Howard. *The High Court of Parliament and Its Supremacy: An Historical Essay on the Boundaries Between Legislation and Adjudication in England.* New Haven, Conn.: Yale University Press, 1910. 408 pp.

1293. Marshall, Geoffrey. "Parliament and the Prerogative of Mercy." *Public Law* (Spring 1961):8–25.

1294. Morton, F.D. "Dual Function of the House of Lords: The Courts of England." *American Bar Association Journal* 35 (November 1949):889–892, 966–969.

1295. Perceval, R.W. "Impeachment." *The Table* 42 (1974):31–33.
1296. Schuyler, Robert L. *Parliament and the British Empire: Some Constitutional Controversies Concerning Imperial Legislative Jurisdiction.* New York: Columbia University Press, 1929. 279 pp.
1297. Smith, S.A., de. "Boundaries Between Parliament and the Courts." *Modern Law Review* 18 (May 1955):281–286.
1298. Smith, T.B. "House of Lords as Supreme Court of Appeals Address." *Scots Law Times* 1950 (May 1950):97–99.
1299. Spielman, Danila Cole. "Impeachments and the Parliamentary Opposition in England, 1621–1641." Ph.D. dissertation, University of Wisconsin, 1959. 234 pp.
1300. Stevens, Robert B. "Judicial Legislation and the Law Lords: Four Interpretations." *The Irish Jurist* 10 (Summer and Winter 1975): 1–23, 216–254.
1301. Stevens, Robert B. "The Role of a Final Appeal Court in A Democracy; the House of Lords Today." *Modern Law Review* 28 (September 1965):509–539.
1302. Tite, Colin G.C. *Impeachment and Parliamentary Judicature in Early Stuart England.* London: Athlone Press, 1974. 249 pp.

Press

1303. Bromhead, Peter A. "Parliament and the Press." *Parliamentary Affairs* 16 (Summer 1963):279–292.
1304. Bush, Henry C. "British Press and Parliamentary Opinion About the Soviet Union, 1946–1950." Ph.D. dissertation, University of Chicago, 1954. 451 pp.
1305. Hidayatullah, M. "Parliamentary Privileges: the Press and the Judiciary." *Journal of Constitutional and Parliamentary Studies* 2 (April/June 1968):1–33.
1306. Lindsay, Thomas F. *Parliament From the Press Gallery.* London: Macmillan, 1967. 176 pp.
1307. MacDonagh, Michael. *The Reporter's Gallery.* London: Hodder and Stoughton, 1913. 452 pp.
1308. Schwoerer, Lois G. "Press and Parliament in the Revolution of 1689." *Historical Journal* 20 (September 1977):545–567.
1309. Thomas, Peter D.G. "Beginning of Parliamentary Reporting in Newspapers, 1768–1774." *English Historical Review* 74 (October 1959):623–636.
1310. Waller, Ian. "Pressure Politics: M.P. and P.R.O." *Encounter* 19 (August 1962):3–15.

Lobbyists

1311. Finer, Samuel Edward. "The Lobbies." *Twentieth Century* 162 (October 1957):371–377.
1312. Kogan, Maurice. *Educational Policy-making: A Study of Interest Groups and Parliament.* London: Allen and Unwin, 1975. 262 pp.
1313. Pym, Bridget A. "Pressure Groups on Moral Issues." *Political Quarterly* 43 (July/September 1972):317–327.
1314. Ramage, Jean Hunter. "The English Woolen Industry and Parliament, 1750–1830: A Study in Economic Attitudes and Political Pressure." Ph.D. dissertation, Yale University, 1970. 378 pp.
1315. Richardson, J.J.; Jordan, A.G.; and Kimber, R.H. "Lobbying Administrative Reform and Policy Styles: The Case of Land Drainage." *Political Studies* 26 (March 1978):47–64.
1316. Robinson, Eric. "Matthew Boulton and the Art of Parliamentary Lobbying." *Historical Journal* 7 (1964):209–229.
1317. Stewart, John D. *British Pressure Groups: Their Role in Relation to the House of Commons.* Oxford: Clarendon Press, 1958. 273 pp.
1318. Wood, David. "Parliamentary Lobby." *Political Quarterly* 36 (July 1965):309–322.

Reform of Parliament

General Studies

1319. Adelman, Paul. "The Second Reform Act of 1867." *History Today* 17 (May 1967):317–325.
1320. Andrews, George Gordon. *Parliamentary Reform in England, 1830–1832.* London: Crofts, 1927. 59 pp.
1321. Alderson, Stanley. "The Need for Greater Parliamentary Production." *Manager* 25 (December 1957):971–974.
1322. Atkins, Elsie M. "The Tory Attitude Towards Parliamentary Reform (1815–1832)." Master's thesis, University of London, King's College, 1931.
1323. Bentham, Jeremy. *Plan of Parliamentary Reform, in the Form of a Catechism, with Reasons for Each Article: With an Introduction, Showing the Necessity of Radical, and the Inadequacy of Moderate Reform.* New York: AMS Press, (1818), 1977. 156 pp.
1324. Black, Eugene Carlton. *The Association: British Extraparliamentary Political Organization, 1769–1793.* Cambridge, Mass.: Harvard University Press, 1963. 344 pp.

1325. Boyer, Barton Lee. "Reform and Revolution: the Parliamentary Debates on the Reform Bill of 1832." Ph.D. dissertation, Claremont Graduate School, 1977. 288 pp.
1326. Brand, Carl Fremont. "The Movement for Parliamentary Reform in England from 1832 to 1867." Ph.D. dissertation, Harvard University, 1923. 470 pp.
1327. Brock, Michael. *The Great Reform Act.* London: Hutchinson, 1973. 411 pp.
1328. Bromhead, Peter A. "How Should Parliament be Reformed." *Political Quarterly* 30 (July 1959):272–282.
1329. Buckley, J.K. "Joseph Parkes of Birmingham and the Part Which He Played in Radical Reform Movements from 1825 to 1845." London: Methuen, 1926. 207 pp.
1330. Butler, James R.M. *The Passing of the Great Reform Bill.* London: Longmans, Green, 1914. 454 pp.
1331. Cahill, Gilbert A., comp. *The Great Reform Bill of 1832: Liberal or Conservative?* Lexington, Mass.: Heath, 1969. 94 pp.
1332. Cahill, Gilbert A. "Popular Movement for Parliamentary Reform, 1829–1932: Some Further Thoughts." *Historian* 37 (May 1975): 436–452.
1333. Cannadine, David. "Economy, Society and Parliamentary Reform, 1820–33: Birmingham Evidence and Westminster Reaction." *Institute of Historical Research Bulletin* 52 (November 1979): 187–199.
1334. Cannon, John A. *Parliamentary Reform, 1640–1832.* Cambridge: Cambridge University Press, 1973. 333 pp.
1335. Chadwick, Mary E.J. "Role of Redistribution in the Making of the Third Reform Act." *Historical Journal* 19 (September 1976): 665–683.
1336. Christie, Ian Ralph. *Wilkes, Wyvill and Reform: The Parliamentary Reform Movement in British Politics, 1760–1785.* London: Macmillan, 1963. 247 pp.
1337. Churgin, Neomi Helen. "Major John Cartwright, a Study in Radical Parliamentary Reform, 1774–1824." Ph.D. dissertation, Columbia University, 1963. 512 pp.
1338. Conacher, J.B. *The Emergence of British Parliamentary Democracy in the Nineteenth Century; the Passing of the Reform Acts of 1832, 1867, and 1884–1885.* New York: Wiley, 1971. 182 pp.
1339. Cook, G.H. "The Evolution of the Franchise in England, with Special Reference to the Reform Act of 1869, and to the Political Influence of Organized Christianity." Master's thesis, University of London, 1922.
1340. Cottenham, Earl of. "Parliamentary Reform—The Urgent Need." *English Review* 59 (July/August 1934):29–39, 163–174.

1341. Cowling, Maurice. *1867: Disraeli, Gladstone and Revolution: the Passing of the Second Reform Bill.* Cambridge: Cambridge University Press, 1967. 451 pp.

1342. Crick, Bernard R. "The Prospects of Parliamentary Reform." *Political Quarterly* 36 (June/September 1965):333–346.

1343. Crick, Bernard R. *The Reform of Parliament.* 2d rev. ed. London: Weidenfeld and Nicolson, 1970. 325 pp.

1344. Cripps, Richard Stafford. *Democracy Up-To-Date: Some Practical Suggestions for the Reorganization of the Political and Parliamentary System.* 2d ed. London: Allen and Unwin, 1944. 108 pp.

1345. Dalton, H. "Labour Party's Proposals for the Reform of Parliamentary Procedure." *Political Quarterly* 5 (October 1934): 469–479.

1346. Davis, Richard W. "Deference and Aristocracy in the Time of the Great Reform Act." *American Historical Review* 81 (June 1976):532–539.

1347. Davis, Richard W. "The Whigs and the Idea of Electoral Deference: Some Further Thoughts on the Great Reform Act." *Durham University Journal* 67 (December 1974):79–91.

1348. Derry, John Wesley. *Parliamentary Reform.* London: Macmillan, 1966. 74 pp.

1349. Dinwiddy, John Rowland. *Christopher Wyvill and Reform, 1790–1820.* York: St. Anthony's Press, 1971. 32 pp.

1350. Elia, R.L. "T.B. Macaulay and W.M. Praed (Reform Act of 1832)." *Notes and Queries* 22 (September 1975):406–407.

1351. Finer, H. "Reform of British Central Government, 1945–1949; Parliamentary Reform." *Journal of Politics* 12 (May 1950):211–222.

1352. Finer, Samuel Edward. *Adversary Politics and Electoral Reform.* London: Wigram, 1975. 372 pp.

1353. Flick, Carlos T. *The Birmingham Political Union and the Movements for Reform in Britain, 1830–1839.* Hamden, Conn.: Archon Books, 1978. 206 pp.

1354. Flick, Carlos T. "Class Character of the Agitation for British Parliamentary Reform." *South Atlantic Quarterly* 68 (Winter 1969):39–55.

1355. Foster, John Galway. *Industry and Electoral Reform.* London: Arms for Freedom and Enterprise, 1975. 8 pp.

1356. Frankle, Robert John. "Parliamentary Crown and Reform, 1689–1701." Ph.D. dissertation, University of Wisconsin, 1970. 304 pp.

1357. Grey, H.G.G. *Parliamentary Government Considered with Reference to Reform, Containing Suggestions for our Representative*

System, and Reform Bills of 1859 and 1861. London: J. Murray, 1864. 360 pp.

1358. Guttsman, W.L. *A Plea for Democracy: An Edited Selection from the 1867 "Essays and Reform" and "Questions for a Reformed Parliament."* London: MacGibbon And Kee, 1967. 304 pp.

1359. Hampsher-Monk, Iain. "Civic Humanism and Parliamentary Reform: the Case of the Society of the Friends of the People." *Journal of British Studies* 18 (Spring 1979):70–89.

1360. Hannay, Robert. *History of the Representation of England, Drawn from Records; and of the Jurisdiction of the House of Commons to Reform Abuses in the Representation, Without the Aid of Statute Law.* London: Longman, Rees, Orme, Brown, and Green, 1831. 290 pp.

1361. Hansard Society for Parliamentary Government. *Parliamentary Reform, A Survey of Recent Proposals for the Commons.* London: Hansard Society, 1967. 208 pp.

1362. Hansard Society for Parliamentary Government. *Parliamentary Reform, 1933–1960: A Survey of Suggested Reforms.* London: Cassel, 1961. 193 pp.

1363. Hansard Society for Parliamentary Government. *The Report of the Hansard Society Commission on Electral Reform, June 1976.* London: Leagrave Press, 1976. 54 pp.

1364. Hardie, Frank M. "Parliamentary Reform in Great Britain: A Critical Analysis of Existing Proposals, with Constructive Comments." Ph.D. dissertation, Oxford University, 1937.

1365. Hardy, Stuart Baxter. "The Political Thought of Walter Bagehot: An Elitist's Critique of Parliamentary Reform." Ph.D. dissertation, Georgetown University, 1974. 343 pp.

1366. Herrick, F.H. "Reform Bill of 1867 and the British Party System." *Pacific Historical Review* 3 (June 1934):216–233.

1367. Hughes, Emrys. *Parliament and Mumbo-Jumbo.* London: Allen and Unwin, 1966. 212 pp.

1368. Hunt, W.K. "The Effects of the Reform Bill of 1832 on Liverpool, and the Contrast Provided by Manchester, 1830–1842." Master's thesis, University of Manchester, 1924.

1369. Jennings, William Ivor. *Parliament Must be Reformed: A Programme for Democratic Government.* London: K. Paul Trench, Trubner, 1941. 64 pp.

1370. Jennings, William Ivor. *Parliamentary Reform.* London: Gollancz, 1934. 175 pp.

1371. Jones, Andrew. *The Politics of Reform, 1884.* Cambridge: Cambridge University Press, 1972. 218 pp.

1372. Lakeman, Enid. "A Case for Electoral Reform." *Contemporary Review* 217 (August 1970):57–62.

1373. Lewis, G.C. "History and Prospects of Parliamentary Reform." *Edinburgh Review* 103 (1856):305–357.

1374. Lindsay, Thomas F. "Is Parliament Out of Date?" *Wiseman Review* 494 (Winter 1962/1963):309–321.

1375. McCabe, Joseph. *The Taint of Politics: A Study in the Evolution of Parliamentary Corruption.* New York: Dodd, Mead, 1920. 288 pp.

1376. McCord, Norman. "Some Difficulties of Parliamentary Reform." *Historical Journal* 10 (1967):376–390.

1377. Mackintosh, John P. "What is Wrong with British Parliamentary Democracy." *Westminster Bank Review* (May 1968):20–35.

1378. Maehl, William Henry. *The Reform Bill of 1932: Why Not Revolution?* New York: Holt, Rinehart & Winston, 1967. 122 pp.

1979. Main, J.M. "The Movement for Parliamentary Reform in Manchester, 1825–1832." Ph.D. dissertation, Oxford University, 1951.

1380. Marshall, Geoffrey. "Parliament and the Constitution." In *Crisis in British Government,* edited by W.J. Stankiewicz, pp. 40–50. London: Collier-Macmillan, 1967.

1381. Marshall, Geoffrey. "Reforming the Parliamentary Commissioner." *Public Administration* 55 (Winter 1977):465–468.

1382. Miller, N.C. "John Cartwright and Radical Parliamentary Reform, 1808–1819." *English Historical Review* 83 (October 1968):705–728.

1383. Miller, N.C. "Major John Cartwright and the Founding of the Hampden Club." *Historical Journal* 17 (September 1974):615–619.

1384. Milton-Smith, John. "Earl Grey's Cabinet and the Objects of Parliamentary Reform." *Historical Journal* 15 (March 1972): 55–74.

1385. Mitchell, Austin. "The Whigs and Parliamentary Reform Before 1830." *Historical Studies: Australia and New Zealand* 12 (October 1965):22–42.

1386. Molesworth, William Nassau. *The History of the Reform Bill of 1832.* London: Chapman and Hall, 1865. 354 pp.

1387. Moonman, Eric. "Electoral Reform." *Parliamentarian* 57 (October 1976):242–249.

1388. Moore, David Cresap. "Sociological Premises of the First Reform Act: A Critical Note." *Victorian Studies* 14 (March 1971):321–337.

1389. Moore, T.C.R. "Reform of Parliament." *English Review* 61 (December 1935): 657–664.

1390. Morris, Homer Lawrence. "Parliamentary-Franchise Reform in England From 1885 to 1918." Ph.D. dissertation, Columbia University, 1921, 208 pp.

1391. Osborne, J.W. "Henry Hunt's Career in Parliament." *Historian* 39 (November 1976):24–39.

1392. Park, Joseph Hendershot. *The English Reform Bill of 1867.* New York: Columbia University, 1920. 285 pp.

1393. Parssinen, T.M. "Association, Convention and Anti-Parliament in British Radical Politics, 1771–1848." *English Historical Review* 88 (July 1973):504–533.

1394. Pollard, Robert S.W. *How to Reform Parliament.* London: Forum Press, 1944. 48 pp.

1395. Reed, R.L. "The Reform Bills of 1884 and 1885." Master's thesis, University of Wales, 1949.

1396. Rogaly, Joe. *Parliament for the People: A Handbook of Electoral Reform.* London: Temple Smith, 1976. 181 pp.

1397. Rose, Hannan. "The Liberal Party and Institutional Reform." *Political Quarterly* 45 (October/December 1974):449–460.

1398. Samuel, H. "Defects and Reforms of Parliament." *Political Quarterly* 2 (July 1931):305–318.

1399. Seymour, Charles. "The Development of Democracy in England Since 1832, as Shown in the Reform of the Representative System." Ph.D. dissertation, Yale University, 1911. 304 pp.

1400. Smith, Francis B. "Democracy in the Second Reform Debates." *Historical Studies: Australia and New Zealand* 11 (October 1964):306–323.

1401. Smith, Francis B. *The Making of the Second Reform Bill.* Cambridge: Cambridge University Press, 1966. 298 pp.

1402. "Some Proposals Towards Constitutional Reform." *English Review* 58 (April 1934):408–414.

1403. Stacey, Frank. *British Government 1966 to 1975: Years of Reform.* London: Oxford University Press, 1975. 243 pp.

1404. Strachey, J., and Joad, C.E.M. "Parliamentary Reform: The New Party's Proposals." *Political Quarterly* 2 (July 1931):319–336.

1405. Study of Parliament Group. *Aspects of Parliamentary Reform.* London: H.M.S.O. 1973. 63 pp.

1406. Sullivan, A.M. "Reform of Parliament." *English Review* 51 (July 1930):28–35.

1407. Trevelyan, George Macaulay. *Lord Grey of the Reform Bill, Being the Life of Charles, Second Earl Grey.* Westport, Conn.: Greenwood Press, 1970. 413 pp.

1408. Turton, Robin H. "Reform of Parliamentary Procedure." *Parliamentarian* 53 (January 1972):69–74.

1409. Veitch, George S. "Genesis of Parliamentary Reform." *American Political Science Review* 9 (May 1915):401–405.

1410. Veitch, George S. *The Genesis of Parliamentary Reform.* London: Constable, 1913. 397 pp.

1411. Vig, N.J., and Walkland, S.A. "Science Policy, Science Administration and Parliamentary Reform." *Parliamentary Affairs* 19 (Summer 1966):281–294.

1412. Vijay, K.I. "Declaration of Interests by MPs: An Analysis of the Current Campaign for Reform." *Political Quarterly* 44 (October 1973):478–486.

1413. Vincent, John R. "The Effect of the Second Reform Act in Lancashire." *Historical Journal* 11 (1968):84–94.

1414. Wade, E.C.S. "The Machinery of Law Reform." *Modern Law Review* 24 (January 1961):3–17.

1415. Wager, David A. "Welsh Politics and Parliamentary Reform 1780–1832." *Welsh History Review* 7 (December 1975):427–449.

1416. Walker, Ernestein. *Struggle for the Reform of Parliament, 1853–1867.* New York: Vantage Press, 1977. 212 pp.

1417. Walkland, S.A. "The Politics of Parliamentary Reform." *Parliamentary Affairs* 29 (Spring 1976):190–200.

1418. Walpole, Spencer. "Great Britain, Last Years of Whiggism, Parliamentary Reform (1856–68)." In *The Cambridge Modern History,* edited by Lord Acton, et al. Cambridge: Cambridge University Press, 1902–1926.

1419. Whale, G.B.M. "The Causes of the Movement for Radical Parliamentary Reform in England, Between 1763 and 1789, with Special Reference to the Influence of the So-Called Rational Protestants." Ph.D. dissertation, Oxford University, 1930.

1420. Winter, James Hannibal. "Cave of Adullam and Parliamentary Reform." *English Historical Review* 81 (January 1966):38–55.

1421. Winter, James Hannibal. "The Liberal Party and Parliamentary Reform: 1852–1867." Ph.D. dissertation, Harvard University, 1961. 304 pp.

1422. Wiseman, Herbert B. "Parliamentary Reform." *Parliamentary Affairs* 12 (Spring 1959):240–254.

1423. Woodbridge, George. *The Reform Bill of 1832.* New York: Cromwell, 1970. 104 pp.

1424. Worlock, David. *Parliament and the People, 1780–1970.* London: Nelson, 1970. 32 pp.

Reform of the House of Commons

1425. Crick, Bernard R. *Reform of the Commons.* London: Fabian Society, 1959. 39 pp.

1426. Cromwell, Valerie. *The Great Reform Bill, 1832, With a Note on Hayter's Picture of the Reformed House of Commons, 1833.* London: H.M.S.O., 1973. 40 pp.

1427. Drewry, Gavin. "Reforming House of Commons Procedures: Another Episode." *Modern Law Review* 42 (January 1979):80–87.

1428. Hanson, Albert Henry. "The Labour Party and House of Commons Reform I." *Parliamentary Affairs* 10 (Autumn 1957):454–468.

1429. Hanson, Albert Henry. "The Labour Party and House of Commons Reform II." *Parliamentary Affairs* 11 (Winter 1957/1958): 39–56.

1430. Mackintosh, John P. "Reform of the House of Commons: the Case for Specialization." In *Modern Parliaments, Change or Decline?*, edited by Gerhard Loewenberg, pp. 33–63. Chicago: Aldine-Atherton, 1971.

1431. Radice, Lisanne. *Reforming the House of Commons.* London: Fabian Society, 1977. 18 pp.

1432. Swinhoe, K. "Richard Crossman and Reform of the Commons." *Political Quarterly* 45 (July 1974):360–364.

Reform of the House of Lords

1433. Bolt, W.J. "House of Lords Reform." *Justice of the Peace* 121 (February 1957):96–98.

1434. Boyd-Carpenter, Lord. "Reform of the House of Lords—Another View." *Parliamentarian* 59 (April 1978):90–93.

1435. Burrows, Henry. "House of Lords—Change or Decay?" *Parliamentary Affairs* 17 (Autumn 1964):403–417.

1436. Chalfont, Lord. "Reform of the House of Lords." *Parliamentarian* 58 (October 1977):233–239.

1437. Chase, E.P. "House of Lords Reform Since 1911." *Political Science Quarterly* 44 (December 1929):569–590.

1438. Chorley, Robert Samuel Theodore. *Reform of the Lords.* London: Fabian Publications, 1954. 41 pp.

1439. Close, David H. "Collapse of Resistance to Democracy: Conservatives, Adult Suffrage, and Second Chamber Reform, 1911–1928." *Historical Journal* 20 (December 1977):893–918.

1440. Clough, Owen. "A Reformed House of Lords: The Dangers of Single-Chamber Government." *Commonwealth Empire Review* (July 1950):46–52.

1441. Comyn-Platt, T. "The House of Lords Reform." *Empire Review* 56 (December 1932):343–348.

1442. Crick, Bernard R. "Tackling the Lords. The Prospects for Parliamentary Reform." In *Crisis in the British Government,* edited by W.J. Stankiewicz, pp. 120–140. London: Collier-Macmillan, 1967.

1443. Denny, E.M.C. "Reform of the House of Lords." *English Review* 49 (October 1929):424–435.
1444. FitzGerald, R.C. "House of Lords and Its Reform." *Current Legal Problems* 1 (1948):69–88.
1445. Hannay, P. "Portrait of Lord Althorp, 1782–1845." *History Today* 27 (December 1977):796–804.
1446. "The House of Lords: Reform Proposals." *Solicitors' Journal* 80 (May 1936):416–417.
1447. Johari, J.C. "Proposals for Reform of the House of Lords." *Indian Journal of Political Science* 31 (April/June 1970):153–166.
1448. Leach, W. "Revisionism in the House of Lords: the Bastion of Rigid 'stare decisis' Falls." *Harvard Law Review* 80 (February 1967): 797–805.
1449. Liberal Party. Working Group on Reform of the House of Lords. *Reform of the House of Lords: Interim report of a Liberal Party Working Group.* London: Liberal Publications Department, 1978. 7 pp.
1450. Lindsay, Martin. *Shall We Reform 'the Lords'?* London: Falcon Press, 1948. 71 pp.
1451. Longford, Earl of. "House of Lords Reform." *Wiseman Review* 494 (Winter 1962/1963):322–326.
1452. McKechnie, William S. *The Reform of the House of Lords, with a Criticism of the Report of the Select Committee of 1908.* Glasgow: J. MacLehose, 1909. 136 pp.
1453. Merrivale, Henry Edward. *The House of Lords: Its Record and Prospects: An Essay on Possible Reforms.* London: Murray, 1935. 67 pp.
1454. Morgan, J.H. "House of Lords Reform. E. Remnant; Hunsdon." *English Review* 45 (August 1927):127–143.
1455. Perceval, R.W., and Gordon, C.A.S.S. "Reform of the House of Lords and the Life Peers Bill." *The Table* 22 (1953):46–51.
1456. Pine, L.G. "Reform of the House of Lords." *Law Journal* 105 (September 1955):583–584.
1457. Ponsonby, Arthur. "The Farce of House of Lords Reform." *Labour Monthly* 11 (December 1932):339–340.
1458. Raglan, Lord. "House of Lords Reform." *English Review* 46 (January 1928):14–18.
1459. Raikes, V. "House of Lords Reform." *English Review* 57 (November 1933):487–493.
1460. "Reform of the House of Lords." *Dublin Review* 192 (January 1933):123–125.
1461. Ross, John. "The Reform of the Second Chamber." *Empire Review* 44 (July 1926):23–27.

1462. Rudlin, W.A. "Report on House of Lords Reform in Great Britain." *American Political Science Review* 27 (April 1933):243–249.

1463. Sainty, John Christopher. "The Joint Committee on House of Lords Reform and the Peerage Bill." *The Table* 31 (1962):13–25.

1464. Schiller, F.C.S. "Eugenical Reform of the House of Lords." *Eugenics Review* 20 (January 1929):237–244.

1465. Smith, S.A. de. "Reform of the Lords. Report of the Joint Committee on House of Lords Reform." *Modern Law Review* 26 (May 1963):288–292.

1466. Smith, Trevor A. *Anti-Politics: Consensus, Reform and Protest in Britain.* London: C. Knight, 1972. 200 pp.

1467. Stevens, Robert B. "The Final Appeal: Reform of the House of Lords and Privy Council, 1867–1876." *Law Quarterly Review* 80 (July 1964):343–369.

1468. Stone, F.G. "The Parliament Act and Second Chamber Reform." *Nineteenth Century* 98 (November 1925):639–656.

1469. Temple-Morris, Peter. *Secundus inter pares: Some New Proposals for Reform of the House of Lords.* London: Bow Publications, 1977. 6 pp.

1470. Wheeler-Booth, M.A.J. "The Attempted Reform of the House of Lords 1964–69." *The Table* 38 (1969):85–109.

1471. Wise, A.R. "House of Lords Reform." *Empire Review* 59 (June 1934):339–343.

Parliament and the Electorate

Elections: General

1472. Abrams, M. "Public Opinion Polls and the British General Election." *Public Opinion Quarterly* 14 (Spring 1950):40–52.

1473. Alexander, J.J. "Dates of Early County Elections." *English Historical Review* 40 (January 1925):1–12.

1474. Ashby, C.; Kirkwood, D.; and Horner, J. "Future of British Politics." *Labour Monthly* 26 (May 1944):137–140.

1475. Belloc, Hilaire, and Chesterton, Cecil. *The Party System.* London: S. Swift, 1911. 226 pp.

1476. Bennett, A. "Elections and the Democratic Idea." *English Review* 4 (February 1910):552–560.

1477. Bonham, J. "Middle Class Revolt." *Political Quarterly* 33 (July 1962):238–246.

1478. "British General Election: Democracy and Inflation." *Round Table* 254 (April 1974):123–132.
1479. Butler, David E., and Stokes, Donald. *Political Change in Britain: The Evolution of Electoral Choice.* 2d ed. New York: St. Martin's Press, 1975. 500 pp.
1480. Cantwell, Frank V. "Meaning of the British Election: Issues, Not Brilliant Leadership, the Important Feature." *Public Opinion Quarterly* 9 (1945):145–157.
1481. Coleman, A.M., and Pountney, I. "Voting Paradoxes: A Socratic Dialogue." *Political Quarterly* 46 (April/July 1975):186–190.
1482. Cook, Hartley K. *The Free and the Independent: The Trials, Temptations and Triumphs of the Parliamentary Elector.* London: Allen and Unwin, 1949. 191 pp.
1483. Dickson, A.D.R. "When Rejects Re-Run: A Study in Independency." *Political Quarterly* 46 (July/September 1975):271–279.
1484. Dutt, R.P. "General Election and British Foreign Policy." *Labour Monthly* 6 (January 1924):17–28.
1485. "Economy and the Electorate." *English Review* 44 (May 1927): 531–536.
1486. Edwards, John Goronwy. "The Emergence of Majority Rule in English Parliamentary Elections." *Royal Historical Society Transactions* 14 (1964):175–196.
1487. Emden, Cecil S. *The People and the Constitution.* 2d ed. Oxford: Clarendon Press, 1956. 339 pp.
1488. Fitzsimons, M.A. "British Elections." *Review of Politics* 14 (January 1952):102–120.
1489. Gibbons, J. "Humours of the Polling Booth." *English Review* 44 (May 1927):564–569.
1490. Hart, Vivien. *Distrust and Democracy: Political Distrust in Britain and America.* Cambridge: Cambridge University Press, 1978. 251 pp.
1491. Hermens, F.A. "Electoral Systems and Political Systems: Recent Developments in Britain." *Parliamentary Affairs* 29 (Winter 1976):47–59.
1492. Holt, Robert R., and Turner, John E. *Political Parties in Action: The Battle of Baron's Court.* New York: Free Press, 1968. 311 pp.
1493. Ionescu, G. "Underlying Question in the British General Election." *Government and Opposition* 13 (Autumn 1978):389–398.
1494. Jessop, Bob. *Traditionalism, Conservatism and British Political Culture.* London: Allen and Unwin, 1974. 287 pp.
1495. Johnson, Nevil. "Servicemen and Parliamentary Elections." *Parliamentary Affairs* 16 (Spring 1963):207–212.

1496. Johnson, Nevil. "Servicemen and Parliamentary Elections 2." *Parliamentary Affairs* 16 (Autumn 1963):440–444.

1497. Jones, Colin. *The University Vote.* London: Bow Group, 1953. 32 pp.

1498. King, Joseph, and Raffety, F.W. *Our Electoral System: The Demand for Reform.* London: T. Murby, 1912. 153 pp.

1499. Krehbiel, E. "Geographic Influences in British Elections." *Geographical Review* 2 (December 1916):419–432.

1500. Lakeman, Enid. "Voice and a Choice: Purpose of the Poll." *Contemporary Review* 208 (May 1966):225–233.

1501. Lane, Peter. *Elections.* London: Batsford, 1973. 96 pp.

1502. Layton-Henry, Z. "Race Electoral Strategy and the Major Parties." *Parliamentary Affairs* 31 (Summer 1978):268–281.

1503. Leonard, Richard L. *Elections in Britain.* London: Van Nostrand, 1968. 102 pp.

1504. Leonard, Richard L. *Guide to the General Election.* London: Pan Books, 1964. 256 pp.

1505. Levy, H.P. "Old Time Elections." *Contemporary Review* 190 (July 1956):38–42.

1506. "List of Opposed Elections on Taking Office." *English Historical Review* 26 (January 1911):139–148.

1507. Lo, Lung-Chi. "The Conduct of Parliamentary Elections in England." New York: J. Lewin, 1928. 186 pp.

1508. Lucas, John R. *Democracy and Participation.* Harmondsworth: Penguin, 1976. 290 pp.

1509. McLean, Iain. *Elections.* London: Longman, 1976. 102 pp.

1510. Martin, L.W. "Bournemouth Affair: Britain's First Primary Election." *Journal of Politics* 22 (November 1960):654–681.

1511. Milnor, Andrew J. "Representation in the Single-Member Districts." In *Elections and Political Stability—An Analytic Study,* pp. 31–45. Boston: Little, Brown, 1969.

1512. Mond, A. "Elections and After." *English Review* 4 (March 1910): 719–728.

1513. Mott, R.L. "Retrospect on the British Election." *Southwestern Political and Social Science Quarterly* 11 (December 1930):260–277.

1514. Mughan, Anthony. "Electorial Change in Britain: The Campaign Reassessed." *British Journal of Political Science* 8 (April 1978): 245–253.

1515. Ogg, F.A. "British Parliamentary Elections." *American Political Science Review* 13 (February 1919):108–114.

1516. "Parliamentary Elections in Britain." *Journal of Constitutional and Parliamentary Studies* 4 (1970):641–658.

1517. "Parliamentary Elections: Who Can Be Elected." *Law Notes* 33 (April 1929):10–14.

1518. Pollitt, H. "General Election and the Class Struggle." *Labour Monthly* 11 (May 1929):273–277.

1519. Potter, A.M. "English Conservative Constituency Association." *Western Political Quarterly* 9 (June 1956):363–375.

1520. Punnett, R.M. "The British Electoral System." *Quarterly Review* 301 (January 1963):11–19.

1521. Ranney, Austin. *Pathways to Parliament: Candidate Selection in Britain.* Madison: University of Wisconsin Press, 1965. 298 pp.

1522. Rasmussen, Jorgen Scott. "Implication of Safe Seats for British Democracy." *Western Political Quarterly* 19 (September 1966): 516–529.

1523. "Recruiting of Parliament." *Round Table* 32 (September 1942): 456–462.

1524. Reynolds, F.M.B. "Election Distributed." *Law Quarterly Review* 86 (July 1970):318–347.

1525. Robinson, H.J. "Weight of the Electorates." *English Review* 6 (August 1910):163–177.

1526. Rose, Richard. *The Problem of Party Government.* London: Macmillan, 1974. 502 pp.

1527. Ross, James Frederick Stanley. *Elections and Electors: Studies in Democratic Representation.* London; Eyre and Spottiswoode, 1955. 480 pp.

1528. Ross, James Frederick Stanley. "Incidence of Election Expenses." *Political Quarterly* 23 (April 1952):175–181.

1529. Slack, P.A. "An Election to the Short Parliament." *Institute of Historical Research Bulletin* 46 (May 1973):108–114.

1530. Watt, D. "Westminster Scene." *Political Quarterly* 45 (April/July 1974):232–242, 346–355.

1531. Williams, Philip M. "Two Notes on the British Electoral System." *Parliamentary Affairs* 20 (Winter 1966/1967):13–30.

Elections: Origins to 1700

1532. Beddard, R.A. "The Sussex General Election of 1695: A Contemporary Account by Robert Middleton, Vicar of Cuchfield." *Sussex Archaeological Collections* 106 (1968):145–157.

1533. Bohannon, M.E. "Essex Election of 1604." *English Historical Review* 48 (July 1933):395–413.

1534. Cherry, George L. "Influence of Irregularities in Contested Elections Upon Election Policy During the Reign of William III." *Journal of Modern History* 27 (June 1955):109–124.

1535. Davis, G. "Election of Richard Cromwell's Parliament, 1658-9." *English Historical Review* 62 (October 1945):488-501.
1536. Edwards, P.S. "The Mysterious Parliamentary Election at Cardigan Borough in 1547." *Welsh History Review* 8 (1976):172-187.
1537. Elton, Geoffrey R. *The Body of the Whole Realm: Parliament and Representation in Medieval and Tudor England.* Charlottesville: University Press of Virginia, 1969. 57 pp.
1538. Farnham, E. "Somerset Election of 1614." *English Historical Review* 46 (October 1931):579-599.
1539. Frear, Mary Reno. "Election at Great Marlow in 1640." *Journal of Modern History* 14 (December 1942):433-448.
1540. George, M.D. "Elections and Electioneering, 1679-81." *English Historical Review* 45 (October 1930):552-578.
1541. George, R.H. "Parliamentary Elections and Electioneering in 1685." *Royal Historical Society Transactions* 19 (1936):167-195.
1542. Golby, John. "The Great Electioneer and His Motives: The Fourth Duke of New Castle." *Historical Journal* 8 (1965):201-218.
1543. Grosvenor, Ian D. "Catholics and Politics: The Worcestershire Election of 1604." *Recusant History* 14 (May 1978):149-162.
1544. Gruenfelder, John K. "The Parliamentary Election for Shrewsbury, 1604." *Shropshire Archaeological Society Transactions* 59 (1973/1974):272-277.
1545. Gruenfelder, John K. "The Parliamentary Election in Northamptonshire, 1626." *Northamptonshire Past and Present* 4 (1968/1969):159-165.
1546. Gruenfelder, John K. "The Spring Parliamentary Election at Hastings, 1640," *Sussex Archaeological Collections* 105 (1967):49-55.
1547. Gruenfelder, John K. "The Spring, 1640, Parliamentary Election at Abingdon." *Berkshire Archaeological Journal* 65 (1970):41-47.
1548. Gruenfelder, John K. "Yorkshire Borough Elections, 1603-1640." *Yorkshire Archaeological Journal* 49 (1977):101-114.
1549. Hoffman, W.J. "Thurloe and the Elections of 1654 and 1656." *Historian* 29 (May 1967):323-342.
1550. Houghton, K.N. "A Document Concerning the Parliamentary Election at Shrewsbury in 1478." *Shropshire Archaeological Society Transactions* 57 (1962/63):162-165.
1551. Houghton, K.N. "Theory and Practice in Borough Elections to Parliament During the Later Fifteenth Century." *Institute of Historical Research Bulletin* 39 (November 1966):130-140.
1552. Illsley, J.S. "Parliamentary Elections in the Reign of Edward I." *Institute of Historical Research Bulletin* 49 (May 1976):24-40.
1553. Jalland, P. "Influence of the Aristocracy on Shire Elections in the

North of England, 1450-70." *Speculum* 47 (July 1972):483-507.

1554. Jessup, Frank W. "The Kentish Election of March, 1640." *Archaeologia Cantiana* 86 (1971):1-10.

1555. Jones, Madeline V. "Election Issues and the Borough Electorates in Mid-Seventeenth Century Kent." *Archaeologia Cantiana* 85 (1970):19-27.

1556. Lewis, N.B. "Re-election to Parliament in the Reign of Richard II." *English Historical Review* 48 (July 1933):364-394.

1557. Lipson, E. "Elections to the Exclusion Parliaments 1679-1681." *English Historical Review* 28 (January 1913):59-85.

1558. Munden, R.C. "The Defeat of Sir John Fortescue: Court Versus Country at the Hustings?" *English Historical Review* 93 (October 1978):811-816.

1559. Neale, John E. "More Elizabethan Elections." *English Historical Review* 61 (January 1946):18-44.

1560. Neale, John E. "Three Elizabethan Elections." *English Historical Review* 46 (April 1931):209-238.

1561. Pinckney, Paul Jan. "The Cheshire Election of 1656." *Bulletin of John Rylands Library* 49 (Spring 1967):387-426.

1562. Plumb, J.H. "The Growth of the Electorate in England From 1600 to 1715." *Past and Present* 45 (November 1969):90-116.

1563. Pole, Jack R. *The Seventeenth Century: The Sources of Legislative Power.* Charlottesville: University Press of Virginia, 1969. 73 pp.

1564. Rogers, Alan. "Parliamentary Elections in Grimsby in the Fifteenth Century." *Institute of Historical Research Bulletin* 42 (November 1969):212-220.

1565. Rogers, Alan. "Parliamentary Electors in Lincolnshire in the Fifteenth Century." *Lincolnshire History and Archaeology* 5 (1970):47-58.

1566. Rogers, Alan. "Parliamentary Electors in Lincolnshire in the Fifteenth Century." *Lincolnshire History and Archaeology* 6 (1971):67-81.

1567. Schafer, R.G. "Robert Harley and the Weobley By-Election of 1691." *Woolhope Naturalists Field Club Transactions* 39 (1969): 456-466.

1568. Seddon, P.R. "The Nottinghamshire Elections for the Short Parliament of 1640." *Thoroton Society Transactions* 80 (1976): 63-68.

1569. Seddon, P.R. "A Parliamentary Election at East Retford, 1624." *Thoroton Society Transactions* 76 (1972):26-34.

1570. Stone, L. "Electoral Influence of the Second Earl of Salisbury, 1614-68." *English Historical Review* 71 (July 1956):384-400.

1571. Swales, R.J.W. "The Howard Interest in Sussex Elections 1529-1558." *Sussex Archaeological Collections* 114 (1976):49–60.
1572. Underdown, David. "The Ilchester Elections, February 1646." *Somersetshire Archaeological and Natural History Society Proceedings* 110 (1966):40–51.
1573. Underdown, David. "Party Management in the Recruiter Elections, 1645–1648." *English Historical Review* 83 (April 1968):235–264.
1574. Virgoe, Roger. "The Cambridgeshire Election of 1439." *Institute of Historical Research Bulletin* 46 (May 1973):95–101.
1575. Virgoe, Roger. "Three Suffolk Parliamentary Elections of the Mid-Fifteenth Century." *Institute of Historical Research Bulletin* 39 (November 1939):185–194.
1576. Williams, C.H. "Norfolk Parliamentary Election, 1461: with Sheriff's Return." *English Historical Review* 40 (January 1925): 79–86.

Elections: 1700s

1577. Cannon, John A. "Polls Supplementary to the History of Parliament Volumes 1715–90." *Institute of Historical Research Bulletin* 47 (May 1974):110–116.
1578. Christie, Ian Ralph. "George III and the Debt of Lord North's Election Account, 1780–1784." *English Historical Review* 78 (October 1963):715–724.
1579. Christie, Ian Ralph "Private Patronage Versus Government Influence: John Buller and the Contest for Control of Parliamentary Elections at Saltash, 1780–1790." *English Historical Review* 72 (April 1956):249–255.
1580. Christie, Ian Ralph. "The Wilkites and the General Election of 1774." *Guildhall Miscellany* 2 (October 1962):155–164.
1581. Dickinson, H.T. "Henry St. John, Wootton Bassett, and the General Election of 1708." *Wiltshire Archaeological Magazine* 64 (1969):107–111.
1582. George, E. "Fox's Martyrs: the General Election of 1784." *Royal Historical Society Transactions* 21 (1939):133–168.
1583. Harrison, Carl. "Radcliffe Steeple Fell in 1792: Or Did It?" *Thoroton Society Transactions* 80 (1976):69–72.
1584. Jenkins, A.P. "Two Shropshire Elections in the Late 18th and Early 19th Centuries." *Caradoc and Severn Valley Field Club Transactions* 16 (November 1968):124–128.
1585. Jennings, R.W. "The Cirencester Contest and Its Aftermath: 1754." *Bristol and Gloucester Archaeological Society Transactions* 92 (1973):157–168.

1586. Kelly, Paul. "Radicalism and Public Opinion in the General Election of 1784." *Institute of Historical Research Bulletin* 45 (May 1972):73–88.

1587. Kerr, Barbara. "Thomas Hyde of Arne and the Poole Election of 1768." *Dorset Natural History and Archaeological Society Proceedings* 89 (1967):282–296.

1588. Laprade, W.T. "Public Opinion and the General Election of 1784." *English Historical Review* 31 (April 1916):224–237.

1589. McLeod, William Reynolds. "Parliamentary Elections in the Home Countries, 1713–1715; a Comparative Study." Ph.D. dissertation, University of Maryland, 1970. 555 pp.

1590. Mayhew, George. "Swift's Political 'Conversion' and His 'Lost' Ballad on the Westminster Election of 1710." *John Rylands Library Bulletin* 53 (Spring 1971):397–427.

1591. Nelson, Allan. "The Parliamentary Election Influence and Activities of the Third Duke of Partland, 1760–1780." Ph.D. dissertation, Fordham University, 1974. 332 pp.

1592. Nulle, S.H. "Duke of Newcastle and the Election of 1727." *Journal of Modern History* 90 (March 1937):1–22.

1593. O'Gorman, Frank. "The General Election of 1784 in Chester." *Chester Archaeological Society Journal* 57 (1970/1971):41–50.

1594. Phillips, N.C. "The British General Election of 1780: A Vortex of Politics." *Political Science* 11 (September 1959):3–22.

1595. Plumb, J.H. "Elections to the House of Commons in the Reign of William III." Ph.D. dissertation, Cambridge University, 1936.

1596. Richards, James Olin. "English Parliamentary Elections and Party Propaganda in the Early Eighteenth Century." Ph.D. dissertation, University of Illinois at Urbana-Champaign, 1962. 287 pp.

1597. Rudé, G. "John Wilkes and the Middlesex Election." *History Today* 11 (February 1961):128–135.

1598. Rudé, G. "Middlesex Electors of 1768–1769." *English Historical Review* 75 (October 1960):601–617.

1599. Shriver, David Perry. "The Problem of Corruption in British Parliamentary Elections, 1750–1860." Ph.D. dissertation, Case Western Reserve University, 1974. 260 pp.

1600. Smith, E.A. "Earl Fitzwilliam and Malton: A Proprietary Borough in the Early Nineteenth Century." *English Historical Review* 80 (January 1965):51–69.

1601. Smith, E.A. "The Election Agent in English Politics, 1734–1832." *English Historical Review* 84 (January 1969):12–35.

1602. Speck, William A. "The General Election of 1715." *English Historical Review* 90 (July 1975):507–522.

1603. Speck, William A. "Londoners at the Polls Under Anne and George I." *Guildhall Studies in London History* 1 (April 1975):253–262.

1604. Speck, William A. *Tory and Whig: The Struggle in the Constituencies, 1701-1715.* London: Macmillan, 1970. 164 pp.

1605. Swanson, R.N. "The Second Northamptonshire Election of 1701." *Northamptonshire Past and Present* 6 (1978):29-31.

1606. Toy, H.S. "Eighteenth-Century Elections of Freemen and Aldermen at Helston, Cornwall." *English Historical Review* 46 (July 1931):452-457.

1607. Turner, J.S.T. "An Augustan Election: The 1710 General Election in the County of Surrey." *Surrey Archaeological Collections* 68 (1971):131-151.

1608. Underdown, P.T. "Henry Cruger and Edmund Burke: Colleagues and Rivals at the Bristol Election of 1774." *William and Mary Quarterly* 15 (January 1958):14-34.

1609. Walcott, Robert R. "East India Interest in the General Election of 1700-1701." *English Historical Review* 71 (April 1956):223-239.

Elections: 1800s

1610. Auchmuty, James J. "Acton's Election as an Irish Member of Parliament." *English Historical Review* 61 (September 1946):394-405.

1611. Blewett, Neal. "The Franchise in the United Kingdom, 1885-1918." *Past and Present* 32 (December 1965):27-56.

1612. Cooke, Alistair B. "Gladstone's Election for the Leith District of Burghs, July 1886." *Scottish Historical Review* 49 (October 1970):172-194.

1613. Douglas, Roy. "The Background to the 'Coupon' Election Arrangements." *English Historical Review* 86 (April 1971):318-336.

1614. Douglas, W.W. "Wordsworth in Politics: The Westmorland Election of 1818." *Modern Language Notes* 63 (November 1948):437-449.

1615. Dunbabin, John P.D. "Parliamentary Elections in Great Britain, 1868-1900: A Psephological Note." *English Historical Review* 81 (January 1966):82-99.

1616. Flick, Carlos T. "The Bedford Election of 1830." *Bedfordshire Historical Record Society* 49 (1970):160-170.

1617. Gash, Norman. "Influence of the Crown at Windsor and Brighton in the Elections of 1832, 1835, and 1837." *English Historical Review* 54 (October 1939):653-663.

1618. Green, David Bonnell. "Wordsworth in the Westmorland Election of 1818: A New Letter to John Taylor." *Modern Language Review* 62 (October 1967): 606-607.

1619. Hanham, Harold J. *Elections and Party Management: Politics in the Time of Disraeli and Gladstone*. London: Longmans, 1959. 468 pp.

1620. Hamer, David A. *The Politics of Electoral Pressure: A Study in the History of Victorian Reform Agitations*. Hassocks, Eng.: Harvester Press, 1977. 386 pp.

1621. Hargreaves, John. "The New Urban Constituencies of 1867." *Local Historian* 13 (August 1979):416–424.

1622. Harvey, Caroline. "The Dorset County Election of 1857." *Dorset National History and Archaeological Society Proceedings* 98 (1976):11–14.

1623. Hechter, M. "Persistence of Regionalism in the British Isles, 1885-1966." *American Journal of Sociology* 79 (September 1973): 319–342.

1624. Hobbs, John L. "John Frail, Election Agent." *Caradoc and Severn Valley Field Club Transactions* 15 (1957/1960):133–140.

1625. Hogarth, C.E. "Derby and Derbyshire Elections, 1837–47." *Derbyshire Archaeological Journal* 95 (1975):48–58.

1626. Hogarth, C.E. "The Derbyshire Parliamentary Elections of 1832." *Derbyshire Archaeological Journal* 89 (1969):68–85.

1627. Hogarth, C.E. "The 1835 Elections in Derbyshire." *Derbyshire Archaeological Journal* 94 (1974):45–59.

1628. Hoppen, K. Theodore. "Tories, Catholics and the General Election of 1859." *Historical Journal* 13 (March 1970):48–67.

1629. Howard, C.H.D. "Parnell Manifesto of 21 November 1885, and the Schools Question." *English Historical Review* 62 (January 1947):42–51.

1630. Howarth, Janet. "The Liberal Revival in Northamptonshire, 1880-1895: A Case Study in the Late Nineteenth Century Elections." *Historical Journal* 12 (1969):78–118.

1631. Hurst, Michael. "Liberal Versus Liberal: The General Election of 1874 in Bradford and Sheffield." *Historical Journal* 15 (December 1972):669–713.

1632. Jasper, R.C.D. "Edward Eliot and the Acquisition of Grampound." *English Historical Review* 58 (October 1943):475–481.

1633. Jowitt, J.A. "A Crossroads in Halifax Politics: Election of 1847." *Halifax Antiquarian Society Transactions* (1973/1974):19–35.

1634. Jupp, Peter. *British and Irish Elections, 1784–1831*. New York: Barnes and Noble, 1973. 212 pp.

1635. Lloyd, Trevor Owen. "Uncontested Seats in British General Elections, 1852–1910." *Historical Journal* 8 (1965):260–265.

1636. McCready, H.W. "British Election of 1874: Frederic Harrison and the Liberal-Labour Dilemma." *Canadian Journal of Economics* 20 (May 1954):166–175.

1637. McQuiston, Julian R. "Farmers' Revolt: The North Shropshire By Election of 1876." *Shropshire Archaeological Society Transactions* 59 (1971/1972):170–180.

1638. McQuiston, Julian R. "Sussex Aristocrats and the County Election of 1820." *English Historical Review* 88 (July 1973):534–558.

1639. Menzies, E.M. "The Freeman Voter in Liverpool, 1802–1835." *Historic Society of Lancashire and Cheshire Transactions* 124 (1972):85–107.

1640. Moore, David Cresap. *The Politics of Deference: A Study of the Mid-Nineteenth Century English Political System.* Hassocks, Eng.: Harvester Press, 1976, 529 pp.

1641. Nossiter, Thomas J. *Influence, Opinion and Political Idioms in Reformed England: Case Studies From the North-East, 1832–74.* New York: Barnes and Noble, 1975, 255 pp.

1642. Nossiter, Thomas J. "Recent Work on English Elections, 1832–1925." *Political Studies* 18 (December 1970):525–528.

1643. O'Leary, Cornelius. *The Elimination of Corrupt Practices in British Elections, 1868–1911.* Oxford: Clarendon Press, 1962. 253 pp.

1644. Olney, R.J. "The Battle of Epworth, 3rd June, 1852." *Lincolnshire History and Archaeology* 5 (1970):39–45.

1645. Pettman, J.C. "The Reform Bill and the Hertford Elections: the Election of 1830." *Hertfordshire Past and Present* 13 (1973): 30–40.

1646. Pettman, J.C. "The Reform Bill and the Hertford Elections, 2. The Election of 1831." *Hertfordshire Past and Present* 14 (1974): 60–72.

1647. Preston, R.A. "W.E. Gladstone and His Disputed Election Expenses at Newark, 1832–1834." *Thoroton Society Transactions* 80 (1976):72–79.

1648. Sanderson, G.N. "Swing of the Pendulum in British General Elections, 1832–1966." *Political Studies* 14 (October 1966):349–360.

1649. Schenkman, A.S. "The British Election Agent." *Parliamentary Affairs* 5 (Autumn 1952):449–454.

1650. Seymour, Charles. *Electoral Reform in England and Wales: The Development and Operation of the Parliamentary Franchise, 1832–1885.* Hamden, Conn.: Archon Books, 1970. 564 pp.

1651. Seymour, Charles. "Electoral Reform in England and Wales: the Development and Operation of the Parliamentary Franchise, 1832–1885." *American Political Science Review* 10 (February 1916):168–171.

1652. Simon, Alan. "Church Disestablishment as a Factor in the General Election of 1885." *Historical Journal* 18 (December 1975): 791–820.

1653. Smith, E.A. "Bribery and Disfranchisement: Wallingford Elections, 1820–1832." *English Historical Review* 75 (October 1960):618-630.

1654. Sutherland, John. "Thackeray, the Oxford Election and the Sunday Question." *Bodleian Library Record* 9 (June 1977):274-279.

1655. Taffs, Winifred A. "General Election of 1868." *Contemporary Review* 188 (September 1955):178-182.

1656. Thompson, A.F. "Gladstone's Whips and the General Election of 1868: Based Largely on the Gladstone Papers." *English Historical Review* 63 (April 1948):189-200.

1657. Veitch, George S. "William Huskisson and the Controverted Elections at Liskeard in 1802 and 1804." *Royal Historical Society Transactions* 13 (1930):205-228.

1658. Vincent, John R. *Pollbooks: How Victorians Voted.* Cambridge: Cambridge University Press, 1967. 194 pp.

1659. Williams, Jeanie. "Bristol in the General Elections of 1818 and 1820." *Bristol and Gloucestershire Archaeological Society Transactions* 87 (1968):173-201.

1660. Woodall, Robert. "The Ballot Act of 1872." *History Today* 24 (July 1974):464-471.

1661. Wright, D.G. *Democracy and Reform, 1815–1885.* London: Longmans, 1970. 160 pp.

Elections: 1900s

1662. Abrams, M. "Opinion Polls and the 1970 British General Election." *Public Opinion Quarterly* 34 (Fall 1970):317-324.

1663. Abrams, M. "Press, Polls and Votes in Britain Since the 1955 General Election." *Public Opinion Quarterly* 21 (Winter 1957/1958):543-547.

1664. Alt, James, et al. "Angels in Plastic: The Liberal Surge in 1974." *Political Studies* 25 (September 1977):343-368.

1665. Alt, James, et al. "Partisanship and Policy Choice: Issue Preferences in the British Electorate, February 1974." *British Journal of Political Science* 6 (July 1976):273-290.

1666. Andrews, William G. "Social Change and Electoral Politics in Britain: A Case Study of Basingstoke, 1964 and 1974." *Political Studies* 22 (September 1974):325-336.

1667. Anwar, Muhammad. "Asian Participation in the October 1974 General Election." *New Community* 4 (Autumn 1975):76-83.

1668. Anwar, Muhammad. "Pakistani Participation in the 1973 Rochdale Local Elections." *New Community* 3 (Winter/Spring 1974):62-72.

1669. Bagley, C.R. "Does Candidates' Position on the Ballot Influence Voters' Choice? A Study of the 1959 and 1964 British General Elections." *Parliamentary Affairs* 19 (Spring 1966):162–174.

1670. Bealey, F. "The Parish Council Elections of Newcastle-Under-Lyme Rural District, May 1961." *North Staffordshire Journal of Field Studies* 11 (1971):81–93.

1671. Bealey, F., and Dyer, M. "Size of Place and the Labour Vote in Britain, 1918–1966." *Western Political Quarterly* 24 (March 1971):84–113.

1672. Beloff, Max. "Reflections on the British General Election of 1966." *Government and Opposition* 1 (August 1966):529–534.

1673. Berrington, Hugh B., and Bedeman, Trevor. "The February Election (1974)." *Parliamentary Affairs* 27 (Autumn 1974):317–332.

1674. Birch, A.H., et al. "Popular Press in the British General Election of 1955." *Political Studies* 4 (October 1956):297–306.

1675. Blewett, Neal. *The Peers, the Parties and the People: the General Elections of 1910.* London: Macmillan, 1972. 548 pp.

1676. Booth, W. "Liberals and the 1923 General Election." *Contemporary Review* 206 (May/June 1965):247–253; 312–315.

1677. Brand, C.F. "British General Election of 1950." *South Atlantic Quarterly* 50 (October 1951):478–498.

1678. Brand, C.F. "British General Election of 1951." *South Atlantic Quarterly* 53 (January 1953):29–53.

1679. Brand, C.F. "British General Election of 1955." *South Atlantic Quarterly* 55 (June 1956):289–312.

1680. Brand, C.F. "British General Election of 1959." *South Atlantic Quarterly* 59 (Fall 1960):521–542.

1681. Brand, C.F. "British General Election of 1964." *South Atlantic Quarterly* 64 (Summer 1965):332–350.

1682. Brand, C.F. "British General Election of 1966." *South Atlantic Quarterly* 66 (Spring 1967):131–147.

1683. Brand, C.F. "British General Election of 1970." *South Atlantic Quarterly* 70 (Summer 1971):350–364.

1684. Butler, David E. *The Electoral System in Britain, 1918–1951.* Oxford: Clarendon Press, 1953. 222 pp.

1685. Cleary, E.J., and Pollins, H. "Liberal Voting at the General Election of 1951." *Sociological Review* 1 (December 1953):27–41.

1686. "Comparative Study of the British Vote, 1918, 1922, and 1923." *Foreign Affairs* 2 (March 1924):504.

1687. Cook, Chris. *The Age of Alignment: Electoral Politics in Britain, 1922–1929.* Toronto: University of Toronto Press, 1975. 367 pp.

1688. Deakin, N., and Bourne, J. "Powell, the Minorities and the 1970 Election." *Political Quarterly* 41 (October 1970):399–415.

1689. Douglass, M.F. "Note on the Recent British General Elections." *Science and Society* 25 (Winter 1961):54–58.
1690. Eatwell, Roger. "Munich, Public Opinion, and Popular Front." *Journal of Contemporary History* 6 (1971):122–139.
1691. Eldersveld, S.J. "British Polls and the 1950 General Election." *Public Opinion Quarterly* 15 (Spring 1951):115–132.
1692. Fox, A.D. "Attitudes to Immigration: A Comparison of Data From the 1970 and 1974 General Election Surveys." *New Community* 4 (Summer 1975):167–178.
1693. "The General Election 1955: Some Impressions by Members of Parliament and Others." *Parliamentary Affairs* 8 (Autumn 1955): 467–481.
1694. Godfrey, J.L. "Onward From Success: the Tory Victory." *Virginia Quarterly Review* 31 (Fall 1955):526–539.
1695. Greenwald, N. "Labour's Reading Victory: A Technical Examination." *Southwestern Social Science Quarterly* 37 (September 1956):111–121.
1696. Harrison, L.H., and Crossland, F.E. "British Labour Party in the General Elections, 1906–1945." *Journal of Politics* 12 (May 1950):383–404.
1697. Hill, A.P. "The Effect of Party Organization: Election Expenses and the 1970 Election." *Political Studies* 22 (June 1974):215–217.
1698. Jaensch, Dean. "The Scottish Vote 1974: A Realigning Party System?" *Political Studies* 24 (September 1974):306–319.
1699. Jenkins, P. "Electoral Post-Mortem." *Encounter* 35 (August 1970): 12–17.
1700. Johnson, R.W. "The Nationalisation of English Rural Politics: Norfolk Southwest, 1945–1970." *Parliamentary Affairs* 26 (Winter 1972/1973):8–55.
1701. Just, Marion R. "Causal Models of Voter Rationality, Great Britain 1959 and 1963." *Political Studies* 21 (March 1973):45–56.
1702. Lakeman, Enid. "British General Election, 1959." *Contemporary Review* 196 (November 1959):206–207.
1703. Laski, Harold J. "General Election, 1935." *Political Quarterly* 7 (January 1936):1–15.
1704. Lemieux, P.H. "Political Issues and Liberal Support in the February 1974, British General Election." *Political Studies* 25 (September 1977):323–342.
1705. Livingston, W.S. "Minor Parties and Minority M.P.'s, 1945–1955." *Western Political Quarterly* 12 (December 1959):1017–1137.
1706. McCallum, R.B. "Thoughts on the General Election." *Contemporary Review* 196 (December 1959):263–269.

1707. McEwen, J.N. "The Coupon Election of 1918 and Unionist Members of Parliament." *Journal of Modern History* 34 (September 1962):294-306.

1708. Mackie, Thomas T., and Rose, Richard. "United Kingdom—Election to the House of Commons, 28th February and 10th October 1974." *European Journal of Political Research* 3 (September 1975):326-327.

1709. McKitterick, T.E.M. "Radicalism After 1964." *Political Quarterly* 36 (January 1965):52-58.

1710. Macmahon, A.W. "British General Election of 1931." *American Political Science Review* 26 (April 1932):333-345.

1711. Miller, William. "Cross-Voting and the Dimensionality of Party Conflict in Britain During the Period of Realignment: 1818-31." *Political Studies* 19 (December 1971):455-461.

1712. Miller, William L. *Electoral Dynamics in Britain Since 1918.* London: Macmillan, 1977. 242 pp.

1713. Miller, William L. "Religious Alignment in England at the General Elections of 1974." *Parliamentary Affairs* 30 (Summer 1977): 258-268.

1714. Miller, William L., and Raab, Gillian. "The Religious Alignment at English Elections Between 1918 and 1970." *Political Studies* 25 (January 1977):227-251.

1715. Morgan William Thomas. "British Elections of December 1923." *American Political Science Review* 18 (May 1924):331-340.

1716. Morgan, William Thomas. "British General Election of 1935; Study of British Public Opinion as Expressed in Ten Daily Newspapers." *South Atlantic Quarterly* 37 (April 1938):108-131.

1717. Morgan, William Thomas. "British General Election of 1945." *South Atlantic Quarterly* 45 (July 1946):297-312.

1718. Morgan, William Thomas. "British Political Debacle in 1931: A Study of Public Opinion." *Southwestern Social Science Quarterly* 13 (September 1932):135-160.

1719. Morse, A.J. "Effect of Popular Opinion on Campaign Slogans—an Illustration." *Public Opinion Quarterly* 13 (Fall 1949):507-510.

1720. Norman, C.H. "Political Defeat of the Working Class." *Labour Monthly* 7 (March 1925):172-179.

1721. Penniman, Howard R., ed. *Britain at the Polls: The Parliamentary Elections of 1974.* Rev. ed. Washington, D.C.: American Enterprise Institute for Public Policy Research, 1975. 256 pp.

1722. Pickles, W. "Psephology Reconsidered: the 1964 General Election Study." *Political Quarterly* 36 (October 1965):460-470.

1723. Pollitt, H. "Communist Party and the Election." *Labour Monthly* 27 (July 1945):197-201.

1724. Pollock, J.K. "English General Election of 1929." *National Municipal Review* 18 (August 1929):505–508.
1725. "Post-Mortem on Voting at the Election; a Mass Observation Report." *Quarterly Review* 284 (January 1946):57–68.
1726. Pugh, Martin. "New Light on Edwardian Voters: the Model Elections of 1906–1912." *Institute of Historical Research Bulletin* 51 (May 1978):103–110.
1727. Rex, Millicent B. "University Constituencies in the Recent British Election." *Journal of Politics* 8 (May 1946):201–211.
1728. Richards, Peter G. "General Election (1950)." *Political Quarterly* 21 (April 1950):114–121.
1729. Richards, Peter G. "Labour Victory: Election Figures." *Political Quarterly* 16 (October 1945):350–356.
1730. Richards, Peter G. "Political Temper; Analysis of By-Election Returns Since 1935." *Political Quarterly* 16 (January 1945):57–66.
1731. Richardson, W.C. "British People Versus Churchill and Co., Ltd." *Southwestern Social Science Quarterly* 31 (September 1950):99–107.
1732. Robertson, James. "The British General Election of 1935." *Journal of Contemporary History* 9 (January 1974):149–164.
1733. Rose, Richard. *The Polls and the 1970 Election.* Glasgow: University of Strathclyde, 1970. 67 pp.
1734. Rowe, E.A. "Broadcasting and the 1929 General Election." *Renaissance and Modern Studies* 12 (1968):108–119.
1735. Russell, Alan K. *Liberal Landslide; the General Election of 1906, Newton Abbot, David and Charles.* Hamden, Conn.: Archon Books, 1973. 260 pp.
1736. Steed, Michael. "National Front Vote." *Parliamentary Affairs* 31 (Summer 1978):282–293.
1737. Studlar, Donley T. "Policy Voting in Britain: the Colored Immigration Issue in the 1964, 1966, and 1970 General Elections." *American Political Science Review* 72 (March 1978):46–64.
1738. Taylor, A.H. "Effect of Party Organization: Correlation Between Campaign Expenditure and Voting in the 1970 Election." *Political Studies* 20 (September 1972):329–331.
1739. "United Kingdom: the Political Situation." *Round Table* 13 (December 1922):130–137.
1740. Wald, K.D. "Class and the Vote Before the First World War." *British Journal of Political Science* 8 (October 1978):441–457.
1741. Wallace, William. "The British General Election of 1970—Impressions of an Academic Candidate." *Government and Opposition* 6 (Winter 1971):36–57.
1742. Wilson, T. "Coupon and the British General Election of 1918." *Journal of Modern History* 36 (March 1964):28–42.

By-Elections

1743. Anwar, Muhammad. "Pakistani Participation in the 1972 Rochdale By-Election." *New Community* 2 (Autumn 1973):418–423.
1744. Buck, P.W. "By-Elections in Parliamentary Careers, 1918–1959." *Western Political Quarterly* 14 (June 1961):432–435.
1745. Butler, David E. "Trends in British By-Elections." *Journal of Politics* 11 (May 1949):396–407.
1746. Cook, Chris, and Ramsden, John, eds. *By-Elections in British Politics.* New York: St. Martin's Press, 1973. 406 pp.
1747. Hill, C.J., and Hazell, P.F. "The 1805 By-Election in Hertfordshire." *Hertfordshire Past and Present* 6 (1966):16–18.
1748. Kenworthy, J.M. "Central Hull By-Election." *English Review* 28 (May 1919):433–435.
1749. Laing, L.H. "Fifty British By-Elections." *Canadian Journal of Economics* 16 (May 1950):222–227.
1750. Rae, S.F. "Oxford By-Election: A Study in the Strawvote Method." *Political Quarterly* 10 (April 1939):268–279.
1751. Richards, Peter G. "Study of By-Elections." *Parliamentary Affairs* 27 (Spring 1974):197–199.
1752. Rossi, John Patrick. "Home Rule and the Liverpool By-Election of 1880." *Irish Historical Studies* 19 (September 1974):156–168.
1753. Rush, Michael. "Timing of By-Elections." *Parliamentary Affairs* 27 (Winter 1973/1974):44–66.
1754. Scammon, R.M. "British By-Elections." *Journal of Politics* 18 (February 1956):83–94.
1755. Scammon, R.M. "British By-Elections, 1952." *American Political Science Review* 47 (June 1953):533–536.
1756. Stannage, C.T. "The East Fulham By-Election, 25 October 1933." *Historical Journal* 14 (1971):165–200.
1757. Steed, Michael. "My Own By-Election." *Government and Opposition* 9 (Summer 1974):345–358.

Electoral Reform

1758. Brett, S.R. "Electoral Reform as a Means to Parliamentary Democracy." *Quarterly Review* 284 (October 1946):457–468.
1759. Driberg, Tom. "Speaker's Conference on the British Electoral Law." *Parliamentarian* 48 (October 1967):213–216.
1760. Gwyn, William B. *Democracy and the Cost of Politics in Britain.* London: Athlone Press, 1962. 256 pp.
1761. Humphreys, John H. *Proportional Representation: A Study in Methods of Elections.* London: Methuen, 1911. 400 pp.

1762. Lakeman, E. "Case of Electoral Reform." *Contemporary Review* 217 (August 1970):57–62.

1763. Mayhew, Christopher P. *The Disillusioned Voter's Guide to Electoral Reform.* London: Arrow Books, 1976. 63 pp.

1764. Newman, R., and Cranshaw, S. "Towards a Closed Primary Election in Britain." *Political Quarterly* 44 (October 1973):447–452.

1765. Park, Joseph Hendershot. "England's Controversy Over the Secret Ballot." *Political Science Quarterly* 46 (March 1931):51–86.

1766. Paterson, Peter. *The Selectorate: The Case for Primary Election in Britain.* London: MacGibbon and Kee, 1967. 190 pp.

1767. Roberts, Geoffrey K. "Point of Departure? The Blake Report on Electoral Reform." *Government and Opposition* 12 (Winter 1977):42–59.

1768. Rogaly, Joe. *Parliament for the People: A Handbook of Electoral Reform.* London: Temple Smith, 1976. 181 pp.

1769. Walkland, S.A. "Adversary Politics and Electoral Reform: A Review." *Political Quarterly* 47 (January 1976):52–58.

1770. Walkland, S.A. "Report of the Hansard Society Commission on Electoral Reform." *Parliamentary Affairs* 29 (Autumn 1976): 450–454.

1771. Winterton, E.M. "Speakers' Conference on Electoral Reform." *Labour Monthly* 26 (March 1944):83–87.

Voting Behavior

1772. Abrams, M. "Social Trends and Electoral Behavior." *British Journal of Sociology* 13 (September 1962):228–242.

1773. Abrams, P., and Little, A. "Young Voter in British Politics." *British Journal of Sociology* 16 (June 1965):95–110.

1774. Allen, A.J. "Voting Recollections and Intentions in Reading: An Opinion Poll Experiment." *Parliamentary Affairs* 20 (Spring 1967):170–177.

1775. Barnett, Malcolm Joel. "Aggregate Models of British Voting Behaviour." *Political Studies* 21 (June 1973):121–134.

1776. Bealey, F. "Electoral Arrangement Between the Labour Representation Committee and the Liberal Party." *Journal of Modern History* 28 (December 1956):353–373.

1777. Bonham, John. *The Middle Class Vote.* London: Faber and Faber, 1954. 210 pp.

1778. Brown, J.C. "Local Party Efficiency as a Factor in the Outcome of British Elections." *Political Studies* 6 (June 1958):174–178.

1779. Butler, D. "Voting Behavior and Its Study in Britain." *British Journal of Sociology* 6 (June 1955):93-103.
1780. Cain, Bruce E. "Dynamic and Static Components of Political Support in Britain." *American Journal of Political Science* 22 (November 1978):849-866.
1781. Cain, Bruce E. "Strategic Voting in Britain." *American Journal of Political Science* 22 (August 1978):639-655.
1782. Clarke, P.F. "Electoral Sociology of Modern Britain." *History* 57 (February 1972):31-55.
1783. Daudt, Hans. *Floating Voters and the Floating Vote: A Critical Analysis of American and English Election Studies.* Leiden: H.E. Stenfert Kroese, 1961. 176 pp.
1784. Davies, P., and Newton, K. "Aggregate Data Analysis of Turnout and Party Voting in Local Elections." *Sociology* 8 (May 1974): 213-231.
1785. Denver, D.T., and Hands, H.T.G. "Differential Party Votes in Multi-Member Electoral Divisions." *Political Studies* 23 (December 1975):486-490.
1786. Denver, D.T., and Hands, H.T.G. "Marginality and Turnout in British General Elections." *British Journal of Political Science* 4 (January 1974):17-35.
1787. Fishbein, Martin; Thomas, Kerry; and Jaccard, James J. *Voting Behaviour in Britain: An Attitudinal Analysis.* London: Social Science Research Council, 1976. 19 pp.
1788. Francis, J.G., and Reele, G. "Reflections on Generational Analysis: Is There a Shared Political Perspective Between Men and Women?" *Political Studies* 26 (September 1978):363-374.
1789. Goldthorpe, John H., et al. *The Affluent Worker: Political Attitudes and Behavior.* Cambridge: Cambridge University Press, 1968. 94 pp.
1790. Hampton, William. "Electoral Response to a Multi-Vote Ballot." *Political Studies* 16 (June 1968):266-272.
1791. Harrop, M. "Beliefs, Feelings and Votes: the British Case." *British Journal of Political Science* 7 (July 1977):301-320.
1792. Himmelwelt, Hilde T. "Memory for Past Vote: Implications of a Study of Bias in Recall." *British Journal of Political Science* 8 (July 1978):365-375.
1793. McLean, Iain. "Problem of Proportionate Swing." *Political Studies* 21 (March 1973):57-63.
1794. Milne, R.S., and MacKenzie, H.C. "Floating Vote." *Political Studies* 3 (February 1955):65-68.
1795. Mosley, P. "Images of the Floating Voter: or, the Political Business Cycle Revisited." *Political Studies* 26 (September 1978):375-394.

1796. Nordlinger, Eric A. *The Working-Class Tories: Authority, Deference and Stable Democracy.* London: MacGibbon and Kee, 1967. 276 pp.

1797. Pear, R.H. "Liberal Vote." *Political Quarterly* 33 (July 1962):247–254.

1798. Ragin, C. "Class, Status, and Reactive Ethnic Cleavages: the Social Bases of Political Regionalism." *American Sociological Review* 42 (June 1977):438–450.

1799. Rallings, C.S. "Two Types of Middle-Class Labour Voter?" *British Journal of Political Science* 5 (June 1975):107–112.

1800. Rose, Richard. *Influencing Voters: A Study of Campaign Rationality.* London: Faber, 1967. 288 pp.

1801. Rose, Richard, and Mossawir, H. "Voting and Elections: A Functional Analysis." *Political Studies* 15 (June 1967):173–201.

1802. Speck, William A.; Gray, W.A.; and Hopkinson, R. "Computer Analysis of Poll Books: A Further Report." *Institute of Historical Research Bulletin* 48 (May 1975):64–90.

1803. Tate, C.N. "Individual and Contextual Variables in British Voting Behavior: An Exploratory Note." *American Political Science Review* 68 (December 1974):1656–1662.

1804. Taylor, A.H. "Measuring Movements Off Electors Using Election Results." *Political Studies* 22 (June 1974):204–209.

1805. Upton, G.J.G. "Diagrammatic Representation of Three-Party Contests." *Political Studies* 24 (December 1976):448–454.

1806. Upton, G.J.G., and Brook, D. "Importance of Positional Voting Bias in British Elections." *Political Studies* 22 (June 1974):178–190.

1807. Vincent, John R. "Electoral Sociology of Rochdale." *Economic History Review* 16 (August 1963):76–90.

1808. Wald, K.D. "Rise of Class-Based Voting in London." *Comparative Politics* 9 (January 1977):219–229.

1809. Weiner, S.L. "Competition for Certainty: The Polls and the Press in Britain." *Political Science Quarterly* 91 (Winter 1976/1977): 673–696.

Representation

1810. Bechhofer, F., and Elliott, B. "Voice of Small Business and the Politics of Survival." *Sociological Review* 26 (February 1978): 57–88.

1811. Bell, Herbert C. "Palmerston and Parliamentary Representation." *Journal of Modern History* 4 (June 1932):186–213.

1812. Benewick, R.J., et al. "Floating Voter and the Liberal View of Rep-
      resentation." *Political Studies* 17 (June 1969):177–195.

1813. Books, J.W., and Reynolds, J.B. "Note on Class Voting in Great
      Britain and the United States." *Comparative Political Studies* 8
      (October 1975):360–376.

1814. "Boundary Commission and the Courts." *Law Journal* 105 (Feb-
      ruary 1955):83–85.

1815. Bromhead, Peter A., and Bromhead, Marjorie Anne. "Malrepresen-
      tation of the People: 1974 Model." *Parliamentary Affairs* 29
      (Winter 1976):7–26.

1816. Butler, David E. "The Redistribution of Seats." *Public Adminis-
      tration (London)* 33 (Summer 1955):125–147.

1817. Carroll, Roy. "The Parliamentary Representation of Yorkshire,
      1625–1660." Ph.D. dissertation, Vanderbilt University, 1964.
      446 pp.

1818. Caunt, George. *Essex in Parliament.* Chelmsford, Eng.: Essex Ar-
      chaeological and Historical Congress, Essex Record Office,
      1969. 147 pp.

1819. Clark, E.V. "Proportional Representation and the Party Machine."
      English Review 52 (January 1931):40–47.

1820. Conniff, J. "Burke, Bristol and the Concept of Representation."
      Western Political Quarterly 30 (September 1977):329–341.

1821. Craig, J.T. "Parliament and Boundary Commissions." *Public Law*
      1959. (Spring 1959):23–45.

1822. Cruickshank, C.G. "Parliamentary Representation of Tournal."
      English Historical Review 83 (October 1968):775–776.

1823. Dann, W.S. "Parliamentary Representation in the Sixteenth Cen-
      tury." Master's thesis, University of London, 1911.

1824. Dean, A.P. "The Concept of Parliamentary Representation in
      Great Britain, 1850–1918. A History of Its Development." B.
      Litt., Oxford University, 1951.

1825. De Villiers, Evangeline. "Parliamentary Boroughs Restored by the
      House of Commons, 1621–41." *English Historical Review* 67
      (April 1952):175–202.

1826. Doyle, Patrick J. "The General Election of 1841: The Representa-
      tion of South Staffordshire." *South Staffordshire Archaeolog-
      ical and Historical Society Transactions* 12 (1970/1971):57–61.

1827. Edwards, P.S. "The Parliamentary Representation of Welsh Bor-
      oughs in the Mid-Sixteenth Century." *Bulletin of the Board of
      Celtic Studies* 27 (1977):425–439.

1828. Elton, Geoffrey R. *The Body of the Whole Realm: Parliament and
      Representation in Medieval and Tudor England.* Charlottesville:
      University of Virginia Press, 1969. 57 pp.

1829. Fieldhouse, R.T. "Parliamentary Representation in the Borough of Richmond." *Yorkshire Archaeological Journal* 44 (1972): 207–216.

1830. Franklin, Mark Newman, and Mughan, Anthony. "Decline of Class Voting in Britain: Problems of Analysis and Interpretation." *American Political Science Review* 72 (June 1978):523–534.

1831. Fulford, Roger. *The Member and His Constituency.* Purley Surrey, Eng.: The Ramsey Muir Educational Trust, 1957. 20 pp.

1832. Gash, Norman. *Politics in the Age of Peel: A Study in the Technique of Parliamentary Representation, 1830–1850.* 2d ed. Hassocks, Eng.: Harvester Press, 1977. 496 pp.

1833. Gooder, Arthur. "The Parliamentary Representation of the County of York from the Earliest Parliaments to 1601. Ph.D. dissertation, University of Leeds, 1933.

1834. Grant, Raymond. *The Parliamentary History of Glamorgan, 1542–1976.* Swansea: C. Davies, 1978. 315 pp.

1835. Haskins, George Lee. *The Growth of English Representative Government.* Philadelphia: University of Pennsylvania Press, 1948. 131 pp.

1836. Havill, E.E. "The Parliamentary Representation of Monmouthshire and the Monmouth Boroughs, 1536–1832." Master's thesis, University of Wales, 1949.

1837. Humberstone, T.L. "University Representation in Parliament." *English Review* 27 (July 1918):49–53.

1838. James, Christopher John. *M.P. for Dewsbury: One Hundred Years of Parliamentary Representation.* Brighouse, Yorkshire: C.J. James, 1970. 348 pp.

1839. Jasper, R.C.D. "The Parliamentary Representation of Grampound." Master's thesis, University of Leeds, 1940.

1840. John, L.B. "The Parliamentary Representation of Glamorgan, 1536–1832." Master's thesis, University of Wales, 1934.

1841. Kermode, D.B. "Legislation Without Representation: the Application of U.K. Legislation to the Isle of Man." *Parliamentary Affairs* 27 (Winter 1973/1974):67–81.

1842. Lively, J.F. "Ideas of Parliamentary Representation in England, 1815–1832." Ph.D. dissertation, Cambridge University, 1957.

1843. McKay, D.H., and Patterson, S.C. "Population Equality and the Distribution of Seats in the British House of Commons." *Comparative Politics* 4 (October 1971):59–76.

1844. Mackintosh, John P. "The Member of Parliament as Representative or as Delegate." *Parliamentarian* 52 (April 1971):14–21.

1845. McKisack, May. "Borough Representation in Richard II's Reign." *English Historical Review* 39 (October 1924):511–525.

1846. McKisack, May. "Parliamentary Representation of King's Lynn Before 1500." *English Historical Review* 42 (October 1927): 583–589.

1847. McKisack, May. *Parliamentary Representation of the English Boroughs During the Middle Ages.* London: Oxford University Press, 1932. 180 pp.

1848. March, J.G. "Party Legislative Representation as a Function of Election Results." *Public Opinion Quarterly* 21 (Winter 1957/1958):521–542.

1849. Mayer, J.P. "Post-War Machinery of Government; Problems of Parliamentary Representation." *Political Quarterly* 15 (April 1944):113–123.

1850. Melton, Frank Tompkins. "London and Parliament: An Analysis of a Constituency, 1661–1702." Ph.D. dissertation, University of Wisconsin, 1969. 379 pp.

1851. Miller, John J. "The Rise of Labor Representation in Parliament." Ph.D. dissertation, University of Iowa, 1943. 204 pp.

1852. Mishler, William, and Mughan, Anthony. "Representing the Celtic Fringe: Devolution and Legislative Behavior in Scotland and Wales." *Legislative Studies Quarterly* 3 (August 1978):377–408.

1853. Park, Godfrey Richard. *Parliamentary Representation of Yorkshire; From the Earliest Representative Parliament on Record to the Dissolution of the Twenty-Second Parliament.* Hull: Barnwell, 1886. 331 pp.

1854. "Parliamentary Representation of the Universities of Great Britain." *Nature* 127, 31 January 1931, pp. 183–184.

1855. Parry, O. "The Parliamentary Representation of Wales and Monmouthshire During the Nineteenth Century—But Mainly Till 1870." Master's thesis, University of Wales, Bangor, 1924.

1856. Pulzer, Peter G.J. *Political Representation and Elections in Britain.* London: Allen and Unwin, 1975. 176 pp.

1857. Richardson, Henry Gerald. "John of Gaunt and the Parliamentary Representation of Lancashire; with Text of Documents." *John Rylands Library Bulletin* 22 (April 1938):175–222.

1858. Robinson, J.J. "Science and Parliamentary Representation." *Nature* 102, 24 October 1918, pp. 144–146.

1859. Rose, M.A. "Petitions in Parliament Under the Lancastrians, From, or Relating to, Towns." Master's thesis, University of London, 1926.

1860. Ross, James Frederick Stanley. *Parliamentary Representation.* 2d ed. London: Eyre and Spottiswoode, 1948. 245 pp.

1861. Runciman, W.G. "'Embourgeoisement', Self-Related Class and Party Preference." *Sociological Review* 12 (July 1964):137–154.

1862. Schwarz, John E. "Impact of Constituency on the Behavior of British Conservative MP's: An Analysis of the Formative Stages of Issue Development." *Comparative Political Studies* 8 (April 1975):75–89.

1863. Skinner, J. "John Bright and the Representation of Manchester in the House of Commons, 1847–57." Master's thesis, University of Wales, Cardiff, 1965.

1864. Snow, Vernon F. "Proctorial Representation and Conciliar Management During the Reign of Henry VIII." *Historical Journal* 9 (1966):1–26.

1865. Sullivan, G.D. "Irish Parliamentary Representation, 1800–1830." B. Litt., University of Dublin, Trinity College, 1950.

1866. Taffs, Winifred A. "The Borough Franchise in the First Half of the Seventh Century." Master's thesis, University of London, 1926.

1867. Taylor, Peter J., and Gudgin, Graham. "A Fresh Look at the Parliamentary Boundary Commissions." *Parliamentary Affairs* 28 (Autumn 1975):405–415.

1868. Taylor, Peter J., and Gudgin, Graham. "The Myth of Non-Partisan Cartography: Electoral Biases in the English Boundary Commission's Redistribution for 1955–1970." *Urban Studies* 13 (February 1976):13–25.

1869. Webber, Richard J. *Parliamentary Constituencies: A Socio-Economic Classification.* London: Office of Population Censuses and Surveys, 1978. 58 pp.

1870. Williams, John F. *Proportional Representation and British Politics.* London: J. Murray, 1914. 99 pp.

1871. Williams, Philip M. "Politics of Redistribution." *Political Quarterly* 39 (July 1968):239–254.

1872. Wood-Legh, K.L. "County Representatives in the Parliaments of Edward III." B. Litt., Oxford University, 1929.

1873. Woolley, S.F. "The Comparative Study of Parliamentary Representation in the New Borough Constituencies Created in 1832." Master's thesis, University of London, External Degree, 1937.

Parties

1874. Adams, William H.D. *English Party Leaders and English Politics.* London: Tinsley, 1878. 2 vols.

1875. Adelman, Paul. *Gladstone, Disraeli and Later Victorian Politics.* Harlow, Longman, 1970. 119 pp.

1876. Alderman, R.K. "The Conscience Clause of the Parliamentary Labour Party." *Parliamentary Affairs* 19 (Spring 1966):224–232.

1877. Alderman, R.K. "Parliamentary Party Discipline in Opposition; the Parliamentary Labour Party 1951-1964." *Parliamentary Affairs* 21 (Spring 1968):124-156.

1878. Allen, A.J. *The English Voter.* London: English Universities Press, 1964. 258 pp.

1879. Alington, Cyril A. *Twenty Years: Being a Study in the Development of the Party System Between 1815-1835.* Oxford: Clarendon Press, 1921. 207 pp.

1880. Bailey, Sydney D., ed. *The British Party System.* London: Hansard Society, 1953. 211 pp.

1881. Bassett, Reginald. *The Essentials of Parliamentary Democracy.* London: Macmillan, 1935. 259 pp.

1882. Beales, Derek E.D. "Parliamentary Parties and the 'Independent' Member, 1810-1860." In *Ideas and Institutions of Victorian Britain: Essays in Honour of George Kitson Clark,* edited by Robert Robson, pp. 1-19. London: Bell, 1967.

1883. Beattie, Alan J., comp. *English Party Politics.* London: Weidenfeld and Nicholson, 1970. 2 vols.

1884. Beattie, Alan J. "Two-Party Legend." *Political Quarterly* 45 (July 1974):288-299.

1885. Beer, Samuel H. *British Politics in the Collectivist Age.* New York: Knopf, 1935. 434 pp.

1886. Beer, Samuel H. *Modern British Politics: A Study of Parties and Pressure Groups.* 2d ed. London: Faber and Faber, 1969. 432 pp.

1887. Brewer, John. *Party Ideology and Popular Politics at the Accession of George III.* Cambridge: Cambridge University Press, 1976. 382 pp.

1888. Brittan, Samuel. *Left or Right: the Bogus Dilemma.* London: Secker and Warburg, 1968. 191 pp.

1889. Bulmer-Thomas, Ivor. *The Growth of the British Party System.* New York: Humanities Press, 1966. 2 vols.

1890. Bulmer-Thomas, Ivor. *The Party System in Great Britain.* London: Phoenix House, 1953. 328 pp.

1891. Burton, Ivor F. *Political Parties in the Reigns of William III and Anne.* London: Athlone Press, 1968. 72 pp.

1892. Butler, David E.; Stevens, Arthur; and Stokes, Donald. "The Strength of the Liberals Under Different Electoral Systems." *Parliamentary Affairs* 22 (Winter 1968/1969):10-15.

1893. Cole, Leonard A. "The Parliamentary Left Wing of the British Labour Party: 1964-1968." Ph.D. dissertation, Columbia University, 1970. 406 pp.

1894. Comfort, George O. *Professional Politicians: A Study of British Party Agents.* Washington: Public Affairs Press, 1958. 69 pp.

1895. Crewe, Ivor, et al. "Partisan Dealignment in Britain, 1964–1974." *British Journal of Political Science* 7 (April 1977):129–190.

1896. Crick, Bernard R. "The Future of the Labour Government." *Political Quarterly* 38 (October/December 1967):375–388.

1897. Cripps, Richard Stafford. "Democracy and Dictatorship." *Political Quarterly* 4 (October 1933):467–481.

1898. Davidson, A. "Why Labour Lost." *Contemporary Review* 217 (August 1970):63–64.

1899. Davidson, John Morrison. *Eminent English Liberals In and Out of Parliament.* London: W. Stewart, 1880. 300 pp.

1900. Davis, Henry W.C. *The Age of Grey and Peel.* Oxford: Clarendon Press, 1929. 347 pp.

1901. Drucker, Henry M. "Leadership Selection in the Labour Party." *Parliamentary Affairs* 29 (Autumn 1976):378–395.

1902. Drucker, Henry M., ed. *Multi-Party Britain.* New York: Praeger, 1979. 242 pp.

1903. Epstein, Leon D. "Cohesion of British Parliamentary Parties." *American Political Science Review* 50 (June 1956):360–377.

1904. Fair, John D. *British Interparty Conferences: A Study of the Procedure of Conciliation in British Politics, 1867–1921.* Oxford: Clarendon Press, 1980. 354 pp.

1905. Finer, Samuel Edward. *The Changing British Party System, 1945–1979.* Washington: American Enterprise Institute for Public Policy Research, 1980. 244 pp.

1906. Finer, Samuel Edward. "Parties at the Parliamentary and Governmental Level." In his *The Changing British Party System, 1945–1979,* pp. 3–31. Washington, D.C.: American Enterprise Institute for Public Policy Research, 1980.

1907. Foord, Archibald Smith. *His Majesty's Opposition, 1714–1830.* Oxford, Clarendon Press, 1964. 494 pp.

1908. Frasure, Robert Conway. "Factionalism in British Parliamentary Parties." Ph.D. dissertation, Duke University, 1970. 250 pp.

1909. Gunn, John A.W. *Factions No More: Attitudes to Party in Government and Opposition in Eighteenth Century England.* London: Cass, 1972. 275 pp.

1910. Hamilton, James Cook. "Parties and Voting Patterns in the Parliament of 1874–1880. Ph.D. dissertation, University of Iowa, 1968. 400 pp.

1911. Harris, William. *The History of the Radical Party in Parliament.* London: K. Paul, Trench, 1885. 510 pp.

1912. Harvey, A.D. "The Third Party in British Politics, 1818–21." *Institute of Historical Research Bulletin* 51 (November 1978):146–159.

1913. Haxey, Simon. *Tory, M.P.* London: Gollancz, 1939. 263 pp.

1914. Hill, Brian W. "Fox and Burke: the Whig Party and the Question of Principles, 1784–1789." *English Historical Review* 89 (January 1974):1–24.

1915. Hill, Brian W. *The Growth of Parliamentary Parties, 1689–1742.* London: Allen & Unwin, 1976. 265 pp.

1916. Jones, G.F. Trevallyn. "Composition and Leadership of the Presbyterian Party in the Convention." *English Historical Review* 79 (April 1964):307–354.

1917. Kenyon, John P. *Revolution Principles: the Politics of Party, 1689–1720.* Cambridge: Cambridge University Press, 1977. 248 pp.

1918. King, Anthony Stephen, ed. *British Politics: People, Parties, and Parliament.* Boston: Heath, 1966. 180 pp.

1919. Kornberg, Allan, and Frasure, Robert Conway. "The Management of Cohesion in British Parliamentary Parties." *Journal of Constitutional and Parliamentary Studies* 6 (1972) 9–33.

1920. Lees, John David, ed. *Political Parties in Modern Britain: An Organizational and Functional Guide.* London: Routledge and Kegan Paul, 1972. 288 pp.

1921. McCabe, Joseph. *The Taint in Politics: A Study in the Evolution of Parliamentary Corruption.* New York: Dodd, Mead, 1920. 288 pp.

1922. McGill, B. "Parliamentary Parties, 1868–1885." Ph.D. dissertation, Harvard University, 1953. 367 pp.

1923. McKenzie, Robert T. *British Political Parties: The Distribution of Power within the Conservative and Labour Parties.* 2d ed. London: Mercury Books, 1964. 694 pp.

1924. Money, L.C. "Impending Triumph of Labour." *English Review* 28 (February 1919):126–133.

1925. Morgan, William Thomas. *English Political Parties and Leaders in the Reign of Queen Anne, 1702–1710.* New Haven, Conn.: Yale University Press, 1920, 427 pp.

1926. Norton, Philip. *Conservation Dissidents: Dissent Within the Parliamentary Conservative Party, 1970–74.* London: Temple Smith, 1978. 331 pp.

1927. Pike, Edgar R. *Political Parties and Policies.* 3d ed. London: I. Pitman, 1948. 101 pp.

1928. "Political Parties and the Alternative Vote." *Political Quarterly* 2 (April 1931):251–256.

1929. Pollitt, H. "Communist Party and the Whitechapel By-Election." *Labour Monthly* 13 (January 1931):29–34.

1930. Quinault, R.E. "Fourth Party and the Conservative Opposition to Bradlaugh 1880–1888." *English Historical Review* 91 (April 1976):315–340.

1931. Rasmussen, Jorgen Scott. "Government and Intra-Party Opposition: Dissent Within the Conservative Parliamentary Party in the 1930's." *Political Studies* 19 (June 1971):172–183.

1932. Rees, Mogg, W.; McKitterick, T.E.M.; and Skelsey, P. "The Selection of Parliamentary Candidates." *Political Quarterly* 30 (July/September 1959):215–229.

1933. Richards, Peter G. "A Study in Political Apprenticeship." *Parliamentary Affairs* 9 (Summer 1956):353–357.

1934. Roberts, Geoffrey K. *Political Parties and Pressure Groups in Britain.* London: Weidenfeld and Nicolson, 1970. 203 pp.

1935. Rodden, Brian William. "Anatomy of the 1886 Schism in the British Liberal Party: A Study of the Ninety-Four Liberal Members of Parliament Who Voted Against the First Home Rule Bill." Ed.D. dissertation, Rutgers University, State University of New Jersey, 1968. 728 pp.

1936. Rush, Michael. *The Selection of Parliamentary Candidates.* London: Nelson, 1969. 307 pp.

1937. Russell, Conrad S.R. *Parliaments and English Politics 1621–1629.* London: Oxford University Press, 1979. 453 pp.

1938. Sack, James J. *The Grenvillities, 1801–29: Party Politics and Factionalism in the Age of Pitt and Liverpool.* Urbana: University of Illinois Press, 1979. 244 pp.

1939. Seyd, P. "Democracy Within the Conservative Party?" *Government and Opposition* 10 (Spring 1975):219–237.

1940. Smellie, Kingsley B. *A Hundred Years of English Government.* London: Macmillan, 1937. 468 pp.

1941. Smiley, Donald Victor. "A Comparative Study of Party Discipline in the House of Commons of the United Kingdom and Canada and in the Congress of the United States." Ph.D. dissertation, Northwestern University, 1954. 252 pp.

1942. Snyder, Henry L. "Party Configurations in the Early Eighteenth-Century House of Commons." *Institute of Historical Research Bulletin* 45 (May 1972):38–72.

1943. Stephens, Hugh W., and Brady, David W. "The Parliamentary Parties and the Electoral Reforms of 1884–85 in Britain." *Legislative Studies Quarterly* 1 (November 1976):491–510.

1944. Thomis, Malcolm I. "Conscription and Consent: British Labour and the Resignation Threat of January 1916." *Australian Journal of Politics and History* 23 (April 1977):10–18.

1945. Thornhill, W. "Parliament: the People and Party." *Yorkshire Bulletin of Economic and Social Research* 16 (May 1964):42–51.

1946. Tibbetts, Margaret Joy. "Parliamentary Parties Under Oliver Cromwell." Ph.D. dissertation, Bryn Mawr College, 1944. 254 pp.

1947. Urbanski, Stephen William. "Parliamentary Politics, 1796–1832,

In An Industrializing Borough: Preston, Lancashire." Ph.D. dissertation, Emory University, 1976. 164 pp.

1948. Walcott, Robert R. *English Politics in the Early Eighteenth Century.* Cambridge, Mass.: Harvard University Press, 1956. 291 pp.

1949. Wilson, David H. *Power and Party Bureaucracy in Britain: Regional Organization in the Conservative and Labour Parties.* Farnborough, Hants.: Saxon House, 1975. 171 pp.

1950. Wood, David. "The Westminster Scene." *Political Quarterly* 43 (July/September 1972):328–339.

Members of Parliament

General Studies

1951. Allyn, Emily. *Lords Versus Commons: A Century of Conflict and Compromise, 1830–1930.* London: The Century Co., 1931. 266 pp.

1952. Brady, H. "The Personnel of Parliament, 1571." Master's thesis, University of Manchester, 1927.

1953. Brunk, Gerald Robert. "The Bishops in Parliament, 1559–1601." Ph.D. dissertation, University of Virginia, 1968. 185 pp.

1954. Cherry, George L. *The Convention Parliament, 1689: A Biographical Study of Its Members.* New York: Bookman Associates, 1966. 218 pp.

1955. Chrimes, S.B. "House of Lords and House of Commons in the Fifteenth Century," *English Historical Review* 49 (July 1934):494–497.

1956. Commonwealth Parliamentary Association. *Salaries and Allowances of Commonwealth Parliaments 1973.* London: The Association, 1973. 62 pp.

1957. Cross, J.A. "Reviewing the Pay of Members of Parliament." *Parliamentarian* 47 (October 1966):273–276.

1958. Davey, C.M. "The Personnel of Parliament, 1597." Master's thesis, University of Manchester, 1927.

1959. Fetter, Frank W. *The Economist in Parliament, 1780–1868.* Durham, N.C.: Duke University Press, 1980. 306 pp.

1960. Fletcher, M.A. "A Study of the Knights of the Shire Returned to Parliament by Bedfordshire During the Middle Ages." Master's thesis, University of London, University College, 1933.

1961. Glynn, J.K. "The Private Member of Parliament, 1833–1868." Ph.D. dissertation, London School of Economics, 1949.

1962. Grant, John. *Member of Parliament.* London: Joseph, 1974. 190 pp.
1963. Hamilton, William W. "Members and Outside Interests." *Parliamentarian* 56 (October 1975):227-231.
1964. Harvey, A.D. "The Ministry of All the Talents: The Whigs in Office, February 1806 to March 1807." *Historical Journal* 15 (December 1972):619-648.
1965. Heasman, D.J. "Parliamentary Paths to High Office." *Parliamentary Affairs* 16 (Summer 1963):315-330.
1966. Hill, Brian W. "Man and Parliament in the Eighteenth Century." *History* 57 (June 1972):234-240.
1967. Houghton, Douglas. "Financial Interests of Members of Parliament." *Parliamentarian* 55 (January 1974):1-8.
1968. Judd, Gerrit D. *Members of Parliament, 1734-1832.* New Haven, Conn.: Yale University Press, 1955. 389 pp.
1969. Kerr, David. "Health Hazards of Members." *Parliamentarian* 51 (July 1970):166-169.
1970. Kerr, David. "The Health of Members of Parliament." *Parliamentarian* 49 (July 1968):133-137.
1971. King, Anthony Stephen. *British Members of Parliament: A Self-Portrait.* London: Macmillan Press, 1974. 128 pp.
1972. Kinnear, Mary. "Pro-Americans in the British House of Commons in the 1770's." Ph.D. dissertation, University of Oregon, 1973. 321 pp.
1973. Mackie, John D. *Cavalier and Puritan.* Rev. ed. London: T. Nelson, 1936. 316 pp.
1974. McClintic, Elizabeth Knight. "The Jacobites in the Parliament of 1715." Ph.D. dissertation, Radcliffe College, 1941. 330 pp.
1975. Matthews, H. "Personnel of the Parliament of 1584-85." Ph.D. dissertation, Universtiy of London, University College, 1948.
1976. "Members' Salaries." *Justice of the Peace* 118 (June 1954):389-390.
1977. Molyneaux, John Leroy. "Clientage Groups in the English Parliaments of the 1620's." Ed.D. dissertation, University of Virginia, 1968. 159 pp.
1978. Muir, J.W. "The Personnel of Parliament Under Henry IV." Master's thesis, University of London, 1924.
1979. Noel-Baker, Francis. "'The Grey Zone': The Problem of Business Affiliations of Members of Parliament." *Parliamentary Affairs* 15 (Winter 1961/1962):87-93.
1980. Nuttall, Geoffrey F. "Nonconformists in Parliament, 1661-1689." *Congregational Historical Society Transactions* 20 (May 1970): 334-340.
1981. Platt, Franklin Dewitt. "The English Parliamentary Radicals— Their Collective Character, Their Failure to Become a Party, and Their Failure to Find a Leader: A Study in the Psycho-Socio-

logical Source of Radical Behavior, 1833–1841." Ph.D. dissertation, University of Washington, 1969. 710 pp.

1982. Popofsky, Linda Seltzer. "The Lawyers and the Crown: The Political Leadership of the Barristers in the Parliament of 1628–1629." Ph.D. dissertation, University of California at Berkeley, 1970. 434 pp.

1983. Putnam, R.D. "Studying Elite Political Culture: The Case of 'Ideology'." *American Political Science Review* 65 (September 1971):651–681.

1984. Ranlett, John. "Railway Members of the House of Commons, 1841–1847: A Cross-Section of the Political Nation." Ph.D. dissertation, Harvard University, 1967. 2 vols.

1985. Ranney, Austin. "Inter-Constituency Movement of British Parliamentary Candidates." *American Political Science Review* 58 (March 1964):36–41.

1986. Rex, Millicent B. *University Representation in England, 1604–1690.* London: Allen & Unwin, 1954. 408 pp.

1987. Richardson, Henry Gerald, and Sayles, George O. "Clergy in the Easter Parliament, 1285: with Text of Minutes." *English Historical Review* 52 (April 1937):220–234.

1988. Richardson, Henry Gerald, and Sayles, George O. "King's Ministers in Parliament, 1272–1377." *English Historical Review* 46 (October 1931):529–550; 47 (April/July 1932):194–203, 377–397.

1989. Rogers, George. "Parliamentary Artists." *Parliamentarian* 48 (October 1967):217–219.

1990. Ryle, Michael. "Overseas Travel by Select Committees of the United Kingdom Parliament." *The Table* 47 (1979):124–127.

1991. Shmidman, Miriam. "A Minority's Right is Achieved: A Study of the Admission of Jews to Parliament in Great Britain." Ph.D. dissertation, New York University, 1975. 386 pp.

1992. Sturgis, James Laverne. "British Parliamentary Radicalism, 1846–1852." Ph.D. dissertation, University of Toronto, 1972. 425 pp.

1993. Sutcliffe, Anthony. "The British Member of Parliament and Local Issues." *Parliamentarian* 51 (April 1970):87–95.

1994. Trafford, E.E. "Personnel of the Parliament of 1593." Master's thesis, University of London, University College, 1948.

1995. Vince, C.A. "Latin Poets in the British Parliament." *Classical Review* 46 (July 1932):97–104.

1996. Willey, Frederick T. "The Declaration and Registration of Members' Interests." *Parliamentarian* 56 (July 1975):167–170.

1997. Willson, F.M.G. "The Parliamentary Executive, 1868–1914, and After." *Public Administration* 52 (Autumn 1974):263–283.

1998. Wilson, Robert Sydney. "A House Divided: British Evangelical Par-

liamentary Influence in the Latter Nineteenth-Century, 1860-1902." Ph.D. dissertation, University of Guelph, 1973.
1999. Winnifrith, C.B. "Members' Interests." *The Table* 43 (1975):30–35.
2000. Witmer, Helen E. *The Property Qualifications of Members of Parliament.* New York: Columbia University Press, 1943. 245 pp.
2001. Wood-Legh, K.L. "Knights' Attendance in the Parliaments of Edward III." *English Historical Review* 47 (July 1932):389–413.
2002. Woolley, S.F. "Personnel of the Parliament of 1833." *English Historical Review* 53 (April 1938):240–262.
2003. Zellick, Graham. "The Imprisonment of Members of Parliament." *Public Law* (Spring 1977):29–47.

Members of the House of Commons

2004. Butler, David E. "Local Government in Parliament." *Public Administration (London)* 31 (Spring 1953):46–47.
2005. Cain, Bruce E.; Ferejohn, John A.; and Fiorina, Morris P. "The House is Not a Home: British MPs in Their Constituencies." *Legislative Studies Quarterly* 4 (November 1979):501–524.
2006. Clendenin, Thurman Barrier. "The Common Lawyers in Parliament and Society: A Social and Political Study of the Common Lawyers in the First Jacobean Parliament." Ph.D. dissertation, University of North Carolina at Chapel Hill, 1975. 386 pp.
2007. Crocket, D.G. "The MP and His Constituents." *Parliamentary Affairs* 20 (Summer 1967):280–284.
2008. Dickson, A.D.R. "MP's Readoption Conflicts: Their Causes and Consequences." *Political Studies* (March 1975):62–70.
2009. Ellis, John, and Johnson, R.W. *Members From the Unions.* London: Fabian Society, 1974. 29 pp.
2010. Ellis, Nesta Wyn. *Dear Elector: The Truth About M.P.s.* London: Coronet, 1974. 236 pp.
2011. Epstein, Leon D. "British M.P.s and Their Local Parties: The Suez Cases." *American Political Science Review* 54 (June 1960):374–390.
2012. Escott, Thomas H.S. *Gentlemen of the House of Commons.* London: Hurst and Blackett, 1902. 2 vols.
2013. Fetter, Frank W. "Influence of Economists in Parliament on British Legislation From Ricardo to John Stuart Mill." *Journal of Political Economy* 83 (October 1975):1051–1064.
2014. Frasure, Robert Conway. "Constituency Racial Composition and the Attitudes of British M.P.s." *Comparative Politics* (January 1971):201–210.

2015. Houghton, Douglas. "Trade-Union MPs in the British House of Commons." *Parliamentarian* 49 (October 1968):215–221.

2016. Iredell, G.W. "Lawyers in Parliament." *The Solicitor* 22 (July 1955):163–164.

2017. Mellors, Colin. *The British MP: A Socio-Economic Study of the House of Commons.* Farnborough: Saxon House, 1978. 146 pp.

2018. Mellors, Colin. "Local Government in Parliament—20 Years Later." *Public Administration* 52 (Summer 1974):223–229.

2019. Muller, William Dale. "The Parliamentary Activity of Trade Union M.P.s, 1959–1964." Ph.D. dissertation, University of Florida, 1966. 348 pp.

2020. Muller, William Dale. "Trade Union M.P.s and Parliamentary Specialization." *Political Studies* 20 (September 1972):317–324.

2021. Muller, William Dale. "Trade Union Sponsored Members of Parliament in the Defence Dispute of 1960 1961." *Parliamentary Affairs* 23 (Summer 1970):258–276.

2022. Muller, William Dale. "Union-MP Conflict: An Overview." *Parliamentary Affairs* 26 (Summer 1973):336–355.

2023. Podmore, D. "Too Many Lawyers in Parliament?" *New Law Journal* 128, 26 January 1978, pp. 76–79.

2024. Roth, Andrew; Kerbey, Janice; and Tench, Judy. *The Business Background of MPs.* 7th ed. London: Parliamentary Profiles, 1981. 384 pp.

2025. Schwartz, John E. "Impact of Constituency on the Behavior of British Conservative MPs; An Analysis of the Formative Stages of Issue Development." *Comparative Political Studies* 8 (April 1975):75–89.

2026. Searing, Donald D. "Measuring Politicians' Values: Administration and Assessment of a Ranking Technique in the British House of Commons." *American Political Science Review* 72 (March 1978):65–79.

2027. Willey, Frederick T. *The Honorable Member.* London: Sheldon Press, 1974. 183 pp.

Members of the House of Lords

2028. Attlee, C.R. "Attitudes of M.P.'s and Active Peers." *Political Quarterly* 30 (January 1959):29–32.

2029. Bailey, Sidney D. "Life Peerages." *Parliamentary Affairs* 7 (Winter 1953/1954):109–120.

2030. "Bishops and the House of Lords." *Law Notes* 34 (August 1930): 96–97.

2031. Carpenter, Edward. *British Aristocracy and the House of Lords.* London: A.C. Fifield, 1908. 34 pp.
2032. Phillips, Gregory D. "Diehards and the Myth of the Backwoodsmen." *Journal of British Studies* 16 (Spring 1977):105-120.
2033. Phillips, Melanie. "Changing Composition of the House of Lords." *Contemporary Review* 233 (July 1978):1-6.
2034. Pumphrey, R.E. "Introduction of Industrialists Into the British Peerage: A Study in Adaptation of a Social Institution." *American Historical Review* 65 (October 1959):1-16.
2035. "Representation of Capitalist and Big Business Interests in the House of Lords." *Labour Bulletin of Industrial and Political Information* 4 (October 1928):67-70.
2036. Round, J.H. "Barons and Peers." *English Historical Review* 33 (October 1918):453-471.
2037. Sainsbury, Keith. "Patronage, Honours and Parliament." *Parliamentary Affairs* 19 (Summer 1966):346-350.
2038. St.-George, C.F.L. "The Composition of the House of Lords." *Parliamentary Affairs* 7 (Winter 1953/1954):60-67.

Backbenchers

2039. Barnett, Malcolm J. "Backbench Behavior in the House of Commons." *Parliamentary Affairs* 22 (Winter 1968/1969):38-61.
2040. Berrington, Hugh B. *Backbench Opinion in the House of Commons, 1945-55.* Oxford: Pergamon Press, 1973. 265 pp.
2041. Buck, P.W. "First-Time Winners in the British House of Commons Since 1918." *American Political Science Review* 58 (September 1964):662-667.
2042. Close, David. H. "Growth of Backbench Organisation in the Conservative Party." *Parliamentary Affairs* 27 (Autumn 1974):371-383.
2043. Epstein, Leon D. "New M.P.'s and the Politics of the PLP." *Political Studies* 10 (June 1962):121-129.
2044. Finer, Samuel Edward; Berrington, H.B.; and Bartholomew, D.J. *Backbench Opinion in the House of Commons, 1955-59.* Oxford: Pergamon, 1961. 219 pp.
2045. Franklin, Mark Newman. "Voice of the Backbench: Patterns of Behavior in the British House of Commons." Ph.D. dissertation, Cornell University, 1970. 331 pp.
2046. Franklin, Mark Newman, and Tappin, M. "Early Day Motions as Unobtrusive Measures of Backbench Opinion in Britain." *British Journal of Political Science* 7 (January 1977):49-69.

2047. Hale, Leslie. "The Backbencher." *Parliamentarian* 47 (July 1966): 191–198.

2048. Hornby, R. "The Influence of The Back-Bench II: A Tory View." *Political Quarterly* 36 (July/October 1965):286–294.

2049. Houghton, Douglas. "The Labour Back-Bencher." *Political Quarterly* 40 (October/December 1969):454–463.

2050. Kerr, David. "The Changing Role of the Backbencher." *Parliamentarian* 50 (January 1969):7–11.

2051. Leece, J., and Berrington, H. "Measurements of Backbench Attitudes by Guttman Scaling of Early Day Motions: A Pilot Study, Labor, 1968–69." *British Journal of Political Science* 7 (October 1977):529–541.

2052. Leonard, Richard L., and Herman, Valentine. *The Backbencher and Parliament.* London: Macmillan, 1972. 267 pp.

2053. Lynskey, James J. "Backbench Tactics and Parliamentary Party Structure." *Parliamentary Affairs* 27 (Winter 1973/1974): 28–37.

2054. Lynskey, James J. "Role of British Backbenchers in the Modification of Government Policy." *Western Political Quarterly* 23 (June 1970):333–347.

2055. MacKintosh, John P. *The Influence of the Backbencher, Now and a Hundred Years Ago.* Stockport: Manchester Statistical Society, 1970. 29 pp.

2056. Norton, Philip. "The Influence of the Backbench Member." *Parliamentarian* 58 (July 1977):164–171.

2057. Piper, John Richard. "Backbench Rebellion, Party Government and Consensus Politics: The Case of the Parliamentary Labour Party, 1966–1970." *Parliamentary Affairs* 27 (Autumn 1974): 384–396.

2058. Piper, John Richard. "The Unofficial Opposition: Labour Party Backbenchers in the British House of Commons, 1966–1970." Ph.D. dissertation, Cornell University, 1972. 321 pp.

2059. Richards, Peter G. *The Backbenchers.* London: Faber and Faber, 1972. 248 pp.

2060. Richards, Peter G. *Honourable Members: A Study of the British Backbencher.* 2d ed. London: Faber and Faber, 1964. 294 pp.

2061. Schwartz, John E., and Lambert, Geoffrey. "The Voting Behavior of British Conservative Backbenchers." In *Comparative Legislative Behavior,* edited by Samuel C. Patterson and John C. Wahlke, pp. 65–85. New York: Wiley, 1972.

2062. Wiseman, Herbert V. "Private Members' Opportunities and Standing Order No. 9." *Parliamentary Affairs* 12 (Summer/Autumn 1959):277–291.

Women in Parliament

2063. Brookes, Pamela. *Women at Westminster: An Account of Women in the British Parliament, 1918–1966.* London: P. Davies, 1967. 287 pp.
2064. Clark, E. "Women Suffrage in Parliament." *American Political Science Review* 11 (May 1917):284–309.
2065. George, M.L. "Thirteen Women of Parliament." *Britain* (Fall 1943):35–38.
2066. Iwi, Edward F. "Women and the House of Lords." *Parliamentary Affairs* 7 (Winter 1953/1954):102–108.
2067. Ogg, Frederick A. "Women Members of Parliament." *American Political Science Review* 13 (February 1919):114–115.
2068. Rasmussen, Jorgen Scott. "Role of Women in British Parliamentary Elections." *Journal of Politics* 39 (November 1977):1044–1054.
2069. Stobaugh, Beverly Parker. *Women and Parliament 1918–1970.* Hicksville, N.Y.: Exposition Press, 1978. 152 pp.

Scottish and Irish Members of Parliament

2070. Birrell, W.D. "The Stormont-Westminster Relationship." *Parliamentary Affairs* 26 (Autumn 1973):471–491.
2071. Casada, James A. "The Scottish Representatives in Richard Cromwell's Parliament." *Scottish Historical Review* 51 (October 1972):124–147.
2072. Clark, J.C.D. "Whig Tactics and Parliamentary Precedent: The English Management of Irish Politics 1754–1756." *Historical Journal* 21 (June 1978):275–301.
2073. Dunboyne, Lord. "Irish Representative Peers: Counsel's Opinion 1924." *Public Law* (Winter 1969):314–322.
2074. Hamilton, Charles Louis. "The Covenanters and Parliament, 1640-1646: A Study of Scottish Relations with England During the British Civil War." Ph.D. dissertation, Cornell University, 1959, 330 pp.
2075. Hoppen, K. Theodore. "Politics, the Law, and the Nature of the Irish Electorate 1832–1850." *English Historical Review* 92 (October 1977):746–776.
2076. Horgan, David Thomas. "The Irish Catholic Whigs in Parliament 1847–74." Ph.D. dissertation, University of Minnesota, 1975. 143 pp.
2077. Hughes, Edward. "Scottish Reform Movement and Charles Grey, 1792–94: Some Fresh Correspondence." *Scottish Historical Review* 35 (April 1956):26–41.

2078. James, Francis G. "The Irish Lobby in the Early Eighteenth Century." *English Historical Review* 81 (July 1966):543–557.

2079. Judge, David, and Finlayson, Donald A. "Scottish Members of Parliament: Problems of Devolution." *Parliamentary Affairs* 28 (Summer 1975):278–292.

2080. Keating, Michael J. "Parliamentary Behavior as a Test of Scottish Integration Into the United Kingdom." *Legislative Studies Quarterly* 3 (August 1978):409–430.

2081. Keating, Michael J. *A Test of Political Integration: The Scottish Members of Parliament.* Glasgow: Centre for the Study of Public Policy, University of Strathclyde, 1977. 33 pp.

2082. Kelly, Paul. "British and Irish Politics in 1785." *English Historical Review* 90 (July 1975):536–563.

2083. Lowe, William Curtis, "Bishops and Scottish Representative Peers in the House of Lords, 1760–1775." *Journal of British Studies* 18 (Fall 1978):86–106.

2084. Lyons, F.S.L. *Irish Parliamentary Party, 1890–1910.* London: Faber and Faber, 1951. 284 pp.

2085. Lysaght, C.E. "Irish Peers and the House of Lords." *North Ireland Legal Quarterly* 18 (September 1967):277–301.

2086. McCahill, Michael Woods. "The Scottish Peerage and the House of Lords in the Late Eighteenth Century." *Scottish Historical Review* 51 (October 1972):172–196.

2087. MacQueen, L.E.C. "Odd-Looking Dull Men; a Historical Fallacy." *Scottish Historical Review* 35 (April 1956):1–9.

2088. Maguire, P.R. "Parliament and the Direct Rule of Northern Ireland." *The Irish Jurist* 10 (Summer and Winter 1975):81–92.

2089. Roberts, G. "The Boroughs of North Wales: Their Parliamentary History From the Act of Union to the First Reform Act (1533–1832)." Master's thesis, University of Wales, 1929.

2090. Schuyler, Robert L. "Ireland and the English Parliament." *Political Science Quarterly* 41 (December 1926):489–519.

2091. Thornley, David. "The Irish Home Rule Party and Parliamentary Obstruction, 1874–1887." *Irish Historical Studies* 12 (March 1960):38–57.

Parliamentary Careers

2092. Aspinall, Arthur. *Three Early Nineteenth Century Diaries.* London: Williams and Norgate, 1952. 402 pp.

2093. Barnard, T.C. "Lord Broghill, Vincent Gookin and the Cork Elections of 1659." *English Historical Review* 88 (April 352–365.

2094. Belchem, J.C. "Henry Hunt and the Evolution of the Mass Platform." *English Historical Review* 93 (October 1978):739–773.

2095. Berelson, Ellen Sue. "The Early Career of Thomas Wentworth, First Earl of Strafford: From Parliament to President of the King's Council in the North.' Ph.D. dissertation, Boston University Graduate School, 1975. 428 pp.

2096. Bowyer, Robert. *The Parliamentary Diary of Robert Bowyer, 1606–1607.* New York: Octagon Books, 1971. 423 pp.

2097. Bromhead, Peter. A. "Mr. Wedgewood Benn, the Peerage and the Constitution." *Parliamentary Affairs* 14 (Autumn 1961): 493–506.

2098. Brown, Everett S. "John Henry Barrow and the 'Mirror of Parliament'." *Parliamentary Affairs* 9 (Summer 1956):311–323.

2099. Chase, Lawrence Joseph. "The Parliamentary Career of Eugene Spuller, 1876–1896." Ph.D. dissertation, University of Notre Dame, 1973. 172 pp.

2100. Cope, Esther Sidney. "John Rushworth and the Short Parliament of 1640." *Institute of Historical Research Bulletin* 51 (May 1978):94–98.

2101. Cope, Esther Sidney. "Lord Montagu and His Journal of the Short Parliament." *Institute of Historical Research Bulletin* 46 (November 1973):209–215.

2102. Cowling, Maurice. "Disraeli, Derby and Fusion, October 1865 to July 1866." *Historical Journal* 8 (1964):31–71.

2103. D'Ewes, Simonds. *The Journal of Sir Simonds D'Ewes; From the First Recess of the Long Parliament to the Withdrawal of King Charles From London.* London: Oxford University Press, 1942. 459 pp.

2104. Dinwiddy, John Rowland. "Bentham's Transition to Political Radicalism, 1809–10." *Journal of the History of Ideas* 36 (October 1975):683–700.

2105. Epstein, Joel Jacob. "The Parliamentary Career of Francis Bacon, 1581–1614." Ph.D. dissertation, Rutgers University, State University of New Jersey, 1966. 312 pp.

2106. Foster, Elizabeth Read. *The Painful Labour of Mr. Elsyng.* Philadelphia: American Philosophical Society, 1972. 69 pp.

2107. Gibbs, Mildred E. "Lord John Russell and the Development of Relations Between Parliament, Cabinet and Parties, 1832–52." Master's thesis, University of Manchester, 1928.

2108. Glenski, Zoe. "Lord Ashley in the House of Commons, 1826 1851." Ph.D. dissertation, Fordham University, 1966. 250 pp.

2109. Glow, Lotte. "Pym and Parliament: the Methods of Moderation." *Journal of Modern History* 36 (December 1964):373–397.

2110. Golant, W. "The Emergence of C.R. Attlee as Leader of the Parliamentary Labour Party in 1935." *Historical Journal* 13 (1970): 318–332.

2111. Gray, Francis J. "The Parliamentary Career of Sir George Savile, Bart, 1759–1783." Ph.D. dissertation, Fordham University, 1958. 248 pp.

2112. Hay, C.H. "Making of a Radical: the Case of James Burgh." *Journal of British Studies* 18 (Spring 1979):90–117.

2113. Hemingford, Denis Herbert H. *Back-bencher and Chairman—Some Parliamentary Reminiscenses of Lord Hemingford.* London: J. Murray, 1946. 243 pp.

2114. Horwitz, Henry, ed. *The Parliamentary Diary of Narcissus Luttrell, 1691–1693.* Oxford: Clarendon Press, 1972. 538 pp.

2115. Hume, L.J. "Jeremy Bentham and the Nineteenth-Century Revolution in Government." *Historical Journal* 10 (1967):316 375.

2116. Jones, V.B.P "Lord John Russell and the Leadership of the House of Commons, 1835–1841." Master's thesis, University of Wales, Aberystwyth, 1970.

2117. Kelly, Joseph Michael. "The Parliamentary Career of Joseph Cowen." Ph.D. dissertation, Loyola University of Chicago, 1970.

2118. Laurenzo, Frederick Edward. "The Parliamentary Career of Robert Harley, 1689–1710." Ph.D. dissertation, University of Illinois at Urbana, 1969. 338 pp.

2119. "Lord Hewart and the House of Lords." *Justice of the Peace* 93, 14 December 1929, pp. 789–790.

2120. McCandless, Amy Maureen Thompson. "The Last of the Benthamites: a Study of the Parliamentary Career of Robert Lowe." Ph.D. dissertation, University of Wisconsin, 1972. 322 pp.

2121. MacDonald, Sir Gordon. *Atcofion Seneddol.* London: W. Griffiths, 1949. 83 pp.

2122. MacDonald, William W. "The Early Parliamentary Career of John Pym." Ph.D. dissertation, New York University, 1965. 276 pp.

2123. McKelvey, James Lee. "Lord Bute and George III: The Leicester House Years." Ph.D. dissertation, Nortwestern University, 1965. 311 pp.

2124. Malcolm, Ian Zachary. *Vacant Thrones: A Volume of Political Portraits.* Freeport, N.Y.: Books for Libraries Press, 1967. 204 pp.

2125. Maples, Charles Thomas. "Parliament's Admiral: the Parliamentary and Naval Career of Robert Rich, Second Earl of Warwick, During the Reign of Charles I." Ph.D. dissertation, University of Alabama, 1975. 310 pp.

2126. Menhennet, David. "Erskine May's Private Journal, 1857–1882;

Diary of a Great Parliamentarian." *Contemporary Review* 219 (October 1971):191–195.

2127. Moss, D.J. "Study in Failure: Thomas Attwood, MP for Birmingham, 1832–1839." *Historical Journal* 21 (September 1978): 545–570.

2128. Neale, John E. "Peter Wentworth." *English Historical Review* 39 (January/April 1924):36–54, 175–205.

2129. Neat, Donald R. "The Parliamentary Career of Sir James Mackintosh." Ph.D. dissertation, University of Kentucky, 1965. 233 pp.

2130. Noble, F. "Herefordshire and Simon de Montfort: 1265." *Woolhope Naturalists Field Club Transactions* 38 (1965):111–118.

2131. Petrie, C. "Pioneer of Parliamentary Opposition: William Shippen." *Saturday Review* 153 (January 1932):90–91.

2132. Pflaum, Ann Mitchell. "The Parliamentary Career of Thomas S. Duncombe, 1826–1861." Ph.D. dissertation, University of Minnesota, 1975. 222 pp.

2133. Potter, D.W. "Downright Shippen: The Politician as Philosopher." *History Today* 22 (March 1972):195–203.

2134. Prest, J. "Decline of Lord John Russell." *History Today* 22 (June 1972):394–401.

2135. Rawlins, Sophia Wyndham. *Members of Parliament for the County of Somerset.* Taunton: The Somersetshire Archaeological and Natural History Society, 1939. 203 pp.

2136. Reid, Loren Dudley. "Fox as Orator." *History Today* 19 (March 1969):149–158.

2137. Rempel, Richard A. "Lord Hugh Cecil's Parliamentary Career, 1900–1914: Promise Unfulfilled." *Journal of British Studies* 11 (May 1972):104–130.

2138. Russell, Conrad S.R. "The Examination of Mr. Mallory After the Parliament of 1621." *Institute of Historical Research Bulletin* 50 (May 1977):125–132.

2139. Smith, Cornelia Donovan. "Oliver St. John: Servant to His Parliament and to His Commonwealth." Ph.D. dissertation, Rutgers University, State University of New Jersey, 1975. 484 pp.

2140. Telford, J. "Fifty Years of Parliament, by Earl of Oxford and Asquith." *London Quarterly Review* 147 (January 1927):101–107.

2141. Wedgewood, Josiah C. "John of Gaunt and the Packing of Parliament." *English Historical Review* 45 (October 1930):623–625.

2142. White, Stephen Daniel. *Sir Edward Coke and the Grievances of the Commonwealth, 1621 and 1628.* Chapel Hill: University of North Carolina Press, 1979. 327 pp.

Support and Housing of Parliament

Staff

2143. Alderman, R.K., and Cross, J.A. "Parliamentary Private Secretary—a Danger to the Free Functioning of Parliament?" *Political Studies* 14 (June 1966):199–208.

2144. Bond, Maurice F. "Clerks of the Parliaments, 1509–1953." *English Historical Review* 73 (January 1958):78–85.

2145. Bond, Maurice F. "The Office of Clerk of the Parliaments." *Parliamentary Affairs* 12 (Summer/Autumn 1959):297–310.

2146. Clough, Owen. "Society of Clerks at the Table in Empire Parliaments." *State Government* 20 (June 1947):158–160.

2147. Clyne, A. "A New Clerk at the Table of the House: Laws for Law Makers." *Justice of the Peace* 112, 18 September 1948, p. 512.

2148. Douglas, James. "The British Parliament and Its Clerks." *Inter-Parliamentary Bulletin* 45 (1965):5–12.

2149. Farmer, H.R.M. "The Administration of the Palace of Westminster." *The Table* 34 (1965):11–17.

2150. Gordon, C.A.S.S. "The Fourth Clerk at the Table." *Journal of the Parliaments of the Commonwealth* 46 (January 1965):53–57.

2151. Heasman, D.J. "The Emergence and Evolution of the Office of Parliamentary Secretary." *Parliamentary Affairs* 23 (Autumn 1970):345–365.

2152. Howard, Charles Alfred. "The Serjeant at Arms." *Parliamentary Affairs* 1 (Summer 1948):20–22.

2153. Lambert, Sheila. "The Clerks and Records of the House of Commons, 1600–1640." *Institute of Historical Research Bulletin* 43 (November 1970):215–231.

2154. Lowry, E.C. "Clerical Proctors in Parliament and Knights of the Shire, 1280–1374." *English Historical Review* 48 (July 1933): 443–455.

2155. McKay, W.R. "Mild Drudgery': the Department of the Clerk of the House of Commons in 1905." *The Table* 41 (1972/1973):53–60.

2156. Mackenzie, Kenneth R. "Six Hundred Years of the Clerkship of the House of Commons." *Journal of the Parliaments of the Commonwealth* 44 (October 1963):353–360.

2157. Marsden, Philip Kitson. *The Officers of the Commons, 1363–1978.* London: H.M.S.O., 1979. 262 pp.

2158. Pollard, Albert Frederick. "Clerical Organization of Parliament." *English Historical Review* 57 (January 1942):31–58.

2159. Pollard, Albert Frederick. "Clerk of the Crown." *English Historical Review* 57 (July 1942):312–333.

2160. Pollard, Albert Frederick. "Receivers of Petitions and Clerks of Parliament." *English Historical Review* 57 (April 1942):202–226.

2161. Stacpoole, E.P. "Clerk of the Commons." *Parliament* (December 1946):11–13.

2162. Williams, Orlo C. "The Role of the Clerk in Parliament." *Journal of the Parliaments of the Commonwealth* 42 (April 1961):106–113.

Libraries and Records

2163. Bear, L.W. "Parliamentary Reporting at Westminster (Part I)." *Parliamentarian* 53 (April 1972):118–121.

2164. Bear, L.W. "Parliamentary Reporting at Westminster (Part II)." *Parliamentarian* 53 (July 1972):186–189.

2165. Blogg, C.W. "The House of Lords Official Record (Hansard) 1946–1977." *The Table* (1977):58–60.

2166. Bond, Maurice F. "Computer Applications in the House of Lords." *The Table* 44 (1976):51–58.

2167. Bond, Maurice F. "The Preservation of the Records of Parliament at Westminster." *The Table* 32 (1963):20–25.

2168. Bond, Maurice F. "Records of Parliament at Westminster." *Parliamentarian* 53 (January 1972):15–16.

2169. Bond, Maurice F. "Le Reyne Le Veuit: The Making and Keeping of Acts at Westminster." *History Today* 6 (November 1956):765–773.

2170. Bond, Maurice F. "The Victoria Tower and Its Records." *Parliamentary Affairs* 8 (1955):482–491.

2171. Butcher, R.F.C. "The Reference and Research Divisions of the House of Commons Library." *Parliamentary Affairs* 8 (Summer 1955):388–395.

2172. Chowdharay-Best, George. "Some OED Antedatings from the Early Journals of the English House of Commons." *Notes and Queries* 23 (December 1976):546–550.

2173. Cobb, Henry S. "Sources for Economic History Amongst the Parliamentary Records in the House of Lords Record Office." *Economic History Review* 19 (April 1966):154–175.

2174. Dobson, Christopher. *The Library of the House of Lords: A Short History with An Appendix Listing Its Principal Contents.* London: H.M.S.O. 1972. 24 pp.

2175. Elton, Geoffrey R. "The Early Journals of the House of Lords." *English Historical Review* 89 (July 1974):481–512.

2176. Englefield, D.J.T. "House of Commons Library, London." In *Library Services to the Legislature, A Symposium*, pp. 38–44. Sydney, N.S.W.: Parliamentary Library, 1965.

2177. Ferneyhough, F. "History of Hansard." *Life and Letters To-Day* 44 (February 1945):82–91.

2178. Hamson, Vincent. "The Production of Hansard." *Parliamentary Affairs* 8 (Spring 1955):254–260.

2179. Hansard Society for Parliamentary Government. *Papers on Parliament.* London: The Hansard Society, 1949. 116 pp.

2180. Holland, D.C.L. "Parliamentary Libraries: III—Indexing of Material." *Parliamentarian* 50 (January 1969):28–32.

2181. Holland, D.C.L. "Parliamentary Papers." *Parliamentary Affairs* 8 (Autumn 1955):526–528.

2182. Lambert, Sheila. "Guide to Parliamentary Printing, 1696 1834." *Institute of Historical Research Bulletin* 38 (May 1965)111 117.

2183. Law, William. *Our Hansard: or, the True Mirror of Parliament: A Full Account of the Official Reporting of Debates in the House of Commons.* London: Pitman, 1950. 80 pp.

2184. Menhennet, David. "Parliamentary Libraries: IV—Information and Research Services." *Parliamentarian* 50 (April 1969):111–116.

2185. Neale, John E. "Commons' Journals of the Tudor Period." *Royal Historical Society Transactions* 4 (1920):136–170.

2186. Nottage, R. "Reporting to Parliament on the Nationalized Industries." *Public Administration (London)* 35 (Summer 1957):143–167.

2187. Palmer, John. "Parliamentary Libraries: I—Basic and Essential Holdings." *Parliamentarian* 49 (July 1968):151–155.

2188. Palmer, John. "Parliamentary Libraries: II—The Resources of Larger Libraries." *Parliamentarian* 49 (October 1968):229–233.

2189. Palmer, M.J. "The Publication of Lords' Attendances." *The Table* 38 (1969):110–116.

2190. Somerset, H.V.F. "Burke's Eloquence and Hansard's Reports." *English Review* 52 (March 1931):342–350.

2191. Trewin, John C., and King, E.M. *Printer to the House: the Story of Hansard.* London: Methuen, 1952. 272 pp.

2192. "White Papers." *Modern Law Review* 7 (November 1944):228–229.

2193. Wilding, Norman W. "The House of Commons Library." *Parliamentary Affairs* 1 (Summer 1948):68–72.

2194. Woodall, Robert. "Before Hansard." *History Today* 23 (March 1973):195–202.

Information Services

2195. Barker, Anthony, and Rush, Michael. *The Member of Parliament and His Information.* London: Allen and Unwin, 1970. 443 pp.

2196. Bevins, A.J. "Research Assistance for M.P.'s?" *Political Quarterly* 47 (July 1976):339–341.

2197. Bond, M.F. "The Development of Public Information Services at Westminster." *The Table* 47 (1979):84–103.

2198. Franklin, Mark Newman. "Computers and the Modern Member of Parliament." *Parliamentarian* 54 (April 1973):80–85.

2199. Franklin, Mark Newman. *Using Computers to Analyse the Activities of Members of Parliament.* Glasgow: Survey Research Center, University of Strathclyde, 1971. 23 pp.

2200. King, Horace Maybray. *Before Hansard: A Quaint Collection of Curious Details from the Story of the Mother of Parliaments, Gathered from the Ancient Journals and From the Diaries of Former M.P.s.* London: Dent, 1968. 114 pp.

2201. Menhennet, David. *The Journal of the House of Commons; a Biographical and Historical Guide.* London: H.M.S.O., 1971. 96 pp.

2202. Menhennet, David, and Poole, John B. "Information Services of the Commons Library." *New Scientist* 7 (September 1967): 499–502.

2203. Menhennet, David. "The Library of the House of Commons." *Political Quarterly* 36 (July 1965):323–332.

2204. Poole, John B. "Computers in the House of Commons: Retrospect and Prospect." *Parliamentarian* 54 (October 1973):214–222.

2205. Poole, John B. "Information Services for the Commons: A Computer Experiment." *Parliamentary Affairs* 22 (Spring 1969): 161–168.

2206. Poole, John B.; Scott, Gay; and Ellis, C.W.H. "Information Retrieval From Hansard and Statute Law: The House of Commons Library—IBM Project." *Parliamentary Affairs* 29 (Autumn 1976):421–436.

2207. Poole, John B., and Van Dongen, J.A. "A Computerized Macroeconomic Data Service for Parliament: the MEDHOC Project. *Program* 9 (January 1975):1–22.

2208. Ruch, Michael, and Shaw, Malcolm, eds. *The House of Commons: Services and Facilities.* London: Allen and Unwin, 1974. 302 pp.

2209. Ryle, Michael. "Review of the Administrative Services of the British House of Commons." *The Table* 44 (1976):99–103.

2210. Starr, Joseph Rankin. "The Development of Modes of Communication Between the Two Houses of the English Parliament." Ph.D. dissertation, University of Minnesota, 1930. 162 pp.

2211. Vickery, B.C. *Computer Support for Parliamentary Information Service. A Feasibility Study for the House of Commons Library.* London: Aslib, 1971. 276 pp.

Broadcasting

2212. Bear, L.W. "Parliamentary Recording." *Journal of the Parliaments of the Commonwealth* 42 (April 1961):114–117.
2213. Blumler, Jay. "Parliament and Political TV." *Encounter* 28 (March 1967):52–56.
2214. Davis, A.G. "Broadcasting of Parliament: the Prime Minister's Powers." *New Zealand Law Journal* 35, 24 November 1959, pp. 328–330.
2215. Day, Robin. *The Case for Televising Parliament.* London: The Hansard Society, 1963. 23 pp.
2216. Dewar, D. "Broadcasting the Proceedings of the House of Lords." *The Table* 27 (1968):60–72.
2217. Fletcher, H. Lynton. "A Sound Record of Parliament." *Parliamentary Affairs* 2 (Winter 1948):82–84.
2218. Jensen, J. Vernon. "Should British Parliamentary Debates Be Televised?" *Parliamentarian* 52 (April 1971):22–28.
2219. Scott, P.H. "Live from Westminster: Broadcasting the British Parliament." *European Broadcasting Union, Review* 29 (September 1978):16–20.
2220. Seymour-Ure, Colin. "An Examination of the Proposal to Televise Parliament." *Parliamentary Affairs* 17 (Spring 1964):172–181.
2221. Starks, Michael. "The Sound Broadcasting of Parliament." *Political Quarterly* 49 (April/June 1978):208–216.
2222. "Televising of Parliament, Westminster." *Parliamentarian* 54 (January 1973):13–16.
2223. "Televising Proceedings of the U.K. House of Commons." *Parliamentarian* 47 (October 1966):263–267.
2224. Vernon, Jensen J. "Should British Parliamentary Debates Be Televised?" *Parliamentarian* 52 (January 1971):22–28.
2225. Wober, Mallory. "Public Opinion and Direct Broadcasting as an Aid to the Efficacy of Parliament." *The Political Quarterly* 50 (July/September 1979):316–325.

Architecture

2226. Bailey, Sidney D. "Legislative Buildings of the World." *Parliamentary Affairs* 2 (Summer 1949):259–273.

2227. Brayley, E.W., and Britton, J. *The History of the Ancient Palace and Late Houses of Parliament at Westminster.* London: John Weale, 1836. 476 pp.

2228. Chowdharay-Best, George. "The Colours of the Two Houses of Parliament at Westminster." *Notes and Queries* 16 (March 1969):89.

2229. Craigavon, James Craig. *The Houses of Parliament: the Royal Palace of Westminster.* London: Pitkin Pictorials, 1958. 24 pp.

2230. Gordon Lennox, A.H.C. "Some Security Problems in Parliament." *The Table* 39 (1970):68–70.

2231. Hastings, Maurice. *Parliament House: the Chambers of the House of Commons.* London: The Architectural Press, 1950. 200 pp.

2232. Hawkins, Paul. "Facilities for Members at Westminster." *Parliamentarian* 48 (January 1967):20–22.

2233. Jay, W. "House of Commons and St. Stephen's Chapel." *English Historical Review* 36 (April 1921):225–227.

2234. Junz, Alfred J. "Accommodation at Westminster." *Parliamentary Affairs* 13 (Winter 1959/1960):100–113.

2235. King-Hall, Stephen, and Sheard, Gerald F. *Parliament Viewing Hall.* London: The Hansard Society, 1963. 20 pp.

2236. Mackenzie, Kenneth R. *The Houses of Parliament: An Illustrated Guide to the Parliament of the Palace of Westminster.* 11th ed. Norwich: Jarrold and Sons, 1972. 21 pp.

2237. Pope-Hennessy, James, and Wild, H. *The House of Parliament.* New ed. London: Joseph, 1975. 47 pp.

2238. Port, M.H., ed. *The Houses of Parliament.* New Haven, Conn.: Yale University Press, 1976. 347 pp.

2239. Sainty, John Christopher. "The Meeting Places of the Houses of Parliament at Westminster." *The Table* 44 (1976):95–98.

2240. Saunders, Hilary St. G. *Westminster Hall.* London: Joseph, 1951. 320 pp.

2241. Smith, Denix. "The House of Parliament: Structure and Building Services, 1835–70." *Newcombe Society Transactions* 45 (1972/1973):89–92.

2242. Thorne, Peter F. "Security in a Legislature." *Parliamentarian* 55 (July 1974):162–165.

2243. Thorne, Peter F. *The Mace in the House of Commons.* Rev. ed. London: H.M.S.O., 1971. 11 pp.

2244. Wilcox, J.H. "The Kitchen and Refreshment Rooms of the House of Commons." *Parliamentary Affairs* 3 (Summer 1950):316–320.

Addendum

2245. "Access to Cabinet Papers." *Parliamentarian* 61 (April 1980):94–95.

2246. Alderman, R.K. "Discipline in the Parliamentary Labor Party from the Formation of the Labor Representation Committee in 1900–1964." Ph.D. dissertation, University of London, External Degree, 1972.

2247. Ashford, Douglas E. *Policy and Politics in Britain: The Limits of Consensus.* Oxford: Basil Blackwell, 1981. 346 pp.

2248. Atton, K.J. "Municipal and Parliamentary Politics in Ipswich, 1818-1847." Ph.D. dissertation, University of London, University College, 1980.

2249. Baker, I.F.W. *Politicians and Defence: Studies in the Formulation of British Defence Policy.* Manchester, Eng.: Manchester University Press, 1981. 202 pp.

2250. Ball, Alan. *British Political Parties: The Emergence of a Modern Party System.* London: Macmillan, 1981. 292 pp.

2251. Balsom, Denis, and Ian McAllister. "The Scottish and Welsh Devolution Referenda of 1979: Constitutional Change and Popular Choice." *Parliamentary Affairs* 32 (Autumn 1979):394–409.

2252. Beckett, J.V. "Making of a Pocket Borough: Cockermouth, 1722–1756." *Journal of British Studies* 20 (Fall 1980):140–157.

2253. Behrens, R. *The Conservative Party from Heath to Thatcher: Policies and Politics, 1974-1979.* Farnborough: Saxon House, 1980. 139 pp.

2254. Beith, Alan. "Prayers Unanswered: A Jaundiced View of the Parliamentary Scrutiny of Statutory Instruments." *Parliamentary Affairs* 34 (Spring 1981):165–173.

2255. Bell, Stuart. *How to Abolish the Lords.* London: Fabian Society, 1981. 25 pp.

2256. Bellamy, J.G. "The Parliamentary Representatives of Nottinghamshire, Derbyshire and Staffordshire in the Reign of Richard II." Master's thesis, University of Nottingham, 1962.

2257. Benn, Tony. "The Case for a Constitutional Premiership." *Parliamentary Affairs* 33 (Winter 1980):7–22.

2258. Bermant, C.I. "The Independent Member of Parliament." B. Litt., University of Glasgow, 1962.

2259. Black, C.J. "Administration and Parliamentary Representation of Nottinghamshire and Derbyshire, 1529-1558." Ph.D. dissertation, University of London, Queen Mary College, 1967.

2260. Bogdanor, Vernon. "The 40 per cent Rule." *Parliamentary Affairs* 33 (Summer 1980):249–263.

2261. Bogdanor, Vernon. *The People and the Party System: The Referendum and Electoral Reform in British Politics.* Cambridge: Cambridge University Press, 1981. 283 pp.

2262. Bogdanor, Vernon. "Social Democrats and the Constitution." *Political Quarterly* 52 (July/September 1981):285–294.

2263. Bolton, P.A. "Parliamentary Representation of Yorkshire Boroughs, 1640–85." Master's thesis, University of Leeds, 1966.

2264. Bond, Maurice F. "The Development of a Parliamentary Sound Archive at Westminster." *Society of Archivists Journal* 6 (October 1980):335–344.

2265. Bond, Shelagh. "A List of Windsor Representatives in Parliament, 1302–1966." *Berkshire Archaeological Journal* 62 (1965/1966): 34–44.

2266. Borthwick, R.L. "The Standing Committees of the House of Commons, A Study of Membership, Procedure and Working Between 1945–1959." Ph.D. dissertation, University of Nottingham, 1968.

2267. Boyne, H. *The Houses of Parliament.* London: Batsford, 1981. 95 pp.

2268. Bradley, Ian C. *Breaking the Mould? The Birth and Prospects of the Social Democratic Party.* Oxford: Martin Robertson, 1981. 172 pp.

2269. Bradley, Ian C. "The Politics of Godliness: The Evangelicals in Parliament, 1784 to 1832." D.Phil., Oxford University, 1975.

2270. British Broadcasting Corporation. *The BBC Guide to Parliament.* London: BBC, 1979, 168 pp.

2271. Bromhead, Peter, and Donald R. Shell. "The British Constitution in 1979." *Parliamentary Affairs* 33 (Spring 1980):141–158.

2272. Brower, Charles N.; Bistline, F. Walter; and Loomis, George W. "The Foreign Sovereign Immunities Act of 1976 in Practice." *American Journal of International Law* 73 (April 1979):200–214.

2273. Burton, Ivor F., and Drewry, Gavin. *Legislation and Public Policy: Public Bills in the 1970–74 Parliament.* London: Macmillan, 1981. 322 pp.

2274. Burton, Ivor F., and Drewry, Gavin. "Public Legislation: A Survey of the Sessions 1977/8 and 1978/9." *Parliamentary Affairs* 33 (Spring 1980):173–209.

2275. Butler, David E., and Kavanagh, Dennis. *The British General Election of 1979.* London: Macmillan, 1980. 443 pp.

2276. Cain, Bruce E., and Ritchie, David B. "Assessing Constituency

Involvement: The Hemel Hempstead Experience." *Parliamentary Affairs* 35 (Winter 1982):73–83.

2277. Callcott, M. "Parliamentary Elections in County Durham, 1929–1935." Master's thesis, University of Newcastle Upon Tyne, 1974.

2278. Cameron, R.H. "Parties and Policies in Early Victorian Britain: A Suggestion for Revision." *Canadian Journal of History* 14 (December 1979):375–393.

2279. Cane, Peter. "Standing, Legality and the Limits of Public Law: The Fleet Street Casuals Case." *Public Law* (Autumn 1981):322–339.

2280. Cannon, John A. "The Parliamentary Representation of the Boroughs of Chippenham, Crickdale, Downton, Hindon, Westbury, and Wooton Bassett, in Wiltshire, from 1754–1790." Ph.D. dissertation, University of Bristol, 1959.

2281. Child, J.S. "Procedural Reform in Congress and Parliament, 1964–1970." B. Litt., Oxford University, 1974.

2282. Chisolm, Michael; Devereux, Bernard; and Versey, Roy. "The Myth of Non-Partisan Cartography: The Tale Continued." *Urban Studies* 18 (June 1981):213–218.

2283. Chivers, G.V. "The Members from the Northern Counties in Richard Cromwell's Parliament." Master's thesis, University of Manchester, 1955.

2284. Christianson, Paul. "Obliterated Portions of the House of Lords Journals Dealing with the Attainder of Strafford, 1641." *English Historical Review* 95 (April 1980):339–353.

2285. Clark, J.C.D. "A General Theory of Party, Opposition and Government, 1688–1832." *Historical Journal* 23 (June 1980):295–325.

2286. Clifford, F.A. "The Parliamentary Representation of Northants and Rutland, 1377–1422." Master's thesis, University of Manchester, 1968.

2287. Coates, C.M. "The Course of Party Discipline in Parliament and the Constituencies over the Past Thirty Years, and Its Effect upon the Worth of the Backbencher in British Government." Master's thesis, University of Bristol, 1960.

2288. Colquhoun, Maureen. *A Woman in the House.* Shoreham-by-Sea: Scan, 1981. 224 pp.

2289. Comber, W.M. "The Cornish Borough and Parliamentary Reform, 1800–1832." Master's thesis, University of Exeter, 1976.

2290. Cope, Esther Sidney. "The Earl of Bedford's Notes of the Short Parliament of 1640." *Institute of Historical Research Bulletin* 53 (November 1980):255–258.

2291. Cormack, Patrick. *Westminster Palace and Parliament.* London: Frederick Warne, 1981. 180 pp.

2292. Cox, Andrew, and Kirby, Stephen. "Innovations in Legislative Oversight of Defence Policies and Expenditure in Britain and America." *Parliamentarian* 61 (October 1980):215–229.

2293. Cox, Harvey, and Laver, Michael. "Local and National Voting in British Elections: Lessons from the Synchro-Polls of 1979." *Parliamentary Affairs* 32 (Autumn 1979):383–393.

2294. Craig, F.W.S. *Britain Votes 2: British Parliamentary Election Results 1974–1979.* 2d ed. Chichester: Parliamentary Research Services, 1980. 292 pp.

2295. Cruickshanks, Eveline G.; Hayton, David; and Jones, Clyve. "Divisions in the House of Lords on the Transfer of the Crown and other Issues, 1689–94: Ten New Lists." *Institute of Historical Research Bulletin* 53 (May 1980):56–87.

2296. Crummett, J.B. "The Lay Peers in Parliament, 1640–44." Ph.D. dissertation, University of Manchester, 1972.

2297. Cubie, G. "Devolution within the United Kingdom." *The Table* 48 (1980):80–86.

2298. Cunningham, George. "Emergency Debates—A Problem for Parliaments." *Parliamentarian* 61 (July 1980):185–186.

2299. Dalyell, Tam. "The Sanctions of 'Prestige.'" *Contemporary Review* 237 (July 1980):1–5.

2300. Davies, R.G., and Denton, J.H., eds. *The English Parliament in the Middle Ages.* Philadelphia: University of Pennsylvania Press, 1981. 214 pp.

2301. Daykin, C.W. "The History of Parliamentary Representation in the City and County of Durham, 1675–1832." Master's thesis, University of Durham, 1961.

2302. Dean, K.J. "Parliamentary Elections and Party Organization in Walsall Constituency, 1906–1945." Master's thesis, University of Birmingham, 1970.

2303. Delaume, Georges R. "The State Immunity Act of the United Kingdom." *American Journal of International Law* 73 (April 1979): 185–199.

2304. Dinwiddy, John Rowland. "Parliamentary Reform as an Issue in English Politics, 1800–1810." Ph.D. dissertation, Makerere University College, 1971.

2305. Dinwiddy, John Rowland. "Sir Frances Burdett and Burdettite Radicalism." *History* 65 (February 1980):17–31.

2306. Ditchfield, G.M. "Repeal, Abolition and Reform: A Study in the Interaction of Reforming Movements in the Parliament of 1790–96." In *Anti-Slavery, Religion and Reform: Essays in Memory of Roger Anstey,* edited by C. Bolt and S. Drescher, pp. 101–118. Folkestone: Dawson, 1980.

2307. Ditchfield, G.M. "Scottish Campaign Against the Test Act, 1790–1791." *Historical Journal* 23 (March 1980):37–61.
2308. Ditchfield, G.M. "The Scottish Representative Peers and Parliamentary Politics, 1787–1793." *Scottish Historical Review* 60 (April 1981):14–31.
2309. Dixson, M.C.S. "Parliament and the Aircraft Industry, 1951–1965." D. Phil., Oxford University, 1972.
2310. Doolittle, I.G. "A First-Hand Account of the Commons Debate on the Removal of Sir Robert Walpole, 13 February 1741." *Institute of Historical Research Bulletin* 53 (May 1980):125–140.
2311. Drewry, Gavin. "Outsider and House of Commons Reform: Some Evidence from the Crossman Diaries." *Parliamentary Affairs* 31 (Autumn 1978):424–435.
2312. Drucker, Henry M. "Changes in the Labour Party Leadership." *Parliamentary Affairs* 34 (Autumn 1981):369–392.
2313. Dunbabin, John P.D. "British Elections in the Nineteenth and Twentieth Centuries: A Regional Approach." *English Historical Review* 95 (April 1980):241–267.
2314. Durrans, P.J. "The Discussion of Imperial Affairs in the British Parliament, 1868–80." D.Phil., Oxford University, 1970.
2315. Edwards, P.S. "The Parliamentary Representation of Wales and Monmouthshire, 1542–1558." Ph.D. dissertation, Cambridge University, 1971.
2316. Elis-Williams, D.M. "The Activities of Welsh Members of Parliament, 1660–1688. Master's thesis, University of Wales, 1952.
2317. Elton, Geoffrey R. "Enacting Clauses and Legislative Initiative, 1559–81." *Institute of Historical Research Bulletin* 53 (November 1980):183–191.
2318. Englefield, D.J.T. *Parliament and Information: The Westminster Scene.* London: Library Association, 1981. 132 pp.
2319. Epstein, Leon D. "What Happened to the British Party Model?" *American Political Science Review* 74 (March 1980):9–22.
2320. Ericson, C.G. "Parliament as a Legislative Institution in the Reigns of Edward VI and Mary." Ph.D. dissertation, University of London, Queen Mary College, 1975.
2321. Farrell, Brian. *The Irish Parliamentary Tradition.* Dublin: Gill & Macmillan, 1973. 286 pp.
2322. Ferman, Monica. "The Tragicomedy of the Housing Bill." *New Statesman* (November 1980):8–11.
2323. Fidlon, P.G. "The House of Commons and the Control of the Executive, 1914–1918." Ph.D. dissertation, London School of Economics, 1972.
2324. Flegmann, Vilma. *Called to Account: the Public Accounts Com-*

mittee of the House of Commons, 1965–66, 1977–78. Farnborrough, Eng.: Gower, 1980. 318 pp.

2325. Foster, Elizabeth Read. "The Journal of the House of Lords for the Long Parliament." In *After the Reformation: Essays in Honor of J.H. Hexter,* edited by B. Malament, pp. 129–146. Philadelphia: University of Pennsylvania Press, 1980.

2326. Fox, E. "The Parliamentary Representation of the County of Lancaster in the Reign of Edward II." Master's thesis, University of Manchester, 1957.

2327. Franks, C.E.S. "Parliament and Atomic Energy." D. Phil., Oxford University, 1974.

2328. Fraser, P. "The Conduct of Public Business in the House of Commons, 1812–1827." Ph.D. dissertation, London School of Economics, 1958.

2329. Fuller, M.R. "Parliamentary Voting Patterns on Non-Party Issues." Master's thesis, University of Southampton, 1971.

2330. Gabriel, R.C. "Members of the House of Commons, 1586–87." Master's thesis, University of London, University College, 1954.

2331. Ganz, G. "Parliamentary Accountability of the Crown Agents." *Public Law* (Winter 1980):454–480.

2332. Gibbs, G.C. "Parliament and Foreign Policy, 1715–1731." Master's thesis, University of Liverpool, 1953.

2333. Giles, D.D. "An Analysis of the Parliamentary Opposition to the National Government's Handling of the International Situation, November 1935–May 1940." Ph.D. dissertation, University of Nottingham, 1976.

2334. Gooder, Arthur. *The Parliamentary Representation of the County of York, 1258–1832.* Wakefield, Yorkshire Archaeological Society, 1935–1938. 2 vols.

2335. Goodman, A.E. "The Parliamentary Representation of Bedfordshire and Buckinghamshire, 1377–1422." B. Litt., Oxford University, 1965.

2336. Gordon, Barry J. *Economic Doctrine and Tory Liberalism, 1824–1830.* London: Macmillan, 1979. 181 pp.

2337. Grant, Wyn. "Business Interests and the British Conservative Party." *Government and Opposition* 15 (Spring 1980):143–161.

2338. Graves, M.A.R. "Thomas Norton the Parliament Man: An Elizabethan M.P., 1559–1581." *Historical Journal* 23 (March 1980): 17–35.

2339. Gross, Izhak. "Abolition of Negro Slavery and British Parliamentary Politics, 1832–33." *Historical Journal* 23 (March 1980): 65–85.

2340. Gross, Izhak. "Parliament and the Abolition of Negro Apprenticeship, 1835–1838." *English Historical Review* 96 (July 1981): 560–576.

2341. Gruenfelder, John K. *Influence in Early Stuart Elections, 1604–1640.* Columbus: Ohio State University Press, 1981. 282 pp.

2342. Guthrie, R. "An Enquiry into the Effectiveness of the Contribution to the Region of Northern M.P.'s as Regional Representatives in Parliament, with Special Reference to the Period February 1974 to December 1976." Master's thesis, University of Newcastle Upon Tyne, 1978.

2343. Hagger, M. "Legislating for Direct Elections—The Passage of a Constitutional Bill." *Parliamentary Affairs* 33 (Summer 1980): 271–293.

2344. Hallett, G.F. "The Influence of the House of Lords on Legislation from 1911–1949." Master's thesis, University of London, External Degree, 1956.

2345. Hanham, Harold J. "Ashburton as a Parliamentary Borough, 1640–1868." *Devonshire Association Reports and Transactions* 98 (1966):206–256.

2346. Hanmer, P.H. "The Role of the House of Commons Committee of Public Accounts in Questions of Science and Technology." Master's thesis, University of Manchester, 1979.

2347. Happs, M.E. "The Sheffield Newspaper Press and Parliamentary Reform, 1787–1832." B. Litt., Oxford University, 1974.

2348. Harcourt, F. "Disraeli's Imperialism, 1866–1868: A Question of Timing." *Historical Journal* 23 (March 1980):87–109.

2349. Hassam, S.E. "The Parliamentary Labour Party and Its Relations with the Liberals, 1910–14." Master's thesis, University of Aberdeen, 1967.

2350. Hawkins, A.B. "British Parliamentary Party Politics, 1855 to 1859." Ph.D. dissertation, London School of Economics, 1980.

2351. Hetherington, Alastair. "Parliamentary Select Committees." *Listener* 104 (August 1980):198–199.

2352. Hill, C. "Parliament and People in Seventeenth-Century England." *Past and Present* 92 (August 1981):100–124.

2353. Hills, Jill. "Candidates, The Impact of Gender." *Parliamentary Affairs* 34 (Spring 1981):221–228.

2354. Himelfarb, Sheldon. "Consensus in Committee: The Case of the Select Committee on Race Relations and Immigration." *Parliamentary Affairs* 33 (Winter 1980):54–66.

2355. Himmelweit, Hilde T.; Humphreys, Patrick; Jaeger, Marianne; and Katz, Michael. *How Voters Decide: A Longitudinal Study of Political Attitudes and Voting Extending over Fifteen Years.* London: Academic Press, 1981. 276 pp.

2356. Hogarth, C.E. "Parliamentary Elections in Derby and Derbyshire, 1832–1865." Master's thesis, University of Manchester, 1958.

2357. Holmes, G.S. "The Influence of the Peerage on English Parliamentary Elections, 1702–1713." B. Litt., Oxford University, Pembroke, 1952.

2358. Hope, S.E. "Select Committees of the House of Commons and Agriculture, 1966–1978." Master's thesis, University of Leicester, 1980.

2359. Ingle, Stephen, and Tether, Philip. *Parliament and Health Policy: The Role of MP's, 1970–75.* Farnborough, Hants.: Gower, 1981. 180 pp.

2360. John, E.L.T. "Parliamentary Representation of Norfolk and Suffolk in the Reigns of Richard II, Henry IV, and Henry V." Master's thesis, University of Nottingham, 1960.

2361. Johnson, D.J. "Parliament and the Railways of London in 1863." *London Topographical Record* 24 (1980):147–165.

2362. Johnston, J.A. "Parliament and the Navy, 1688–1714." Ph.D. dissertation, University of Sheffield, 1968.

2363. Johnston, R.J., and Rossiter, D.J. "Shape and the Definition of Parliamentary Constituencies." *Urban Studies* 18 (June 1981): 219–223.

2364. Jones, M.E. "The Parliamentary Representation of Pembrokeshire and Pembroke Boroughs and Haverfordwest, 1535–1761." Master's thesis, University of Wales, 1958.

2365. Jones, Madeline V. "Political History of the Parliamentary Boroughs of Kent, 1642–1662." Ph.D. dissertation, University of London, Royal Holloway College, 1967.

2366. Judge, David. *Backbench Specialisation in the House of Commons.* London: Heinemann Educational, 1981. 288 pp.

2367. Judge, David. "British Representative Theories and Parliamentary Specialisation." *Parliamentary Affairs* 33 (Winter 1980):40–53.

2368. Katz, Richard S. "The Dimensionality of Party Identification: Cross-National Perspectives." *Comparative Politics* 11 (January 1979):147–163.

2369. Kennedy, D.E. "Parliament and the Navy, 1642–1648: a Political History of the Navy During the Civil War." Ph.D. dissertation, Cambridge University, Trinity College, 1960.

2370. Kershaw, Anthony. "The Canadian Constitution and the Foreign Affairs Committee of the U.K. House of Commons, 1980 and 1981. *Parliamentarian* 62 (July 1981):173–182.

2371. King, Anthony Stephen. "Rise of the Career Politician in Britain— and Its Consequences." *British Journal of Political Science* 11 (July 1981):249–285.

2372. Lambert, Sheila. "Procedure in the House of Commons in the Early-

Stuart Period." *English Historical Review* 95 (October 1980): 753–781.

2373. Lankester, R.S. "House of Commons Select Committees Related to Government Departments." *The Table* 48 (1980):29–34.

2374. Lankester, R.S. "The Remodelled Select Committee System of the House of Commons." *Contemporary Review* 238 (January 1981):19–24.

2375. Lanouette, W.J. "Legislative Control of Cannabis: A Comparison of the Use of Information about Cannabis by Members of the U.K. House of Commons and the U.S. House of Representatives in the Course of Legislating for Drug Control, 1969–1971." Ph.D. dissertation, London School of Economics, 1973.

2376. Lawrence, Michael. "The Administrative Organization of the House of Commons." *The Table* 48 (1980):29–34.

2377. Lawson, Philip. "George Grenville and America: The Years of Opposition, 1765 to 1770." *William and Mary Quarterly* 37 (October 1980):561–576.

2378. Lawson, Philip. "Grenville's Election Act, 1770." *Institute of Historical Research Bulletin* 53 (November 1980):218–228.

2379. Leamy, A.R. "Relations Between Lords and Commons in the Reign of Charles II." Master's thesis, University of Leeds, 1967.

2380. Leopold, Patricia M. "Freedom of Speech in Parliament: Its Misuse and Proposals for Reform." *Public Law* (Spring 1981): 30–51.

2381. Leopold, Patricia M. "References in Court to Hansard." *Public Law* (Autumn 1981):316–321.

2382. Liversedge, D. "Parliament and Administration: Four Specialist Select Committees, 1966–1969." Master's thesis, University of Hull, 1974.

2383. Loach, J. "Conservatism and Consent in Parliament, 1547–1559." In *The Mid-Tudor Polity, c. 1540–1560,* ed. by J. Loach and R. Tittler, pp. 9–28. London: Macmillan, 1980.

2384. Lodge, Juliet. "The United Kingdom Parliament and the European Parliament." *Parliamentarian* 62 (April 1981):119–123.

2385. Lowe, J.C. "Parliamentary Elections in Blackburn and the Blackburn Hundred, 1865–80." Master's thesis, University of Lancaster, 1971.

2386. Lowe, J.F.G. "Parliamentary Debates in 1701 from the Reports of Foreign Observers." Master's thesis, University of Liverpool, 1960.

2387. Macartney, W.J. Allen, and Bochel, Jean. *The Referendum Experience, Scotland 1979.* Aberdeen: Aberdeen University Press, 1981. 160 pp.

2388. McCahill, Michael Woods. *Order and Equipoise: the Peerage and the House of Lords, 1783–1806.* London: Royal Historical Society, 1978. 256 pp.

2389. McCarthy, M.A., and Moodie, R.A. "Parliament and Pornography: The 1978 Child Protection Act." *Parliamentary Affairs* 34 (Winter 1981):47–62.

2390. McDonald, J.F. "Parliamentary Interest in British Regional Policy from 1968 to 1976." Master's thesis, University of Wales, Cardiff, 1978.

2391. McKenzie, L.A. "French Revolution and English Parliamentary Reform: Jame Mackintosh and the Vindiciae Gallicae." *Eighteenth-Century Studies* 14 (Spring 1981):264–282.

2392. MacKenzie, R.G.A. "The Parliamentary Representation of Bristol, 1837–59, and the Political Career of Henry Berkeley." Master's thesis, University of Bristol, 1975.

2393. Margach, James D. *The Anatomy of Power: An Enquiry into the Personality of Leadership.* London: W.H. Allen, 1979. 164 pp.

2394. Marquand, David. "Club Government—The Crisis of the Labour Party in the National Perspective." *Government and Opposition* 16 (Winter 1981):19–36.

2395. Marquand, David. "Parliamentary Accountability and the European Community." *Journal of Common Market Studies* 19 (March 1981):221–236.

2396. Marshall, Geoffrey. "United Kingdom Parliament and the British North America Acts." *Alberta Law Review* 19 (1981):352–362.

2397. "Members' Salaries and Allowances." *Parliamentarian* 61 (October 1980):242–243.

2398. Miller, William L. "Class, Region and Strata at the British General Election of 1979." *Parliamentary Affairs* 32 (Autumn 1979):376–382.

2399. Miller, William L. *The End of British Politics? Scots and English Political Behaviour in the Seventies.* Oxford: Clarendon Press, 1981. 281 pp.

2400. "Ministers and Members' Remuneration." *The Table* 48 (1980):154.

2401. Mitchell, John David Bawden. "Sovereignty of Parliament and Community Law: The Stumbling-Block that Isn't There." *International Affairs* 55 (January 1979):33–46.

2402. Moran, Michael. "Parliamentary Control of the Bank of England." *Parliamentary Affairs* 33 (Winter 1980):67–78.

2403. Morgan, Janet P., ed. *The Backbench Diaries of Richard Crossman.* London: Hamish Hamilton and Jonathan Cape, 1981. 1136 pp.

2404. Morgan, Janet P. "The House of Lords in the 1980's." *Parliamentarian* 62 (January 1981):18–26.

2405. Morgan, K.S. "Parliamentary Reporting at Westminster." *Parliamentarian* 61 (July 1980):147–152.

2406. Mort, M.K. "The Personnel of the House of Commons in 1601." Master's thesis, University of London, Royal Holloway College, 1952.

2407. Mullen, R.F. "The House of Lords and the Repeal of the Corn Laws." D. Phil., Oxford University, 1975.

2408. Munroe, R. "The Constituency Role of Members of Parliament, with Particular Reference to the Constituency of Stoke-on-Trent." Master's thesis, University of Keele, 1975.

2409. Newbould, Ian D.C. "Whiggery and the Dilemma of Reform: Liberals, Radicals and the Melbourne Administration." *Institute of Historical Research Bulletin* 53 (November 1980):229-241.

2410. Newman, A.N. "Elections in Kent and Its Parliamentary Representation, 1715-1754." D. Phil., Oxford University, 1958.

2411. Norton, Philip. "The Changing Face of the British House of Commons in the 1970's." *Legislative Studies Quarterly* 1 (1980)333-357.

2412. Norton, Philip. *The Commons in Perspective.* Oxford: Martin Robertson, 1981. 288 pp.

2413. Norton, Philip. "'Dear Minister'—The Importance of MP-to-Minister Correspondence." *Parliamentary Affairs* 35 (Winter 1982)59-72.

2414. Norton, Philip. "The House of Commons and the Constitution: The Challenges of the 1970's."*Parliamentary Affairs* 34 (Summer 1981):253-271.

2415. Norton, Philip. *The House of Commons in the 1970's: Three Views on Reform.* Hull: Department of Politics, University of Hull, 1978. 14 pp.

2416. Norton, Philip, and Aughey, Arthur. *Conservatives and Conservatism.* London: Maurice Temple Smith, 1981. 334 pp.

2417. Oliver, D. "Constitutional Implications of the Reforms of the Labour Party." *Public Law* (Summer 1981):151-163.

2418. Olson, Alison G. "Parliament, Empire and Parliamentary Law, 1776." In *Three British Revolutions, 1641, 1688, 1776,* ed. by J.G.A. Pocock, pp. 289-322. Princeton, N.J.: Princeton University Press, 1980.

2419. Olson, Alison G. "Parliament, the London Lobbies and Provincial Interests in England and America." *Historical Reflections* 6 (Winter 1979):367-386.

2420. Olson, T.K. "Legislative Representation in Great Britain and the U.S.A.: A Comparative Study of Constituent-Legislator Relations." Ph.D. dissertation, London School of Economics, 1965.

2421. O'Neill, M., and Martin, Ged. "Backbencher on Parliamentary Reform, 1831-1832." *Historical Journal* 23 (September 1980): 539-563.

2422. Oppenheimer, M.B.G. "Freedom of Speech in the House of Commons in the Reign of James I." B. Litt., Oxford University, 1955.

2423. Oram, E. "Investigative Select Committees in the 1966 House of Commons: The Effects of an Experiment in Parliamentary Reform upon the House of Commons, the Political Parties, the Executive and the Public." Ph.D. dissertation, University of Strathclyde, 1975.

2424. Pall, R.N. "The Prime Minister and the Cabinet Form of Government: A Case Study of Britain and France." *Journal of Constitutional and Parliamentary Studies* 33 (1979):320–337.

2425. "Parliament and the Scrutiny of Science Policy: The Report of a Study Group of the Commonwealth Parliamentary Association, Lord Sherfield, Chairman." *Parliamentarian* 62 (October 1981): 251–276.

2426. "Parliamentary Developments, January–March 1980." *Parliamentary Affairs* 33 (Summer 1980):243–248.

2427. Parry, Charles Henry. *The Parliament and Councils of England, Chronologically Arranged, from the Reign of William I to the Revolution in 1688*. London: Murray, 1839. 603 pp.

2428. Paterson, D.J. "Compact Politics: The 1868 Parliamentary Election for the Borough of Warwick." Master's thesis, University of Warwick, 1978.

2429. Peck, Linda Levy. "The Earl of Northampton, Merchant Grievances, and the Addled Parliament of 1614." *Historical Journal* 24 (September 1981):533–552.

2430. Pelling, Henry. "The 1945 General Election Reconsidered." *Historical Journal* 23 (June 1980):399–414.

2431. Penniman, Howard R., ed. *Britain at the Polls, 1979: A Study of the General Election*. Washington, D.C.: American Enterprise Institute, 1981. 345 pp.

2432. Phillips, Gregory D. "The Whig Lords and Liberalism." *Historical Journal* 24 (March 1981):167–173.

2433. Phillips, John A. *Electoral Behavior in Unreformed England: Plumpers, Splitters, and Straights*. Princeton, N.J.: Princeton University Press, 1982.

2434. Phillips, John A. "Structure of Electoral Politics in Unreformed England." *Journal of British Studies* 19 (Fall 1979):76–100.

2435. Phillips, Melanie. *The Divided House: Women at Westminster*. London: Sidgwick and Jackson, 1980. 185 pp.

2436. Pitblado, David. "Proposals for Expanded Scrutiny of Public Spending in the United Kingdom." *Parliamentarian* 62 (July 1981):209–218.

2437. Plaskitt, James. "The House of Lords and Legislative Harmonization in the European Community." *Public Administration* 59 (Summer 1981):203-214.

2438. Pocock, J.G.A. "1776: The Revolution Against Parliament." In his *Three British Revolutions: 1641, 1688, 1776,* pp. 265-288. Princeton, N.J.: Princeton University Press, 1980.

2439. Powell, Christopher, and Buller, Arthur. *The Parliamentary and Scientific Committee—The First Forty Years, 1939-1979.* London: Croom Helm, 1980. 102 pp.

2440. Price, F.C. "The Parliamentary Elections in York City, 1754-1790." Master's thesis, University of Manchester, 1958.

2441. Pronay, Nicholas, and Taylor, John. *Parliamentary Texts of the Later Middle Ages.* Oxford: Clarendon Press, 1980. 230 pp.

2442. Pugh, E.L. "John Stuart Mill and the Women's Question in Parliament, 1865-1868." *Historian* 42 (May 1980):399-418.

2443. Pugh, Martin. "Political Parties and the Campaign for Proportional Representation, 1905-1914." *Parliamentary Affairs* 33 (Summer 1980):294-307.

2444. Pulzer, Peter G.J. "The British General Election of 1979: Back to the Fifties or on to the Eighties?" *Parliamentary Affairs* 32 (Autumn 1979):361-375.

2445. Punnett, R.M. "The Operation of the Parliament Acts, 1911 and 1949." Master's thesis, University of Sheffield, 1961.

2446. Purdue, A.W. "Parliamentary Elections in North East England, 1900-1906: The Advent of Labor." Master's thesis, University of Newcastle Upon Tyne, 1974.

2447. "Questions in the House of Commons of the United Kingdom: A Short Introduction to Their History and Procedure by the Clerks in the Table Office of the House of Commons." *Constitutional and Parliamentary Information* (1979):76-84.

2448. Rabb, T.K., and Hirst, D. "Revisionism Revised: Two Perspectives on Early Stuart Parliamentary History." *Past and Present* 92 (August 1981):55-99.

2449. Rasmussen, Jorgen Scott. "Women Candidates in British By-Elections: A Rational Choice Interpretation of Electoral Behavior." *Political Studies* 29 (June 1981):265-274.

2450. Rees, R.D. "Parliamentary Representation of South Wales, 1790-1830." Ph.D. dissertation, University of Reading, 1962.

2451. Roberts, Geoffrey K. "The Development of a Railway Interest, and Its Relation to Parliament, 1830-1868." Ph.D. dissertation, London School of Economics, 1966.

2452. Roberts, J.C. "The Parliamentary Representation of Devon and Dorset, 1559-1601." Master's thesis, University of London, University College, 1959.

2453. Roberts, K. "The English Country Members of Parliament, 1784–1832." B. Litt., Oxford University, 1974.

2454. Robertson, David. "Judicial Ideology in the House of Lords: A Jurimetric Analysis." *British Journal of Political Science* 12 (January 1982):1–26.

2455. Robson, Peter, and Watchman, Paul, eds. *Justice, Lord Denning, and the Constitution.* Farnborough, Hants.: Gower, 1981. 270 pp.

2456. Rogers, Alan. "The Parliamentary Representation of Surrey and Sussex." Master's thesis, University of Nottingham, 1958.

2457. Roots, I.A. "Cromwell Road: The Shortage and Troublesome Reign of Richard IV." *History Today* 30 (March 1980):10–15.

2458. Rose, Paul. *Backbencher's Dilemma.* London: Frederick Muller, 1981. 198 pp.

2459. Rose, Paul. "Cameras in the Chamber in 1980?" *Contemporary Review* 236 (January 1980):12–14.

2460. Rush, Michael. "Parliament and Government: An Annotated Bibliography of Government Publications for the 1977–78 Parliamentary Session." *Parliamentary Affairs* 32 (Autumn 1979): 482–493.

2461. Rush, Michael. *Parliamentary Government in Britain.* London: Pitman, 1981. 288 pp.

2462. Ryan, Mick. "Too Much Study of Parliament?" *Political Quarterly* 51 (April/June 1980):223–226.

2463. Rydz, D.L. *The Parliamentary Agents: A History.* London: Royal Historial Society, 1979. 234 pp.

2464. Ryle, Michael. "The Legislative Staff of the British House of Commons." *Legislative Studies Quarterly* 6 (November 1981):497–520.

2465. Sack, James J. "The House of Lords and Parliamentary Patronage in Great Britain, 1802–1832." *Historical Journal* 23 (December 1980):913–937.

2466. Salt, S.P. "Sir Thomas Wentworth and the Parliamentary Representation of Yorkshire, 1614–1628." *Northern History* 16 (1980):130–168.

2467. Schofield, D.A. "Henry Addington, Speaker of the House of Commons, 1789–1801." Master's thesis, University of Southampton, 1959.

2468. Scholes, P.M. "Parliament and the Protestant Dissenters, 1702–1719." Master's thesis, University of London, University College, 1962.

2469. Schwartz, John E. "Attempting to Assert the Commons Power: Labour Members in the House of Commons, 1974–1979." *Comparative Politics* 14 (October 1981):17–29.

2470. Schwoerer, Lois G. *The Declaration of Rights, 1689.* Baltimore, Md.: Johns Hopkins University Press, 1981. 391 pp.

2471. Scott, Stephen Allan. "Law and Convention in the Patriation of the Canadian Constitution." *Parliamentarian* 62 (July 1981): 183–191.

2472. Scott, Stephen Allan. "Opinion Submitted to the Foreign Affairs Committee of the House of Commons of the United Kingdom on the Role of the United Kingdom Parliament in Relation to the British North America Acts." *McGill Law Journal* 26 (1981): 614–625.

2473. Seagrave, J.R. "The Church of England in Parliament." Ph.D. dissertation, University of Birmingham, 1972.

2474. Seidle, F. Leslie. "State Aid for Political Parties." *Parliamentarian* 61 (April 1980):79–86.

2475. Seymour-Ure, Colin. "The Press and Parliamentary Privilege in Britain During the Twentieth Century." D. Phil., Oxford University, 1969.

2476. Seymour-Ure, Colin. "Press and Referenda: The Case of the British Referendum of 1975." *Canadian Journal of Political Science* 11 (1978):601–615.

2477. Shell, Donald R. "The British Constitution in 1980." *Parliamentary Affairs* 34 (Spring 1981):149–164.

2478. Shell, Donald R. "Parliamentary Developments." *Parliamentary Affairs* 32 (Autumn 1979):355–360.

2479. Smith, Geoffrey. *Westminster Reform: Learning from Congress.* London: Trade Policy Research Center, 1979. 52 pp.

2480. Smith, Geoffrey, and Polsby, Nelson W. *British Government and Its Discontents.* New York: Basic Books, 1981. 202 pp.

2481. Southall, E. "The General Election and Members of the Parliament of 1784–1790." Master's thesis, University of Manchester, 1952.

2482. Southern, David. "Lord Newton, the Conservative Peers and the Parliament Act of 1911." *English Historical Review* 96 (October 1981):834–840.

2483. Speck, William A. "The House of Commons, 1702–14: A Study in Political Organization." D.Phil., Oxford University, 1966.

2484. Spendlove, J.M. "Government and the House of Commons, 1747–1754." B. Litt., Oxford University, 1956.

2485. Stancer, J.D. "A Study of Backbench Members of Parliament Between 1945–1965." Ph.D. dissertation, London School of Economics, 1973.

2486. Storer, Donald. *Conduct of Parliamentary Elections.* 8th ed. London: Labor Party, 1977. 128 pp.

2487. Stray, Stephanie, and Silver, Mick. "Do By-Elections Demonstrate a Government's Unpopularity?'' *Parliamentary Affairs* 33 (Summer 1980):264–270.

2488. Stuart, D.G. 'The Parliamentary History of the Borough of Tamworth, Staffordshire, 1661–1837.'' Master's thesis, University of London, External Degree, 1958.

2489. Studlar, Donely T. ''The Influence of British Political Candidates on Public Attitudes Toward Immigrants.'' *Plural Societies* 10 (Autumn/Winter 1979):103–114.

2490. Study of Parliament Group. *The Commons Today.* Edited by S.A. Walkland and Michael Ryle. Glasgow: Fontana, 1981. 333 pp.

2491. Study of Parliament Group. ''Private Bill Procedure: A Case for Reform.'' *Public Law* (Summer 1981):206–227.

2492. Swales, R.J.W. ''Local Politics and the Parliamentary Representation of Sussex, 1529–1558.'' Ph.D. dissertation, University of Bristol, 1965.

2493. Sweeney, J.M. ''The House of Lords in British Politics, 1830–41.'' D. Phil., Oxford University, 1974.

2494. Swinhoe, K. ''A Study of Opinion About the Reform of House of Commons Procedure, 1945–68.'' Ph.D. dissertation, University of Leeds, 1971.

2495. Szechi, D. ''Some Insights on the Scottish MP's and Peers Returned in the 1710 Election.'' *Scottish Historical Review* 60 (April 1981):61–68.

2496. Taylor, Robert. ''The New Watchdogs of Parliament.'' *New Society* 55 (January 1981):96–98.

2497. Teriotdale, D.A. ''Glasgow Parliamentary Constituency, 1832–1846.'' B. Litt., University of Glasgow, 1962.

2498. Thomas, George, ''Parliamentary Privilege at Westminster.'' *Parliamentarian* 61 (October 1980):212–214.

2499. Thomas, P.R. ''The Attitude of the Labor Party to Reform of Parliament, with Particular Reference to the House of Commons, 1919–1951.'' Ph.D. dissertation, University of Keele, 1975.

2500. Thomas, Peter D.G. ''The Debates of the House of Commons, 1768–1774.'' Ph.D. dissertation, University of London: University College, 1958.

2501. Thomas, Peter D.G. ''New Light on the Commons Debate of 1763 on the American Army.'' *William and Mary Quarterly* 38 (January 1981):110–112.

2502. Thomas, Peter D.G. ''The Parliamentary Representation of North Wales, 1715–1784.'' Master's thesis, University of Wales, 1954.

2503. *The Times Guide to the House of Commons, May 1979.* London: Times Books, 1979. 339 pp.

2504. Tite, Colin G.C. ''The Development of English Parliamentary Judicature, 1604–1626.'' Ph.D. dissertation, University of London, Royal Holloway College, 1970.

2505. Tucker, A.D. "Commons in the Parliament of 1545." D. Phil., Oxford University, 1967.

2506. "The United Kingdom and the Isle of Man." *Parliamentarian* 61 (April 1980):88–90.

2507. Vallance, Elizabeth. *Women in the House—A Study of Women Members of Parliament.* London: Athlone Press, 1979. 212 pp.

2508. Vallance, Elizabeth. "Women in the House of Commons." *Political Studies* 29 (September 1981):407–414.

2509. Vandyk, Neville D. "An End to the House of Lords as Appeal Court?" *Medico-Legal Journal* 48 (1980):111–115.

2510. Virgoe, Roger. "The Parliament of 1449–50." Ph.D. dissertation, University of London, Queen Mary College, 1965.

2511. Wade, A. "Parliamentary Representation of Essex and Hertfordshire, 1377–1422." Master's thesis, University of Manchester, 1967.

2512. Wade, Donald William. "A Bill of Rights for the United Kingdom." *Parliamentarian* 61 (April 1980):65–71.

2513. Wahlstrand, J.M. "The Elections to Parliament in the County of Lancashire 1685–1714." Master's thesis, University of Manchester, 1957.

2514. Walker, I. "An Analysis of Questions in the House of Commons in the Fields of Race Relations and Commonwealth Immigration, 1959–1964." Master's thesis, University of Bradford, 1974.

2515. Ward, P.W.U. "Members of Parliament and Elections in Derbyshire, Leicestershire and Staffordshire between 1660 and 1714." Master's thesis, University of Manchester, 1960.

2516. Watkins, Kenneth, "The British Election of 1979 and Its Aftermath." *Policy Review* 9 (Summer 1979):103–110.

2517. Watson, S.A. "Parliamentary Political Interests in Lancashire and Cheshire in the Late Seventeenth and Early Eighteenth Centuries." Master's thesis, University of Manchester, 1979.

2518. Webb, M.G. "The Parliamentary Representation of Warwickshire and Leicestershire, 1377–1422." Master's thesis, University of Nottingham, 1962.

2519. Williams, Bruce A. "Bureaucracy, Democracy and Class: The Parliamentary Labour Party and the Problem of Voluntary Political Organizations." Ph.D. dissertation, University of Minnesota, 1980. 284 pp.

2520. Willis, K. "Role in Parliament of the Economic Ideas of Adam Smith, 1776–1800. *History of Political Economy* 11 (Winter 1979):505–544.

2521. Wilson, C.E. "First Daily Newspaper in English." *Journalism Quarterly* 58 (Summer 1981):286–288.
2522. Wilson, T. "The Parliamentary Liberal Party in Britain, 1918–1924." D. Phil., Oxford University, 1960.
2523. Winterton, George. "Parliamentary Supremacy and the Judiciary." *Law Quarterly Review* 97 (April 1981):265–274.
2524. Witcombe, D.T. "The Cavalier House of Commons: Court and Country Manoeuvres, 1663–1674." Ph.D. dissertation, University of Manchester, 1964.
2525. Wood, David. "Comparing Parliamentary Voting on European Issues in France and Britain." *Legislative Studies Quarterly* 7 (February 1982):101–117.
2526. Wood, S. "Walpole's Constituency: King's Lynn." *History Today* 30 (April 1980):40–44.
2527. Yardley, D.C.M. "Constitutional Reform in the United Kingdom." *Current Legal Problems* 33 (1980):147–164.
2528. Yarlott, R. "The Long Parliament and the Fear of Popular Pressure, 1640–1646." Master's thesis, University of Leeds, 1964.

Index of Authors

Abbott, W.C., 336
Abel, D., 1149
Abraham, L.A., 100
Abrams, M., 1472, 1662, 1663, 1772
Abrams, P., 1773
Adams, William H.D., 1874
Adelman, Paul, 1319, 1875
Aiken, C., 160
Ajibola, W.A., 1214
Albu, Austen, 1185
Alderman, R.K., 1121, 1122, 1186, 1876, 1877, 2143, 2246
Alderson, Stanley, 1321
Alexander, J.J., 1473
Aligwekwe, Evalyn Cumblidge, 1215
Alington, Cyril A., 1879
Allen, A.J., 1774, 1878
Allen, Agnes, 161
Allen, Carleton Kemp, 587
Allen, E.G., 1084
Allen, F.G., 613
Allison, Lincoln, 614
Allott, Philip, 1270
Allyn, Emily, 1951
Alt, James, 1257, 1664, 1665
Amspoker, Gertrude Joanne, 831
Anderson, Bruce L., 465
Anderson, Clifford B., 337, 1216
Anderson, Ian G., 1
Anderson, Olive, 1020, 1217
Andervont, Carolyn Bancroft, 1169
Andrews, George Gordon, 1320
Andrews, William G., 512, 1666
Antler, Steven D., 338
Anwar, Muhammad, 1667, 1668, 1743
Arnstein, Walter L., 653, 654
Arora, R.S., 1085
Ashby, C., 1474
Ashford, Douglas E., 107, 2247
Aspinall, Arthur, 866–871, 2092
Atkins, Elsie M., 1322
Attlee, C.R., 2028

Atton, K.J., 2248
Auchmuty, James J., 1610
Aughey, Arthur, 2416
Aydelotte, William O., 429, 872, 873
Aylmer, G.E., 339

Bagley, C.R., 1669
Bailey, R.C.J.F., 415, 430
Bailey, Sidney D., 162, 163, 913–915, 1880, 2029, 2226
Bain, G.S., 108
Baker, Arthur, 733
Baker, J.E.W., 2349
Ball, Enid, 874
Ball, Allan, 2250
Balsom, Denis, 2251
Barclay, H.M., 734
Barker, Anthony, 2, 735, 785, 786, 2195
Barlas, R.D., 513, 1086
Barnard, T.C., 2093
Barnett, Malcolm J., 1775, 2039
Barratt, Robin, 514
Barrows, Floyd Dell, 832
Bartholomew, D.J., 2044
Bassett, Reginal, 164, 1881
Bateman, Charles D., 165
Battley, John, 166
Baylen, Joseph O., 91
Bayley, C.C., 271
Bayne, C.G., 814
Beales, Derek E.D., 1882
Bealey, F., 1670, 1671, 1776
Beamish, D.R., 1087
Bear, L.W., 2163, 2164, 2212
Beattie, Alan J., 1883, 1884
Bechhofer, F., 1810
Beckett, J.V., 2252
Beddard, R.A., 1532
Beddow, J.F.H., 340
Bedeman, Trevor, 1673
Beer, Samuel H., 1885, 1886

153

Behrens, R., 2253
Behrman, Cynthia F., 431
Beith, Alan, 2254
Belchem, J.C., 2094
Bell, Herbert C., 1811
Bell, S. Peter, 117
Bell, Stuart, 2255
Bellamy, J.G., 1271, 2256
Belloc, H., 736, 1170, 1475
Beloff, Max, 167, 1672
Benewick, R.J., 1812
Benn, Tony, 2257
Bennett, A., 1042, 1476
Bennett, Edward Earl, 1218
Benstead, C.R., 168
Bentham, Jeremy, 1323
Benyon, John, 614
Berelson, Ellen Sue, 2095
Bermant, C.I., 2258
Berrington, H.B., 875, 1673, 2040,
    2044, 2051
Bevins, A.J., 2196
Bidwell, William Bradford, 341
Birch, A.H., 1674, 1812
Birrell, W.D., 2070
Birt, Phyllis, 235
Bistline, F. Walter, 2272
Black, C.J., 2259
Black, Eugene Charlton, 1324
Blackstone, Tessa, 109
Blewett, Neal, 1611, 1675
Blogg, C.W., 2165
Blom-Cooper, Louis J., 1272, 1273
Bloomfield, Valerie, 58
Blue, R.N., 1187
Blumler, J.G., 1812, 2213
Boardman, Harry, 169
Boardman, Robert, 3
Bochel, Jean, 2387
Bodet, Gerald P., 170
Body, Richard, 1043
Bogdanor, Vernon, 2260–2262
Bohannon, M.E., 1533
Boisvert, H.V., 515
Bolt, W.J., 1433
Bolton, P.A., 2263
Bond, Maurice F., 19, 1088, 1123,

    2144, 2145, 2166–2170, 2197, 2264
Bond, Shelagh, 2265
Bonham, John, 1477, 1777
Books, J.W., 1813
Booth, W., 1676
Borthwick, R.L., 1044–1046, 1072,
    2266
Bossom, Alfred, 655
Bottomley, Arthur, 466, 1089
Boulton, C.J., 787, 1047
Bourne, J., 1688
Bourne, R.C., 737
Bowring, Nona, 662
Bowyer, Robert, 2096
Boyd-Carpenter, John, 1090, 1434
Boyer, Barton Lee, 1325
Boyne, H., 2267
Bradley, Ian C., 2268, 2269
Bradshaw, Kenneth, 467, 656
Brady, David W., 1943
Brady, H., 1952
Brand, C.F., 1326, 1677–1683
Brasher, Norman H., 788, 916, 917
Brayley, E.W., 2297
Brazier, Rodney, 1274
Brendon, John A., 101
Brendon, Keith, 143
Brett, S.R., 342, 1758
Brewer, John, 1887
Bridge, C., 703
Bridge, J.W., 516
British Broadcasting Corporation, 2270
Britain, Herbert, 615
Brittain, J. Michael, 110
Brittan, Samuel, 1888
Britton, J., 2227
Brock, Michael, 1327
Brocklebank-Fowler, Christopher, 171
Bromhead, Marjorie Anne, 1815
Bromhead, Peter A., 604, 657, 738,
    789, 790, 918, 1036, 1303, 1328,
    1815, 2097, 2271
Brook, D., 1806
Brooke, John, 20, 856
Brookes, Pamela, 2063
Brookes, S.K., 679
Brower, Charles N., 2272

Clarke, Maude V., 274
Clarke, P.F., 1782
Clarke, R., 621
Cleary, E.J., 1685
Clendenin, Thurman Barrier, 2006
Clifford, F.A., 2286
Clifford, Frederick, 605
Close, David H., 878, 1439, 2042
Clough, Owen, 529, 530, 1440, 2146
Clyne, A., 2147
Coates, C.M., 2287
Cobb, Henry S., 5, 2173
Cocks, Bernard, 177, 622, 663, 704,
    1221
Cocks, T.G.B., 1054
Coe, Dennis, 922
Cohen, John, 898
Cohen, Lionel H., 1155
Coit, William Baer, 275
Cole, Leonard A., 1893
Coleman, A.M., 1481
Collier, E.G., 1021
Colquhoun, Maureen, 2288
Comber, W.M., 2289
Comford, A.F., 73
Comfort, George O., 1894
Commonwealth Parliamentary
    Association, 1956
Compton, E., 1156
Comyn-Platt, T., 1441
Conacher, J.B., 1338
Cone, C.B., 416
Conference on British Studies, 120–125
Conniff, J., 1820
Cook, Chris, 6, 143–144, 149, 1687,
    1746
Cook, G.H., 1339
Cook, Hartley K., 1482
Cooke, Alistair B., 1612
Coombes, David L., 1091, 1092, 1222
Cooper, J.P., 276
Cooper, Peter, 898
Cope, Esther Sidney, 349, 2100, 2101,
    2290
Cormack, Patrick, 2291
Cornelius, I.V., 22
Cottenham, Earl of, 1340

Cowie, Leonard W., 102
Cowling, Maurice, 1341, 2102
Cox, Andrew, 2292
Cox, Geoffrey, 178
Cox, H., 179
Cox, Harvey, 2293
Cox, M.D., 854
Craig, F.W.S., 59–66, 2294
Craig, J.T., 531, 1821
Craig, Robert, 277
Craigavon, James Craig, 2229
Craik, G.L., 742
Cranshaw, S., 1764
Crawford, P., 350
Crewe, Ivor, 1257, 1895
Crick, Bernard R., 180, 181, 532, 923,
    1342, 1343, 1425, 1442, 1896
Cripps, Richard Stafford, 1344, 1897
Crocket, D.G., 2007
Croessmann, Allen Ward, 833
Croft, Pauline, 834
Cromwell, Valerie, 23, 879, 1426
Cross, J.A., 1122, 1125, 1186, 1957,
    2143
Cross, Rupert, 1276, 1277
Crossland, F.E., 1696
Crowe, Edward W., 743
Cruickshank, C.G., 1822
Cruickshanks, Eveline G., 835, 1171,
    2295
Crummett, J.B., 2296
Cubie, G., 2297
Cumming-Bruce, C.H., 1223
Cumpston, M., 1224
Cunningham, George, 2298
Cuttino, G.P., 278

Dalton, H., 1345
Dalyell, Tam, 2299
Dann, W.S., 1823
Dasent, Arthur Irwin, 1126
Daudt, Hans, 1783
Davenport, E.H., 623
Davey, C.M., 1958
Davidson, A., 1898
Davidson, John Morrison, 1899
Davies, E., 606, 1093, 1190

Hanumanthappa, T.C., 545
Happs, M.E., 2347
Harcourt, F., 2348
Hardie, Frank M., 200, 1176, 1364
Hardy, Stuart Baxter, 1365
Hargrave, O.T., 139
Hargreaves, John, 1621
Harris, J.P., 546, 633
Harris, William, 1911
Harrison, Carl, 1583
Harrison, F., 928
Harrison, J.F.C., 130
Harrison, L.H., 1696
Harriss, G.L., 634, 818
Harrop, M., 1791
Hart, M.C., 1003
Hart, Vivien, 1490
Harvey, A.D., 1912, 1964
Harvey, Caroline, 1622
Harvey, Joan M., 77
Haskins, George Lee, 286, 287, 1835
Hassam, S.E., 2349
Hastings, Maurice, 2231
Hatsell, John, 798
Havill, E.E., 1836
Hawkins, A.B., 2350
Hawkins, Paul, 2232
Hawtry, S.C., 100
Haxey, Simon, 1913
Hay, C.H., 2112
Hayden, R., 669
Hayes, Carlton, 929
Hayter, P.D.G., 670, 1137, 1177
Hayton, David, 835, 2295
Hazell, P.F., 1747
Hazell, R., 930
Headlam, Cuthbert, 931, 932
Heasman, D.J., 1178, 1965, 2151
Heath, Edward, 201
Hechter, M., 1623
Helms, Mary Elizabeth, 359
Hemingford, Denis Herbert H., 202,
    2113
Henderson, W. Craig, 547
Henning, Basil D., 360
Herbert, Alan P., 203, 548, 933, 1057
Herman, Valentine, 549, 799, 2052

Hermens, F.A., 1491
Herr, Elmer Francis, 991
Herrick, F.H., 1366
Hetherington, Alastair, 2351
Heuston, R.F.V., 1024
Hewitt, D.J., 595
Hexter, J.H., 361
Hidayatullah, M., 1305
Higgins, Graham M., 1074, 1075
Higgs, Henry, 114
Higham, Robin, 131
Hill, A.P., 1697
Hill, Andrew, 204
Hill, Brian W., 1914, 1915, 1966
Hill, C., 2352
Hill, C.J., 1747
Hills, Jill, 2353
Himelfarb, Sheldon, 2354
Himmelweit, Hilde T., 1792, 2355
Hinchingbrooke, Viscount, 934
Hirst, D., 705, 837, 2448
Hitchner, D.G., 1128
Hobbs, John L., 1624
Hobson, J.A., 978
Hockin, Thomas A., 751
Hodgson, Patricia, 205
Hodson, J.L., 206
Hoffman, W.J., 1549
Hogarth, C.E., 1625–1627, 2356
Holdsworth, W.S., 899, 1013
Holland, D.C.L., 78, 550, 2180, 2181
Holland, David, 36, 37
Hollis, Christopher, 207–209, 499
Hollis, Daniel Webster, 362
Holmes, G.S., 2357
Holmes, George A., 288
Holt, Robert T., 1492
Hope, S.E., 2358
Hopkinson, R., 1802
Hoppen, K. Theodore, 1628, 2075
Horgan, David Thomas, 2076
Hornby, R., 551, 2048
Horner, J., 1474
Horstman, Allen Henry, 1004
Horwitz, Henry, 363, 420, 846, 2114
Houghton, Douglas, 752, 1967, 2015,
    2049

Jupp, Peter, 1634
Just, Marion R., 1701

Kaberry, Donald, 677
Kanner, Barbara, 133
Katz, Michael, 2355
Katz, Richard S., 2368
Katzenstein, Peter J., 107
Kavanagh, Dennis, 2275
Keating, Michael J., 2080, 2081
Keeler, Mary F., 366
Keeton, George W., 218, 596, 706
Keith, A.B., 707
Kelly, Joseph Michael, 2117
Kelly, Paul, 421, 1586, 2082
Kemp, Betty, 802
Kendall, Maurice, G., 79
Kennedy, A.R., 1058
Kennedy, D.E., 2369
Kennedy, W.P.M., 292
Kenney, Marion L., 1237
Kennon, Andrew, 640
Kenny, R.W., 840
Kent, Joan, 819
Kenworthy, J.M., 1748
Kenyon, John P., 1917
Kerbey, Janice, 96, 2024
Kermode, D.G., 1841
Kerr, Barbara, 1587
Kerr, David, 1969, 1970, 2050
Kersell, John E., 597, 598, 678
Kershaw, Anthony, 2370
Kershaw, R.N., 367, 841
Kilmuir, David Maxwell Fyfe, 708
Kimber, Richard H., 679, 771, 1077
King, Anthony Stephen, 219, 474,
    1918, 1971, 2371
King, E.M., 2191
King, Horace Maybray, 557, 1129,
    2200
King, Joseph, 1498
King-Hall, Stephen, 934, 2235
Kingdon, John W., 709
Kinnear, J.B., 935
Kinnear, Mary, 1972
Kinnear, Michael, 68
Kirby, Stephen, 2292

Kirkwood, D., 1474
Kishlansky, M.A., 368, 369
Koester, C.B., 1078
Kogan, Maurice, 1312
Kolinsky, Martin, 1100
Korah, Valentine, 558
Kornberg, Allan, 1919
Krehbiel, E., 499

Labor Research Department, 936
Lacey, Douglas Raymond, 370
Lachs, P.S., 1238
Laing, L.H., 475, 1749
Lakeman, Enid, 1372, 1500, 1702
Lamb, W.K., 442
Lambert, Geoffrey, 2061
Lambert, Sheila, 559, 1239, 2153,
    2182, 2372
Lampson, E.T., 501
Landau, J.E., 979
Lane, Peter, 1501
Langbein, J.H., 937
Lanham, D.J., 599
Lankester, R.S., 1059, 2373, 2374
Lanouette, W.J., 2375
Laprade, W.T., 1588
Lapsley, Gaillard, Thomas, 293–298
Large, David, 1015, 1025, 1026
Lascelles, F.W., 680
Laski, Harold J., 220, 502, 938, 1703
Latham, R.C., 299
Laundy, Philip, 14, 1130, 1131
Laurence, W.B., 755
Laurenzo, Frederick Edward, 2118
Laver, Michael, 2293
Law, William, 2183
Lawrence, Michael, 2376
Lawson, J., 300
Lawson, Philip, 2377, 2378
Lawton, Richard, 80
Layton-Henry, Z., 1502
Lazar, H., 476
Leach, W., 1448
Leamy, A.R., 2379
Lebeau, Sandra Smith, 443
Lee, Clive H., 81
Lee, J.M., 1101, 1201, 1288

Willy, T.G., 1267
Wilson, C.E., 2521
Wilson, David J., 1949
Wilson, Robert Sydney, 1997
Wilson, T., 1742, 2522
Windlesham, David James, 968
Windreich, Elaine, 1268
Winnifrith, C.B., 1999
Winter, James Hannibal, 1420, 1421
Winterton, E.M., 1771
Winterton, Edward T., 912
Winterton, George, 511, 969, 2523
Wise, A.R., 1471
Wiseman, Herbert V., 668, 701, 1056,
     1120, 1199, 1212, 1422, 2062
Witcomb, D.T., 2524
Witmer, Helen E., 2000
Wittke, Carl, 729
Wober, Mallory, 2225
Wolf-Philips, Leslie, 702
Wolffe, B.P., 584
Wollman, David Harris, 1269
Wood, David, 1318, 1950, 2525
Wood, S., 2526
Wood-Legh, K.L., 1872, 2001

Woodall, Robert, 454, 585, 1660
     2194
Woodbridge, George, 1423
Woolley, S.F., 1873, 2002
Woolrych, Austin, 411
Woolven, G.B., 108
Worden, Blair, 412, 413
Worlock, David, 1424
Wright, A., 268
Wright, D.G., 1661
Wyatt, Woodrow, 784
Wymer, Norman, 269

Yardley, D.C.M., 586, 612, 730,
     1213, 2527
Yarlott, R., 2528
York, Archbishop of, 970
Young, Roland A., 270

Zaller, Robert Michael, 414
Zaring, Philip Brewer, 1035
Zebel, S.H., 1071
Zellick, Graham, 731, 732, 2003
Zimmer, L.B., 455

Index of Subjects

About the Authors

Robert U. Goehlert received the Ph.D. in political science and the M.L.S. from Indiana University, where he is the librarian for economics, political science, and forensic studies. He has written numerous research and reference tools for the study of political science.

Fenton S. Martin received the M.L.S. from Indiana University, where she is the librarian for the research collection in the Department of Political Science. She has extensive experience in the librarianship of political science and is currently working on other major bibliographies in the field of American politics.